SHYNESS

SHYNESS

*How Normal Behavior
Became a Sickness*

Christopher Lane

Yale University Press
New Haven & London

Published with assistance from the Kingsley Trust Association Publication Fund established by the Scroll and Key Society of Yale College.

The information and suggestions contained in this book are not intended to replace the services of your physician or caregiver.

The author has attempted to make this book as accurate and up to date as possible, but it may nevertheless contain omissions or material that is out of date at the time you read it. Neither the author nor the publisher has any legal responsibilities or liability for errors, omissions, out-of-date material, or the reader's application of the medical information or advice contained in this book.

Set in Galliard type by The Composing Room of Michigan, Inc.
Printed in the United States of America by Vail-Ballou Press, Binghamton, New York.

ISBN: 978-0-300-14317-1 (pbk. : alk. paper)
Library of Congress Control Number: 2007925003

A catalogue record for this book is available from the British Library.

This paper meets the requirements of ANSI/NISO Z39.48-1992 (Permanence of Paper).

Might there be a brand of "shyness" serious enough to warrant medical attention? There is. It is "social phobia."

—Murray B. Stein, *The Lancet* (April 1996)

CONTENTS

INTRODUCTION:
BASHFUL NO MORE

When my mother was six years old, she often pretended she was a horse. Painfully shy, she preferred galloping around on "four" legs to the ordeal of talking to strangers on two. The Germans were bombing London and southern England at the time, a source of terror for many children, and my grandparents—concerned about her safety—heightened her anxiety by sending her off to boarding school. Once there, my mother would cavort outside for hours. When that wasn't feasible, she withdrew to a practice room and played the piano with quiet intensity.

No one found her especially odd or recommended medication for her quirky behavior. My grandparents shrugged off her equestrian impressions as the charming eccentricity of a girl blessed with a vivid imagination, and waited patiently for her to change. Years later, still playing the piano and still unconventional, she became a renowned music therapist and lecturer at London's Nordoff-Robins Center for children with learning difficulties.

In my mother's generation, shy people were seen as introverted and perhaps a bit awkward, but never mentally ill. Adults admired their bashfulness, associating it with bookishness, reserve, and a yen for solitude. But shyness isn't just shyness any more. It's a disease. It has a variety of overwrought names, including "social anxiety" and "avoidant personality disorder," afflictions said to trouble millions (almost one person in five, according to some estimates).[1] And since the early 1990s, when the U.S. Food and Drug Administration agreed that powerful psychotropic drugs were suitable ways of treating these conditions, countless Americans and

Britons have daily swallowed large doses of Paxil, Prozac, Zoloft, and other pills for routine emotions that experts now consider medical conditions.

Unlike my countrymen in Britain, Americans are regarded as the most gregarious people on earth. So when large numbers of them say they find talking to a stranger *terrifying* and claim they would rather die than make a public speech, something dramatic is happening.[2] "It is a part of the American character," Thomas Jefferson once enthused, "to consider nothing as desperate—to surmount every difficulty by resolution and contrivance."[3] Nowadays, if we're to believe preeminent psychiatrists and fabulously profitable drug companies, almost 19 percent of the population is so fearful of others' judgments, it shuns activities that would risk incurring them.[4] Gone are the days when we could value exuberance *and* shyness, as well as a vast repertoire of similar moods. Today many psychiatrists and doctors assert that those who aren't sufficiently outgoing may be mentally ill.

One reason for the skyrocketing diagnoses is that doctors and psychiatrists require a very low burden of proof. They say social anxiety runs the gamut from stage fright to paralyzing fears of criticism and embarrassment. (The most common nightmare scenarios are eating alone in restaurants, with fear of hand-trembling a close second, and avoidance of public restrooms third.) Some doctors also include, as symptoms of the disorder, fears of sounding foolish and of being stumped when asked questions in social settings—fears that doubtless afflict almost everyone on the planet.[5] Considering these elastic guidelines, we can grasp quite easily why the "illness" is so widely diagnosed, but it's harder to say why so many take the diagnosis seriously, much less accept its judgment of mental debility.

The transformation of shyness into a disease occurred behind the closed doors of carefully vetted committee meetings. Over the course of six years, a small group of self-selecting American psychiatrists built a sweeping new consensus: shyness and a host of comparable traits were anxiety and personality disorders. And they stemmed not from psychological conflicts or social tensions, but rather from a chemical imbalance or faulty neurotransmitters in the brain.

Beginning in 1980, with much fanfare and confidence in its revised diagnoses, the American Psychiatric Association added "social phobia," "avoidant personality disorder," and several similar conditions to the third edition of its massively expanded *Diagnostic and Statistical Manual of*

Mental Disorders. In this five-hundred-page volume, the bible of psychiatrists the world over, the introverted individual morphed into the mildly psychotic person whose symptoms included being aloof, being dull, and simply "being alone."[6]

The fact that psychiatrists often playfully call this reference manual their bible doesn't offset the reality that they follow its pronouncements chapter and verse. The influence of the *DSM* also extends far beyond psychiatry, to a vast network of healthcare agencies, social services, medical insurers, courts, prisons, and universities. It took the psychiatrists in question just a few years to update their manual and turn routine emotions into medical conditions, but their discussions—detailed here for the first time—rarely dwelled on the lasting consequences of their momentous decisions. Those expecting deep ruminations on what it means to call half the country mentally ill (the chief conclusion of the latest national survey),[7] may be surprised to learn that the psychiatrists' fundamental concerns included how best to keep the Freudians out of the room, how to reward the work of allies, and who should get credit for plucking a term out of a dictionary. Tackling a vast array of human experience, the *DSM* drains it of complexity and boils it down to blunt assertions that daily determine the fate of millions of lives, in this country as in many others.

The fourth edition appeared in 1994 with four hundred more pages and dozens of new disorders. It sold over a million copies, in part because insurance companies require a *DSM* diagnosis before they will authorize reimbursement, while defense attorneys cite it as gospel when trying to explain or mitigate the charges against their clients. Until the 1990s, moreover, the *DSM* competed with a rival diagnostic system: the *International Classification of Diseases* (*ICD*), published by the World Health Organization in Geneva, is more favorably disposed to psychoanalysis and less reliant on ambiguous narrative. Since the publication of *DSM-IV*, however, the European system has lost some of its cachet. The *DSM* has by contrast assumed global authority, an outcome greatly increasing the importance of its once-local arguments about social anxiety and related disorders. Indeed, with managed care and the pharmaceutical industry, this reference manual has begun to transform how the world thinks about mental health. As one psychoanalyst recently lamented to me, "We used to have a word for sufferers of ADHD. We called them *boys*."

When so many behaviors are viewed as disorders, is it possible to live a normal life without hitting up against one or more of them? "Where you thought your friends were just having normal troubles," explain Herb Kutchins and Stuart Kirk, "the developers of the American Psychiatric Association's diagnostic bible raise the possibility that you are surrounded by the mentally ill. Equally disconcerting to you, you may be among them."[8] In *Making Us Crazy*, Kutchins and Kirk largely ignored the many hundreds of letters that circulated behind the scenes to document this controversial chapter of psychiatry, doubtless because neither scholar had access to them. The picture looks even more troubling when one reproduces these discussions, as I do further on, and puts them under an uncompromising microscope.

After the DSM task forces had completed their work, the relabeling of our emotions advanced with lightning speed. Anxiety Disorders clinics soon sprang up at universities across the United States, Canada, and Britain to research and treat the problem. A few experts insisted they wanted to treat only "extreme shyness,"[9] but others admitted they couldn't distinguish between that trait and social anxiety disorder,[10] so they put them on the same hazy continuum. As the coauthors of *Social Anxiety Disorder: A Guide* explain with surprising nonchalance, "Where shyness ends and social anxiety disorder begins isn't clear. Some social anxiety is expected in everyone."[11] A generation ago, they might have insisted, "Some *shyness* is expected in everyone."

Building on this muddle, public relations firms were hired to hype ambiguous data and to raise the profile of the new disorders. And marketing departments spent tens of millions of dollars blurring the lines between social phobia and ordinary shyness so that both would strike us as debilitating conditions.

Wide-eyed health updates in the mass media dutifully reported the canny sound bites and "video news releases" that the drug companies sent them. One of many newspaper articles caught the right tone by warning readers, "You're Not Shy, You're Sick."[12] Even the *Wall Street Journal* succumbed, titling one piece, "Depression Pill May Help Treat the Acutely Shy," and another, "Easing Stage Fright Could Be as Simple as Swallowing a Pill." In both cases they meant more the long-term use of antidepressants like Paxil than the occasional use, before a stressful event, of beta-blockers like Propranolol.[13]

Meanwhile, *Psychology Today* helpfully dubbed the phobia "disorder of the decade,"[14] and estimates of the total U.S. population suffering from it soon swelled from 3.7 percent to as high as 18.7 percent, apparently making it "the third-most-common psychiatry disorder, behind only depressive disorder and alcohol dependence."[15] Murray Stein, the chief author of a study publishing that range and an aggressive proponent of shyness studies at the University of California, San Diego, became a trusted presence on television and in pharmaceutical brochures, urging Americans to seek treatment for their reticence. Few could know his influential article drew from a single study—a random telephone survey of urban Canadians.

For many psychiatrists and healthcare professionals, shyness is now one facet of a bona fide illness. Allegedly it almost rivals in magnitude depression, for which almost 200 million prescriptions are filled every year in this country alone, and apparently has become a pandemic. Lynne Henderson and Philip Zimbardo, colleagues at Stanford and codirectors of the Shyness Institute in Palo Alto, warn of a "public health danger that appears to be heading toward epidemic proportions."[16] And psychiatrists on a DSM working group claim that those "presenting complaints may represent the tip of the social phobic iceberg."[17] They also wonder whether the number of people who loathe giving speeches means that "public speaking phobia should be classified separately from the other Social Phobias."[18]

Meanwhile celebrities, quietly accepting large fees without needing to mention a drug's side effects, lament their social awkwardness (ironically, on television and in magazine interviews) and urge everyone who has felt the same to medicate themselves.[19] Talk shows air programs on topics such as "People Who Are Afraid of People" and invite viewers to "imagine a fear so paralyzing that you can't drive, shop, or even get a haircut."[20] Bookstores are replete with a staggering array of self-help cures for those "dying of embarrassment" and feeling they might even be "diagonally-parked in a parallel universe." All these books tout more or less the same remedies: face your fears, visualize competence, set practical goals in modest increments, but also be yourself.[21]

A representative of the National Institute of Mental Health explains that excessive shyness is "one of the worst neglected disorders of our time."[22] And skeptics are either dismissed or rebuked for putting others' lives at risk and delaying their relief from a severe psychiatric condition: We've scarcely begun to cure this underreported pandemic, they warn, insisting that even more people need to be on Paxil, Zoloft, or a comparable antidepressant. In just eight years (1985–1993), then, shyness ballooned into one of the most common psychiatric diagnoses in the Western world.

How did we get to this point? Were psychiatrists for decades really blind to a crippling illness troubling millions of people? Or did influential psychiatrists, partnering with (and often sponsored by) drug companies, hype a problem still afflicting just a tiny percentage of people in each country? If so, why did both groups depict an ordinary, if difficult, emotional state like shyness as a defect of brain chemistry that had to be treated by drugs? And what other moods and ordinary fears are likely to become major illnesses in the next edition of *DSM*, whose working groups have just begun meeting to discuss the 2011 publication?

In *Shyness: How Normal Behavior Became a Sickness*, I answer these pressing questions. I explain for the first time how social phobia, the most enigmatic and poorly defined anxiety disorder, became *the* psychosocial problem of our age. And I tell this story from several interlocking angles: the DSM task forces that created the disorders; the drug companies that branded them through clever marketing; the fiction and films that satirize both activities before representing our anxieties quite differently; and the larger trends and battles in especially American psychiatry, waged for over a century, to which anxiety is now a much-fought-over cornerstone.

Shyness draws on the American Psychiatric Association's vast archive of unpublished and hitherto unavailable letters, transcripts, and memoranda that were circulated among the leading figures. I also quote previously classified memos circulated among drug company executives; reproduce documents voicing grave concerns about the side effects of drugs that are now household names; and include probing interviews with all the leading psychiatrists in question.

First among these is Robert Spitzer, arguably the most influential psychiatrist in the twentieth century, who chaired the task force that reshaped the entire discipline. In his home by the Hudson River, he described to me how his colleagues devised new psychiatric problems, and shared some of the strategies he used to thwart his opponents. Other figures include his rival, Isaac Marks, a world-renowned phobia specialist in London who first developed the term "social anxiety," but now considers much of the literature about it an "advertising ploy";[23] and David Healy, a leading pharmacologist with close links to SmithKline Beecham and the clinical trials of Paxil, who for years has fought to make us aware of this drug's sometimes devastating side effects.

Aligned with Spitzer, by contrast, are Michael Liebowitz, a preeminent Columbia University psychiatrist who served on the DSM's subcommittee on anxiety disorders and did much to promote social phobia's standing as a "neglected disorder";[24] his frequent coauthor, Richard Heimberg, director of the Adult Anxiety Clinic at Temple University, whose work in the field began with studies on dating anxiety; and David M. Clark, Chair of Psychiatry at the University of London, who once advised the Blair government in Britain about social phobia's best remedies.

The combined effect of all these sources and documents isn't merely another exposé of the pharmaceutical industry, although details about its clever manipulation of our fears are increasingly becoming major news items. It is, after all, well known that the number of Washington lobbyists employed by our drug companies is far greater than the members of Congress, and that in 2005 antidepressants earned these companies $12.5 billion from national sales alone.[25]

Shyness instead presents the compelling inside story of how several eminent psychiatrists and their pharmaceutical sponsors turned a minor condition into a major illness. Part of this story, however, is that the tide is starting to turn. Many writers, pundits, and recovering patients are tired of the avalanche of drug-related ads in the media, and greet the newly publicized syndromes (including "intermittent explosive disorder," a euphemism for road rage) with bemusement, skepticism, and scorn. Skits on *Saturday Night Live* routinely deride the claims of big pharma ("If you're over forty-five and a gay male," they joke, "you could be suffering from queer-loss. . . . Ask your doctor if Gaystrogen® is right for you").[26] A growing list of films, novels, and patient support groups is even more scathing, the latter springing up when drug treatments go horribly wrong.

These forces combine to form a powerful backlash against psychiatry and the pharmaceutical industry. My book not only unites these disparate perspectives, but also launches a deeper investigation into the meaning of shyness and anxiety in earlier times, when neither term implied what it does today. I also consider the philosophical consequences of medicalizing a large number of human emotions. My behind-the-scenes perspective confirms that deep-seated conflicts of interest, buried research data, professional ambition, and fierce marketing campaigns together have grossly exaggerated social phobia and avoidant personality disorder, turning behavior we recently accepted, and even welcomed, into pathologies needing medical treatment.

The unavoidable conclusion is that we've narrowed healthy behavior so dramatically that our quirks and eccentricities—the *normal* emotional range of adolescence and adulthood—have become problems we fear and expect drugs to fix. We are no longer citizens justifiably concerned about our world, who sometimes need to be alone. Our afflictions are chronic anxiety, personality or mood disorders; our solitude is a marker for mild psychosis; our dissent, a symptom of Oppositional Defiant Disorder; our worries, chemical imbalances that drugs must cure.

This conclusion amounts to neither Orwellian paranoia nor an alarmist *Brave New World* scenario whose full effects will unfold generations from now. "Mood brightening" is already pervasive in our culture, driven by endless encouragement to be "up" and "on" around the clock. Performance-enhancing drugs are used in scores of occupations—by athletes, musicians, white-collar workers, and laborers. While voicing concern about the drugs' sometimes worrisome track records, some doctors fear that antidepressants are causing widespread emotional blunting—altering the strength of our attachments, how well we can concentrate, and even how deeply we fall in love.

The sad consequence is a vast, perhaps unrecoverable, loss of emotional range, an impoverishment of human experience. Not so long ago, the reclusive Emily Dickinson could write eloquently about what ensues after great pain ("a formal feeling comes—/ The Nerves sit ceremonious, like Tombs").[27] Nathaniel Hawthorne could transform his reticence into a new way of engaging with the world, which one critic aptly calls a "philosophy of shyness."[28] And Henry David Thoreau could press for solitude by living in a hut some miles from town. Refusing to accept mail or pay his poll tax, he shunned other people in order to "live deliberately."[29] These days, Dickinson would be on Prozac; Hawthorne would be on *Oprah,* lamenting his plight as a social phobe; and Thoreau—arraigned before a judge—would receive a DSM diagnosis for citing civil disobedience as the right to follow his conscience. In the nineteenth century, Thoreau, Hawthorne, Dickinson, and countless others gave us the wisdom that ensues from deep reflection. Today, psychiatrists offer us a pill.

To help account for this fundamental shift in thinking, I take anxiety as a test case, showing how psychiatry and its definitions of illness have changed quite radically since the 1970s. I open with a brief history of anxiety and shyness, contrasting modern perspectives with those of ancient Greece, the Renaissance, and the Victorian period. I then recount in two chapters how the DSM-III task force went about creating 112 new disorders, seven of which involve anxiety. While these chapters examine the ensuing wrangles in scrupulous—and, for some participants, possibly excruciating—detail, the second of them (Chapter 3) focuses on the peculiar fate of "introverted personality disorder" as it evolved into "schizoid personality disorder," a mild form of psychosis.

The story then turns to describing how the drug companies promoted these disorders, spending millions of dollars trying to persuade us that run-of-the-mill behaviors might stem from a chemical imbalance in the brain. As their drug treatments have spawned a litany of side effects, some of them quite dangerous, Chapter 5 explains clearly how the drugs are meant to work and why they often fail. Given the difficulties many patients experience trying to come off these pills, I point to alternative treatments that distinguish chronic anxiety from routine fears. Asking whether "social phobia" and "avoidant personality disorder" may at times represent a type of noncompliance with our culture's demand for extroversion, I invert the discussion in Chapter 6 and examine four satires that constitute a growing backlash against neuropsychiatry and pharmacology: Jonathan Franzen's prize-winning novel *The Corrections,* Zach Braff's film *Garden State,* Alan Lightman's novel *The Diagnosis,* and Will Self's novella *Dr. Mukti.* A final chapter sounds some of the broader diagnostic and ethical issues.

In sum, *Shyness: How Normal Behavior Became a Sickness* provides not only a comprehensive picture of how an ordinary trait became a mental disorder, but also a new and vitally important perspective on anxiety today. Insisting that we're overdiagnosed and overmedicated, it describes in precise detail how psychiatrists, public relations consultants, and drug companies successfully turned shyness, self-consciousness, and even introspection into major psychiatric disorders.

1

THE HUNDRED YEARS' WAR OVER ANXIETY

Anxiety, a famous psychoanalyst once observed, is one of the few things that never deceives.[1] It is also one of those rare elements of psychology that seem constant as it ripples through the ages, tormenting its sufferers with persistent, sometimes grinding dread. Those familiar with the sensation know it feels dreadfully tangible even when the fear in question is often imaginary. But has anxiety always been tied to shyness, or is the connection more recent?

In listing the first recorded use of the word *anxiety*, the *Oxford English Dictionary* names an emotion we're likely to recognize instantly, though its spelling and context will seem slightly foreign: "There dyed he," Sir Thomas More writes in 1525 about Jesus of Nazareth, "without grudge, without anxietie."[2] More used the word to suggest worry or concern rather than illness, but toward the end of the nineteenth century medical lexicons began calling it a morbid "condition of agitation and depression [whose] . . . marked expression . . . forms a dangerous symptom in acute diseases."[3] And somehow it feels right that the word's meaning and history expanded to include extreme states. It might even be odd to have a stress-free definition of *anxiety*.

The word *shyness* also boasts a long history, and in earlier periods had meanings that modern commentators are apt to overlook. When people in the Middle Ages used the adjective *shy*, they meant horses and other animals that were skittish or easily frightened. Only in the seventeenth century did the word cross over to include humans—sometimes, entire peo-

11

ples—who are reticent, suspicious, even untrustworthy.[4] All of these meanings are broadly comparable, yet no two are identical. One might even ponder how the shy slipped into appearing untrustworthy, as if being cautious were so provocative that it entitled strangers to question one's integrity.

In his *Anatomy of Melancholy,* also dating from the seventeenth century, Richard Burton described what can happen when shyness combines or collides with anxiety. He portrays a man Hippocrates found notable, because "through bashfulness, suspicion, and timorousness, [he] will not be seen abroad; 'loves darkness as life, and cannot endure the light,' or to sit in lightsome places; his hat still in his eyes, he will neither see nor be seen by his goodwill. He dare not come in company, for fear he should be misused, disgraced, overshoot himself in gesture or speeches, or be sick; he thinks every man observes him, aims at him, derides him, owes him malice."[5]

Scholars today like mentioning this passage because it strikes them as a perfect example of early social phobia.[6] But is that an accurate comparison or one telling us more about contemporary assumptions? There is, for starters, the small problem of anachronism. The Greeks had no name for social phobia; given their linguistic and philosophical gifts, they doubtless would have coined one (like *xenophobia,* or ξενοφοβία, a deep fear of foreigners) if they had considered social phobia a problem, much less an illness.

True, the Greeks recognized stage fright. According to Burton, they even described the heart-pounding dread that often "amazeth many men that are to speak, or show themselves in public assemblies, or before some great personages, as Tully confessed of himself, that he trembled still at the beginning of his speech; and Demosthenes, that great orator of Greece, before Phillipus."[7] But they credited this fear to known circumstances, not the peculiar symptoms of a mental disorder. They also prized bashfulness, especially in women and younger men, and drew firm distinctions—as our psychiatrists used to do—between chronic anxiety and its more routine counterparts.

"Since ancient times," Isaac Marks confirms in his classic 1969 study, *Fears and Phobias,* cultures have recognized that "minor degrees of social anxiety are, of course, perfectly normal and compatible with excellent function."[8] Despite his key role in grasping why social interactions make some people anxious, Marks now claims that psychiatrists have eroded crucial distinctions between normal and acute anxiety to hype their own research.[9]

Another problem with psychiatrists' notions about the history of our pathologies: Hippocrates's neutral description doesn't attribute the man's behavior to a single cause, much less to a deeply ingrained psychological one. On the contrary, his allusion to misuse suggests that the man's avoidance stems from a justified fear of mistreatment, perhaps because of prejudice, ostracism, or a severe misunderstanding with his neighbors. One of the inflections in the *Oxford English Dictionary* definition of *anxiety* alludes to groups and individuals who are "timidly or cautiously averse to encountering or having to do with some specified person or thing," including fear of invasion or retribution.

Hippocrates's perspective then shifts dramatically by invoking disgrace. Before we rush to call this a malady, we must clarify whether the man's reaction is due to circumstances or to lasting temperament. And we can't really do that, because Hippocrates (echoed in turn by Burton) presents an open-ended sketch, not a straightforward case study. Although he considers the man's behavior notable, he views it more as a foible than as an illness.

How different our perspective is today. Nowadays experts are likely to say the man has a chemical imbalance that needs medical or psychiatric attention. Any hint that his woes may be existential or circumstantial pales before this bedrock explanation: he has low levels of serotonin and needs medication to make him well again. When people are well, after all, we presume they will be sociable.

Still, there are no firm links between health and sociability, and—perhaps more surprising to many—there is no scientific correlation between low serotonin and depression, anxiety, or anger management. Although some psychopharmacologists and drug companies have found it useful to say otherwise, the simplification that low serotonin *causes* anxiety or depression is, in one critic's words, little more than "vacuous biobabble." According to David Healy, author of 12 acclaimed books and more than 120 refereed articles on the topic, the reasons we're anxious or depressed are far more complex; they involve intricate (often unknown) facets of our psychology, biology, society, and even environment.[10] Nurtured by a litany of drug-company advertisements, however, we more often hear the contrary argument about serotonin, because reducing the brain's formidable complexity to a simple metaphor can look like a foolproof explanation for almost anything.

Although simple definitions in the *Oxford English Dictionary* contradict the idea that anxiety and shyness have meant the same thing throughout history, it is useful to add that many lively discussions of shyness and stage fright, including Darwin's *Expression of the Emotions in Man and Animals* (1872), describe these phenomena without any hint of pathology. "Almost every one," Darwin maintains, "is extremely nervous when first addressing a public assembly, and most men remain so throughout their lives; but this appears to depend on the consciousness of a great coming exertion [especially one which is in some way strange to us], with its associated effects on the [nervous] system, rather than on shyness."[11]

The turning point in these discussions came roughly a decade later, when psychiatrists in the 1880s (known at the time as "alienists") began viewing shyness as a morbid condition that bordered on pathology. In historical terms, the battle over how we define or diagnose shyness and similar kinds of anxiety is thus quite recent—it began just over a century ago. But you wouldn't know that from reading much of the literature on the subject. Psychiatrists are adamant that the problems they have unearthed echo through the ages, a claim the mass media generally take very seriously.

One reason psychiatrists cite historical anecdotes is to give their arguments more clout. Adopting this strategy lets them build scholarly consensus around the urgent treatment of a neglected "disorder." If a powerhouse physician like Hippocrates allegedly thought the same way about X or Y, then failing to act promptly on fresh evidence of the same problem looks downright irresponsible, no matter how wide the historical chasm. Skeptics will look painfully obtuse, moreover, if they doubt the connection; the historical comparison will even bring the most intricate debate to a screeching halt. ("You'll have to argue with Hippocrates, I'm afraid; I'm just slightly restating his point.") Best of all, this approach lets the psychiatrist rewrite history: he or she can weave past incidents into recent discoveries and newly revised theories.

"Historical literature is rich in descriptions of persons who probably had intermittent explosive disorder," claims Susan McElroy at the start of a foundational essay on the illness. The *Diagnostic and Statistical Manual of Mental Disorders, 3rd Edition* (DSM-III) first officially recognized this "disorder" in 1980, almost two decades before McElroy's essay appeared, but her strategy is shorthand for asking, "What took them so long?"[12]

The idea here, nicely understated, is that her colleagues have failed to appreciate the magnitude of a problem everyone else knows a great deal about. Just open a classic work of literature or a historical treatise, she implies, and in every century you'll find someone with symptoms almost identical to those listed in DSM-III or DSM-IV. It doesn't matter whether the person was Diogenes, Richard II, Friedrich Nietzsche, or the "angry young men" who rebelled in 1950s Britain (chiefly playwrights John Osborne and Harold Pinter and novelists Alan Sillitoe and John Braine). Nor does it matter if the reasons for that person's anger were vastly different or were, in the end, quite justified. What matters is pronouncing him mentally ill, for doing so shores up the validity of one's diagnosis.

To intellectual historians, this approach looks painfully crude, to say the least. Giving facile explanations for past events lets one glide over incongruities and anachronisms, turning major differences between historical periods and cultures into a single narrative that makes sense today. As Helen Saul puts it in *Phobias,* "Hippocrates saw people with many different phobias over the years, ranging from agoraphobia and social phobia to animal phobias and other fears still common today."[13]

According to Saul, social phobia recedes more or less unchanged from our world to that of ancient Greece. But why stop there? In 2001 a team of psychiatrists in California declared that as Samson, the biblical figure, met at least six of DSM-IV's seven criteria for the illness, he might have suffered from "antisocial personality disorder." Sadly, the psychiatrists didn't appear to be joking. "Recognition of the diagnosis of ASPD for Samson may help in better understanding the biblical story," they opined, "and, in general, may help in instances when a leader has ASPD. Also, we hope it stimulates interest in the history of ASPD." Now it's true that Samson didn't exactly plan ahead or "conform to social norms." His "irritability and aggressiveness" also resulted in a "reckless disregard for safety of self or others," all of these being criteria in the DSM. But the Philistines had gouged out his eyes after Delilah repeatedly betrayed him—factors the scientists either didn't know or conveniently overlooked.[14]

You might think that having one's eyes gouged out after betrayal by a loved one would be reason enough to express a certain amount of fury. However, if your thinking is fixed in a different groove, all such loosely related examples become illustrations—helpfully recovered—of disorders that not only run the gamut of history but do so merely as variations on our current syndromes.

The risks of portraying anxiety, fear, or depression as historical constants should be clear. One loses all sense of what is distinctive about the way different eras and cultures represented these traits; and one drains the emotions in these examples of all complexity, as anyone glancing at, say, Kierkegaard's metaphysical treatise on *The Concept of Anxiety* and hereditary sin will appreciate.[15]

Put another way, the era W. H. Auden later dubbed "The Age of Anxiety," because it encompassed the unsparing atrocities of World War II, the Holocaust, and the use of atomic bombs against the Japanese, doesn't align well with the fear that Thucydides said arose in the fifth century B.C. between the Athenians and Spartans, in *History of the Peloponnesian War.* But it's comforting to say otherwise. Doing so tells us we are less unusual and isolated than we might think; and it empowers us to reimagine our individual and collective destinies, based on a notion that we can alter our brain chemistry effortlessly, with almost surgical precision.

In 1994, at the height of the giddy media coverage of Prozac, *Newsweek* asked readers if they were "Shy? Forgetful? Anxious? Fearful? Obsessed?"—then presented them with a simple cure ("How Science Will Let You Change Your Personality with a Pill"). The idea was that shyness, absentmindedness, and a host of other routine traits were medical conditions best treated by drugs. "For the first time in human history," the neuropsychiatrist Richard Restak announced, "we will be in a position to design our own brain." Pharmacology would let us design brains unafraid of eating alone in restaurants, signing checks in public, and using public rest-rooms (the principal characteristics of social phobia).[16]

Newsweek may not be as exacting as *Clinical Psychopharmacology,* but its coverage is part of a trend offering breathtakingly simple explanations and remedies for our emotional and social problems. Our culture has swal-lowed this trend with few questions or concerns about side effects, perhaps because it's easy to trade quick fixes and the illusion of pain-free remedies for complex, enigmatic problems.

This outcome may also be tied to our distance from sources in the past that had different—often, better—explanations for anxiety and its reme-dies. But pathologizing shyness only aggravates that loss. If the Samson story is merely a parable of antisocial personality disorder, then it is no longer a tale of betrayal, or of man's relation to a higher spiritual authority, or even of his sexual vulnerabilities. Still, if we accept the glib logic of *Newsweek,* all we need undergo is "a kind of psychopharmacological plas-tic surgery."[17]

In his bestseller *Listening to Prozac,* Peter Kramer called aspects of this emerging field "cosmetic psychopharmacology" and worried that they conveyed a strong, perhaps unrealistic demand for mood brightening.[18] But it's doubtful so many Americans would be taking antidepressants for stage fright, fear of public bathrooms, and other routine matters if psychi-atrists and the DSM hadn't first convinced them that these behaviors were aspects of a serious mental illness.

So much for the transhistorical argument. What of the cross-cultural one?

Those saying social phobia is global sometimes point to a short (four-page) essay that Kutaiba Chaleby published in 1987. The piece, "Social Phobia in Saudis," was based on 35 outpatients he observed at the King Faisal Specialist Hospital in Riyadh. And while those apparently "met the DSM-III criteria of social phobia" (which we'll investigate more thor-oughly in the next chapter) Chaleby had to concede, halfway through his paper, that of that group "only 22 (63%) actually *presented* with social pho-bia."[19]

Most people would find it awkward to generalize about a large country from 22 patients. Yet Chaleby has no qualms about writing, two paragraphs later: "The high incidence of social phobia in Saudi Arabia is the first observation worthy of discussion. Is there a genetic predisposition?"

Based on his research, Chaleby swiftly pronounces social phobia more common in Saudi Arabia than in England. "Western literature indicates," he states rather breezily, without references, "that phobia disorders affect less than 1% of a given population . . . However, in Saudi Arabia social phobia occurs more frequently. Our outpatient clinic statistics indicate that it represents about 12–13% of the neurotic disorders seen." Anyone dazzled by this claim must ignore Chaleby's rather painful admission, in the next paragraph, that "four [of his] case records were lost." They also must overlook how small a group 12 percent of his sample represents.

Chaleby does, however, make one key observation, which neither he nor his admirers heed: "The frequency with which a condition presents for treatment is not a good guide to its frequency in the community."[20] This wise point alerts us to the danger of self-fulfilling prophecies: As clinics are never representative samples of a population, one should never try to draw trends from their small, nonrandom population.

Like Chaleby, psychiatry—American psychiatry in particular—has taken such gray areas and turned them into supposedly clear-cut, diagnostic categories encompassing vast swaths of our behavior. Consequently, it is increasingly difficult for psychiatrists to differentiate shyness and social phobia. Many of them simply view the first as a prelude to the second.

A more interesting but still vexed point of comparison lies between Western definitions of social phobia and Japanese-Korean perspectives on *taijin kyofusho,* which approximates to *anthropophobia* and often takes the form of a person's complete withdrawal from society. The psychology underlying such behavior is, however, quite different from that said to cause social phobia. According to specialists, those with social phobia shun activities that might incur criticism and embarrassment to themselves, whereas those afflicted with taijin kyofusho withdraw from society for fear of embarrassing *other people* (especially parents). Western psychiatrists classify social phobia as an anxiety disorder; in Japan and South Korea, taijin kyofusho is closer to a form of shame "thoroughly in concert with Japanese cultural sensibilities," as Arthur Kleinman puts it, "but quite foreign to North American" ones.[21]

Anxiety, then, is an interesting challenge to those seeking black-and-white distinctions, for it tends unerringly to fall between them. Freud called it a "riddle" and Darwin "an extremely obscure subject," because its causes and effects baffle so many who would render them clear.[22] It is almost pointless to discuss the well-known biological consequences of anxiety (a racing heart, shortness of breath, sweaty palms, and so on) without assessing what real or imagined factor causes them. Freud's and Darwin's examples rarely discuss the potential causes, moreover, without hinting at contributing social factors (overweening parental expectations, class shame, sexual guilt, and so on).

Since our psychology is sandwiched unevenly between the social and the biological, it ends up mistranslating many of their varied stimuli, pressures, and cues. We might even think of anxiety as a symptom of that mistranslation, telling us pointedly when the biological, psychological, and social *fail* to align.

After so many still exciting discoveries about the brain, neuroscientists are apt to think they have resolved every aspect of this conundrum. But the more they stress these discoveries, the quicker they forget that anxiety concerns far more than misfiring neurons, shifting levels of serotonin, and genetic configurations. It also involves the mind—which is to say, the strange, unusual turns of our consciousness, themselves in thrall to vivid memories, irrational fantasies, persistent associations, and sometimes-inexplicable impulses.

As these terms can sound quaint and unscientific, neuropsychiatrists often scoff at any mention of them. It's easier (and more tempting) to make bold generalizations about anxiety, as when the authors of a 1997 guide to social phobia say that a "genetic predisposition" is probably the cause. "Just as familiar features such as hair and eye color, facial shape and body size are often recognizable across generations," they state in a questionable comparison, "sensitivity to scrutiny and criticism may be passed on from generation to generation. . . . The child of two shy parents may inherit genetic code which amplifies shyness into social anxiety disorder."[23]

Elliot Valenstein calls such arguments reductive, even insidious, ways of "blaming the brain." That things run in families "by itself is not evidence of a genetic cause," he says pointedly, "as poverty also runs in families." Valenstein provides a list of other devastating rejoinders:

- A person's mental state and experience can modify the brain just as surely as the other way around. When there is a correlation between two events, we should not assume that we always know which way causation flows.
- The drugs used to treat a mental disorder . . . may induce long-lasting biochemical and even structural changes [to the brain], which in the past were claimed to be the cause of the disorder, but may actually be an effect of the treatment.
- Inferring the cause of an illness . . . from the effectiveness of a treatment [is] a form of "*ex juvantibus* reasoning (Latin: from that which produces health)," which may be grossly misleading and turn out to be wildly inaccurate.
- Asserting that a disorder has a biological cause [doesn't mean that] a biological treatment will be most effective. A condition may have a biological origin, but may be best treated by a psychological approach, and the converse is equally true.

And finally:

- [Neuropsychiatrists] assume . . . that anyone who criticizes the chemical theories of mental disorders must be against all biological explanations of behavior. Of course, this need not be the case.[24]

A neuroscientist himself, Valenstein insists he has perspectives on human behavior that are quite different from these.

The authors of *Social Anxiety Disorder* might respond that knowing the brain is responsible for various "malfunctions" is a kindness and relief to patients, because it sidelines any argument about judgment or blame. Narrowing the many possible causes of anxiety to one or two—a "genetic code" or "abnormalities in functioning of some parts of their anxiety apparatus"—might also ensure more rapid and effective treatment.[25] But do neuropsychiatrists really know that "genetic code [may] amplif[y] shyness into social anxiety disorder," or are they simply saying they would like it to be so? And is raising such possibilities more scientific or credible than arguing that anxiety surpasses hereditary factors, engaging aspects of psychology that are still unknown to us?

———————

Since the late 1970s, the tension between biochemical and psychological perspectives has repeatedly boiled over. But the wrangle started roughly a century ago when two German psychiatrists began urging their colleagues to classify, then treat, abnormalities of the brain. In this way they formalized a split with psychologists still stubbornly committed to healing the mind.

One of the earliest proponents of "scientific psychiatry" and holder of the first chair of psychiatry in Germany, Wilhelm Griesinger is famous for asserting, "Mental diseases are diseases of the brain." When his acclaimed *Mental Pathology and Therapeutics* went to a second edition in 1867, he added this ringing declaration: "The first step towards a knowledge of . . . symptoms is their locality—to which organ do the indications of the disease belong? . . . Physiological and pathological facts show us that this organ can only be the brain; we therefore primarily, and in every case of mental disease, recognize a morbid action of that organ."[26]

In similar tones and conviction, his compatriot Emil Kraepelin argued some 40 years later: "The principal requisite in the knowledge of mental diseases is an accurate definition of the separate disease processes. . . . Until this is known we cannot hope to understand the relationship between mental symptoms of disease and the morbid physical processes underlying them, or indeed the causes of the entire disease process."[27] But Kraepelin didn't merely state the importance of this goal. He tried to prove that psychiatric disorders stem exclusively from biological and hereditary causes, so crystallizing the "psychiatric style of reasoning" that led to his being dubbed the father of the profession.[28]

As Kraepelin believed the course of each disorder was predictable, he set about classifying them by common patterns; he is also famous for offering the first sustained analysis of *schizophrenia*, calling it *dementia praecox*. His biological perspective put him at loggerheads with Freud, his contemporary and principal rival, who insisted that psychiatric disorders stem from varied, sometimes unpredictable psychological conflicts. Freud remains more famous, but among professionals Kraepelin is now the guide. His commitment to charting the course, outcome, and prognosis of every known and neglected illness made him immensely popular in his own time, though it also led him to rule out psychological factors in ways that might seem baffling today.

CLASSIFICATION OF MENTAL DISEASES

		LECTURE
INTRODUCTION		I.
MELANCHOLIA		I.
MANIACAL-DEPRESSIVE CONDITIONS	DEPRESSED CONDITIONS	II.
	MANIACAL EXCITEMENT	VII.
	MIXED CONDITIONS	VIII.
DEMENTIA PRÆCOX (OF ADOLESCENCE)	DEMENTIA PRÆCOX	III.
	PARANOIDAL FORMS	XVI.
	FINAL STAGES	XXI.
GENERAL PARALYSIS (OF THE INSANE)	STATES OF DEPRESSION	V.
	STATES OF GRANDEUR	X.
	FINAL STAGES	XX.
KATATONIA	KATATONIC STUPOR	IV.
	KATATONIC EXCITEMENT	IX.
PARANOIA (MONOMANIA, PROGRESSIVE SYSTEMATIZED INSANITY)		XV.
AFTER ACUTE DISEASES (DELIRIUM OF COLLAPSE)		XII.
AFTER HEAD INJURIES (TRAUMATIC)		XXV.
EPILEPTIC		VI.
HYSTERICAL		XXVI.
PUERPERAL		XIV.
ALCOHOLIC	ALCOHOLIC MENTAL DISTURBANCES	XI.
	CHRONIC ALCOHOLISM (COMBINED FORMS)	XVIII.
MORPHINISM, COCAINISM		XIX.
VARIETIES OF IMBECILITY	FROM COARSE BRAIN LESIONS	XXII.
	OLD AGE (SENILE)	XXIII.
	EPILEPTIC	XXIV.
	CONGENITAL	XXVIII.
	CRETINISM	XXX.
VARIETIES OF DELIRIUM		XIII.
VARIETIES OF DELUSIONS		XVII.
IRREPRESSIBLE IDEAS AND IRRESISTIBLE FEARS		XXVII.
MORBID PERSONALITIES		XXIX.
CRETINISM—CONCLUDING REMARKS		XXX.

(Left margin label spanning the table: VARIETIES OF INSANITY.)

Emil Kraepelin's classification of mental diseases (*Lectures on Clinical Psychiatry,* 1904)

At the start of his lecture on melancholia, for instance, Kraepelin insists, "from the medical point of view, it is disturbances in the *physical foundations* of mental life which should occupy most of our attention." Not surprisingly, he groups under "varieties of insanity" even mental illnesses such as depression and "states of grandeur." But a closer examination reveals that these can derive from merely "irrepressible ideas and irresistible fears." Several case studies in his influential *Lectures on Clinical Psychiatry* may also make us wonder how his work could have a comeback in leading psychiatric circles.

"I will first place before you a farmer, aged fifty-nine," he briskly tells colleagues and the reader,

> who was admitted to the hospital a year ago. . . . His expression is dejected. The corners of his mouth are rather drawn down, and his eyebrows drawn together. He usually stares in front of him, but he glances up when he is spoken to. On being questioned about his illness, he breaks into lamentations, saying that he did not tell the whole truth on his admission, but concealed the fact that he had fallen into sin in his youth and practised uncleanness with himself; everything he did was wrong. "I am so apprehensive, so wretched; I cannot lie still for anxiety. O God, if I had only not transgressed so grievously!"

The farmer is married, with four healthy children, adds Kraepelin, and "in all other respects . . . behaves naturally"; but when he recalls masturbating as a youth (as he has felt compelled to do for over a year), the man starts trembling and pants in "broken sentences, interrupted by wailing and groaning," that he'll be "carried off [by] the Evil One."[29]

We might find this case poignant, for by today's standards the man's guilty pleasure would seem normal, even healthy, behavior. That such extreme torment could stem chiefly from masturbation tells us a lot about the religious and social mores of the time. Kraepelin's detached response is, if anything, more staggering. Making no allusion to unwarranted guilt, and doing nothing to alleviate the farmer's grinding anxiety from involuntary recollection of earlier memories, he says the man suffers from melancholia (an "involution psychosis") and blithely adds, "Our first patient only made a rather feeble attempt at suicide." Instead of voicing surprise or pathos, he suggests even a hint of criticism that the man's resolution was too weak to carry out the deed.[30]

"The most striking feature of this clinical picture is the *apprehensive depression,*" Kraepelin avers. He concedes that such behavior might superficially resemble that of a healthy person, but in the farmer's case "the apprehension . . . has lasted for months, with increasing severity. This is the diagnostic sign of its morbidity. It is true that the patient himself refers to the sins of his youth as the cause of the apprehension, but it is clear that, even if they were ever really committed, they did not particularly disturb him before his illness; his conscience has only awakened now."[31]

The clearest sign of the farmer's congenital pathology, apparently, is that he did not recoil from masturbation at the time. That he requires extensive medication and prolonged treatment in an asylum is also seemingly caused by "*delusions of sin,*" which bear no relation to his past.[32] What the man himself says is of no importance, though, so the psychiatrist can dismiss it.

As Kraepelin was wedded to thinking that the farmer, like other patients, has an innate, morbid condition with "*physical foundations,*" the psychological facets of the case make plain the serious limitations of his perspective and the genuine risks of reviving it today. Had he spent a moment considering the man's psychological traits, including the ones he powerfully articulates, Kraepelin might have grasped (as Freud eventually did) how naive and reductive it is to view delays in symptom formation as signs of congenital illness or moral failing. The mind is often traumatized when situations causing horror are *repeated,* sometimes years after the initial shock. "Deferred action" explains why one might emerge psychologically unscathed from a serious car accident, only to experience acute nausea or dread years later, if one is so unfortunate as to have a near miss with a second car.[33]

Despite the literalism of Kraepelin's approach, many neuropsychiatrists praise his desire to establish "an accurate definition of the separate disease processes": Robert Spitzer and his handpicked team on the DSM-III task force tried, in essence, to copy the earlier diagnostic template. So it is crucial to ask whether Kraepelin succeeded in this endeavor. After all, a key problem he and Griesinger faced, which their advocates play down or ignore altogether, is that "mental diseases . . . present but very few lesions that have positively distinctive characteristics, and furthermore there is the extreme difficulty of correlating physical and mental morbid processes." While it is therefore "extremely difficult to ascertain the relationship between the causes and the symptoms" of mental diseases, it is, Kraepelin conceded, "*almost impossible* to establish a fundamental distinction between the normal and the morbid mental state."[34] But that didn't stop him from trying.

No one would dispute that Kraepelin spent hours documenting his patients' "distinctive characteristics." But as we've seen in his clinical work, it is one thing to observe such traits and quite another to establish beyond doubt that they have a clear and exclusive biological cause. Kraepelin wanted above all to prove that psychological symptoms have unambiguous "*physical foundations.*" Nonetheless, his distinction between normal and morbid mental states kept collapsing because the distinction itself was, in his words, "*almost impossible* to establish." He ended up translating the psychological back into the physiological, in ways that were reductive and misleading.

———————

What, then, was the appeal of Victorian psychiatry in the 1970s and 1980s? We need to ask the question because, for many commentators and psychiatrists, the recent turn to Kraepelin inexplicably combines twenty-first-century neuropsychiatry with nineteenth-century methodology. One psychoanalyst remarked: "It's extraordinary. *Kraepelin.* They're going back to Kraepelin."[35] The reasons for this backward glance range from preference to necessity.

Although much of Kraepelin's work is crude, the new disorders that Spitzer's task force created needed empirical and intellectual validation. It wasn't enough merely to pull several different names for them "out of the classificatory hat," as David Healy puts it in *The Antidepressant Era.*[36] The group needed corroborating research and an intellectual tradition that would bolster its sometimes flimsy categories.

Turning to psychoanalysis for guidance would have revived a disciplinary war over the unconscious and repressed memory, so the task force and its later acolytes devised an ingenious alternative. Calling themselves neo-Kraepelinians, they drew a neat but deceptive line from their work to Kraepelin's in the 1900s.[37] Bypassing Freud altogether and thus further marginalizing their Freudian colleagues, they used the categories of Kraepelin and others as a pretext to model anxiety and depression after *pre*-Freudian tenets.

One might say that the neo-Kraepelinians had little choice. For in ridiculing psychoanalysis, they inadvertently pulled the rug out from under their feet. Although Spitzer's task force professed no interest in the causes of each disorder, implicitly the group still needed a theory of pathology and the emotions that would seem quasi-psychological without looking Freudian. So, from this perspective, they had to revive Victorian models of disease as these partisans championed biological explanations for mental disorders.

Alternatively, one could argue—as Spitzer and several other influential neuropsychiatrists did—that Freud, in breaking with Victorian psychiatry, had misconstrued the biological foundations of psychiatric illnesses and taken the profession in the wrong direction. The best way to remedy his mistake, they reasoned, was to return to his precursors and reclassify everything as a medical condition. Biological maladaption therefore supplanted Freud's argument that some of our actions and motivations are unconscious. (Even so, Kraepelin ingeniously smuggled the unconscious back in as "irrepressible ideas and irresistible fears.") Either way, the emphasis on Victorian psychiatry emboldened the task force and its followers to make an end run around psychoanalysis and act as if its legacy and clinical emphases either had vanished or no longer mattered.

Nowadays, if you open a textbook on social phobia and other anxiety disorders you are likely to come across several references to Kraepelin and Griesinger; incredibly, you will find almost nothing on the thousands of books, articles, and treatises that dominated American and European psychiatry for most of its history, from the mid-1890s until the early 1960s. The sixth edition of the *Comprehensive Textbook of Psychiatry* is unusual in granting that "psychoanalytic theories of phobias are now mainly of historical interest but are included for purposes of completeness."[38] In most other textbooks, you would be pressed to find even a paragraph on such theories. The rewriting of psychiatry's history has been so complete, it is as if Freudianism never happened. Consequently, the unconscious can appear as either a biological anomaly or the mad hallucinations of a scientific impostor.

We've already seen glimpses of this revisionist strategy at work. Enthusiasm for it grew so strong that in the mid-1990s an influential psychopharmacologist deeply hostile to what he calls "soft-headed" or "pseudo" psychiatry announced it was time to update Richard Burton's *Anatomy of*

Melancholy in advancing the conceptual value of *humoral theory*.[39] Without blinking, Hagop Akiskal began invoking Aristotle, Galen, Aurelianus, Soranus, and other examples of Greco-Roman medicine in a bewildering attempt to orient 1990s psychiatry around the four temperaments: the sanguine, melancholic, choleric, and phlegmatic. According to Akiskal, himself an ally of Spitzer's, these last two temperaments have such affinities with "borderline" and "avoidant" personality disorders that the Classical and Renaissance concepts have "a very modern ring to them."[40] So while David Barlow and Michael Liebowitz were stating that "psychoanalytic theories of phobias are now mainly of historical interest," their colleagues were engaged in validating theories millennia out of date.[41]

Apart from historical inaccuracy, the other key problem stemming from psychopharmacology's turn to pre-Freudian theory is that Griesinger and Kraepelin had painfully limited notions of what is normal. Consequently, they were quick to call vast amounts of behavior "morbid" and "pathological"—behavior that colleagues with more catholic views thought problematic only if it caused the patient undue stress or misery.

Freud began his work as a neuropsychiatrist steeped in similar hidebound judgments, but one reason many humanists and clinicians still admire him is that he spent the rest of his career questioning, then undoing, such judgments. He did so, moreover, to a point where he not only depathologized vast amounts of behavior, but overturned a coercive, sometimes unethical insistence that individuals should *always* sacrifice and adapt their behavior for the greater good.

These distinctions may seem trivial and academic, but in truth they are neither. The criteria psychiatry adopts when diagnosing mental and mood disorders have enormous implications for the general public. If one accepts Griesinger's and Kraepelin's normative perspectives on character and social phobia, as many neuropsychiatrists have, it makes sense to view even minor departures from them as maladaptive and thus requiring treatment.

One begins from a presumed but unstated norm and diagnoses much or all that fails to accord with it. However, the editors of *Abnormal Psychology and Modern Life* concede that "for psychological disorder[s], . . . we have no ideal, or even universally 'normal,' model of human mental and behavioral functioning to use as a base of comparison. Thus we find considerable confusion and disagreement as to just what is or is not normal, a confusion aggravated by changing values and expectations in society at large."[42]

We could put this slightly differently: Whenever assessments of what is normal are at stake, it is both difficult and momentous to decide what are reasonable and unreasonable departures from it. Most people have silent and sensible notions of what is justifiable anger, for instance, and thus when it is *not* appropriate publicly to express it. But how does one codify those standards in a manual of mental disorders that will go on to sell by the million, determining worldwide standards of mental health? The issue becomes even more vexed when one tries to gauge reasonable amounts of sociability and appropriate degrees of social anxiety—especially when Darwin and Marks insist we are abnormal if we *don't* experience some form of the latter.

Despite immense advances in knowledge between Kraepelin's day and ours, the "extreme difficulty" he experienced in connecting mental effects with physical causes continues. Psychiatrists today can derive patterns to quantify and traits to compute, but major holes in knowledge remain that are unlikely to vanish soon. For starters, the paths to symptom formation vary dramatically from one person to the next and manifest themselves erratically within each lifetime. Many clinicians still insist that our minds form some of these connections unconsciously, through associations that can take months, even years, to fathom.

In short, the belief that psychiatry and psychology can establish precise connections between our mental conflicts and our physical symptoms remains an illusion sustained by misleading metaphors like "chemical imbalance." Although such metaphors give neuropsychiatrists and their public the impression that they've solved the "riddle" of anxiety, major pieces of it remain, because they are so idiosyncratic and unconscious. Scientists dislike conceding these gaps in knowledge, because they have grown used to thinking that there is a biochemical or genetic explanation for every trait and "malfunction." But when it comes to treating anxiety, much less to understanding its causes, one size (or pill) certainly does not fit all.

———————

Before the standoff between neuropsychiatry and psychoanalysis came to a head at the end of the nineteenth century, several quite neutral accounts of shyness and anxiety existed. These include Darwin's fascinating and read-able *Expression of the Emotions in Man and Animals,* published just a few years after Griesinger's second edition of *Mental Pathology.* Darwin began the book in 1838, but let it languish until he'd finished his famous *Descent of Man* in 1871. Influenced by that key text, *Expression* pits evolutionary ar-guments about shyness and anxiety against those of authors such as Thomas Burgess, who claimed a few decades earlier that God had designed both so that "the soul might have sovereign power of displaying in the cheeks the various internal emotions of the moral feelings." Burgess wel-comed such reactions, insisting they "serve as a check on ourselves, and as a sign to others, that [we're] violating rules which ought to be held sa-cred."[43] But Darwin demurred, saying blushing makes the person in ques-tion "suffer and the beholder uncomfortable, without being of the least [moral] service to either of them."[44]

Ultimately, Darwin saw shyness as an adaptive trait tied to socially learned conventions that are not at all universal, but as he didn't find such behavior exceptional he was far from calling it a congenital disorder. His perspective therefore is a refreshing antidote to the pathological and med-ical arguments that filled later treatises, including those returning with a vengeance in the 1970s. In fact, Darwin thought "self-attention" the "es-sential element" in shyness, shame, and modesty, and dubbed the former an "odd state of mind," for he thought it curious that the inferred opinion of others could excite such extreme emotion in us. As he asked quite bluntly but not naively, "Why should the thought that others are thinking about us affect our capillary circulation?"[45]

Charles Bell had argued slightly earlier that blushing is "a provision for expression," whereby the shy communicate in a manner they can't or won't put into words.[46] The best example of surrogate expression in Dar-win's book is a fascinating anecdote of "an extremely shy man" who tries to thank friends at a dinner party given in his honor. In rising to speak, Darwin recalls, the man simply "rehearsed the speech, which he had evi-dently learnt by heart, in absolute silence, and did not utter a single word; but he acted as if he were speaking with much emphasis. His friends, per-ceiving how the case stood, loudly applauded the imaginary bursts of elo-quence, whenever his gestures indicated a pause, and the man never dis-covered that he had remained the whole time completely silent. On the contrary, he afterwards remarked to my friend, with much satisfaction, that he thought he had succeeded uncommonly well."[47]

The anecdote is touching on several counts. Mindful of the fear that grips many a public speaker, without hinting that they have psychiatric symptoms, Darwin uses the example to relay the "confusion of mind" that blushing and anxiety can cause. While his peers would say the man had a congenital pathology, Darwin left his thoughts on shyness impressionistic, conjectural, and free of all condescension: "By what means attention— perhaps the most wonderful of all the wondrous powers of the mind—is effected [in blushing], is an extremely obscure subject." At other points, he calls our associations unconscious and involuntary, in ways rendering him a closer precursor to Freud than to Kraepelin and his particular brand of scientific psychiatry.[48]

If we fast-forward to the end of the century, noting in passing that Carl Westphal inherited Griesinger's mantle by coining the term *agoraphobia* in 1872 and placing such people firmly within the realm of medicine, we find Pierre Janet busy arguing in France that claustrophobics and other neurotics suffer from obsessive ideas that culminate in "psychasthenia."[49] Janet in fact coined the phrase *social phobia* (*phobies sociales*) and drew quite heavily on Paul Hartenberg's 1901 study *Les Timides et la timidité* to detail the varied fears of those with chronic shyness.[50]

Janet did not distinguish between those who dread being in public, such as agoraphobics, and those, like misanthropes, who have a horror of society in general (*des phobies de la société*). Although Hartenberg devotes a chapter to what he calls "pathological shyness," which in one patient apparently blossoms when he falls in love, like Janet he represents even this extreme as an emotional sickness and deficiency that weakens the will.[51]

Hartenberg's interest in pathological shyness is certainly as close as one gets to contemporary studies of social phobia, which makes his near-absence from them rather surprising.[52] The explanation may lie in his willingness to judge the acutely shy as flaunting their cultural and constitutional "degeneracy." *Les Timides et la timidité* is, if anything, a critique of allegedly weak and simpering behavior, not a compassionate bid to recognize a problem beyond the sufferer's control. Unfortunately for modern neuropsychiatrists too, Hartenberg describes even the extreme edge of shyness as but one of the trait's many facets, which include the affected fear of artists, outsized bids for sympathy, and, perhaps most intriguing of all, intellectual timidity.[53]

_____

At virtually the same time, Freud was starting to break with the neurological model he had not only favored, but actively promoted since the start of his career. So it's worth asking why Freud switched tracks, even if neuropsychiatrists—ridiculing him for altering his emphasis—are convinced his work is outdated, inaccurate, and even pernicious.

For starters, Freud's alternative explanations for anxiety made clear that it could be an appropriate, even rational response to external and inner pressure. He also kept the line between the sick and the well suitably open-ended, treating patients according to their distress, rather than reacting to prejudged medical or psychiatric signs of their complaint. Additionally, that his career began where many of his detractors' have ended up makes their hostility to even Freud's early work surprising. Something about this picture rings false and is worth investigating.

Freud outlined his neurological vision in his *Project for a Scientific Psychology,* begun in 1895, but he never published the book. As he realized then, and freely acknowledged to his closest colleagues, its mechanistic arguments did not work. They failed to account for key psychological factors like the often-unconscious way we interpret sensory phenomena—factors Freud soon thought neurology ill equipped to explain. Yet even in 1950, when the *Project* appeared posthumously (and, we can say, against Freud's will) the work was sufficiently polarizing for readers to fall into two camps. As scientists seized on the work, lambasting it as a betrayal of concrete proof, they scoffed that Freud had traded speculation for scientific precision and denounced him as a charlatan. So much for investigating the unknown, sometimes peculiar recesses of our minds.

Strangely, this camp never took seriously the reasons Freud gave for leaving the *Project* unpublished—reasons both logical and honest in revealing his principled commitment to understanding *all* aspects of psychology. By trying to outline how the mind makes sense of phenomena, Freud in fact alighted on what science cannot account for: the blind spots of our consciousness, the strange detours of our fantasies, the baffling irrationality of some of our actions, and aspects of anxiety that we can't reduce to biology because, he stressed, their source is *not* organic.

While none of these elements fits comfortably into a neurological frame-work, they are not sufficiently unusual to be considered pathological. To Freud's supporters, the very failure of the *Project* heralded a fresh way of thinking about the mind, based on less a rejection of scientific method than an urgent need to tackle behavior that follows quite different pre-cepts. Drawing a firm line between normal and aberrant behavior (as Griesinger, Kraepelin, Westphal, and others tried to do) told us most about the psychiatrists' value judgments. As Freud put it in 1894, the rea-son he broke with psychiatry stemmed from his desire to understand a widespread "*estrangement* between the somatic and the psychical."[54]

"It is . . . easy to forget," notes Adam Phillips in a superb essay on anxi-ety, "that worries are imaginative creations, small epics of personal failure and anticipated catastrophe. They are, that is to say, made up."[55] Not every worry, to be sure, but a form of treatment that didn't take this per-sonal theater into account would subtract the mind from its investigations, impoverishing the result. Accordingly, "we cannot approach Freud's con-cepts by appealing to the kinds of diagnostic gestures one finds in the *DSM*, wherein a list of features or phenomenal attributes can be accumulated in order to arrive at a diagnosis (shortness of breath, loss of appetite, in-creased heart rate, and so forth)."[56] Biological explanations for mental symptoms will take us only so far.

The mid-1890s marked a watershed, because Freud found it necessary then to distinguish mechanistic from less rigid psychological explanations for behavior. He published an essay on anxiety whose clinical observations departed radically from his colleagues' biological claims, one reason he called it "The Justification for Detaching from Neurasthenia a Particular Syndrome: The Anxiety-Neurosis." In seeking to "differentiate more sharply than had hitherto been possible between neurasthenia proper and various kinds of pseudo-neurasthenia," Freud hoped to track the unusual paths of melancholia, as well as the "morbid" distress he had witnessed in a slightly different syndrome, "Anxiety-Neurosis." He quickly rattled off the latter's symptoms: general irritability, anxious expectation, pangs of conscience, and attacks accompanied by heart tremors, acute sweating, vertigo, hyperventilating, and insomnia.[57]

After the years they have spent trashing psychoanalysis, neuropsychia-trists might be chastened to see how closely Freud's description of this phenomenon resembles their own "generalized anxiety disorder," cobbled together rather hastily a century later. But, unlike today's backward-looking psychiatrists, Freud's refusal to blend the physiological and the psychical meant he could distinguish affect from physical tension, based on his growing recognition that the mind "translates" these sensations and gives them a life of their own.

Affect is thus a "*dislocated* or *transposed*" version of such sensations, he stressed, adding later in a useful simile that neurotic anxiety is "related to [libido] in the same kind of way as vinegar is to wine."[58] One reason this sour residue flummoxes us, as it did Freud for a while, is because it is oriented by memories and associations of which we're often unconscious or dimly aware.

"I cannot better describe the condition I have in mind," he explains, than "by appending a few examples. A woman who suffers from anxious expectation will imagine every time her husband coughs, when he has a cold, that he is going to have influenzal pneumonia, and will at once see his funeral *in her mind's eye*. If when she is coming towards the house she sees two people standing by her front door, *she cannot avoid the thought* that one of her children has fallen out of the window; if the bell rings, then someone is bringing news of a death, and so on; whereas on all these occasions there is no particular ground for exaggerating a mere possibility."[59]

Is it irrelevant—or precisely the point—that her fears are likely never to materialize? That she can't stop imagining the worst affirms her fatalism, but it also traps her in a net of self-fulfilling prophecies. The resulting anxiety must be exhausting and a cause of great anguish, but it may also have an important, even consoling function: if one can predict a disaster, one might avert it. Blessed or perhaps cursed by a vivid imagination, this woman can always conjure new things to worry about, but her exaggerated perception of her husband's and children's vulnerability may be secondary to the reason she needs such fantasies to clarify her family's roles.

Psychiatrists who are largely interested today in gauging the measurable effects of selective serotonin-reuptake inhibitors are likely to confound these distinctions, leaving a core aspect of their patients' misery untouched or misrecognized. (I say more about this in Chapter 5.) Even if this woman's modern counterpart responds successfully to drugs, that is, and experiences neither side effects nor withdrawal symptoms, psychoanalysts would argue that the woman's altered bodily response to anxiety arguably will not change its "*dislocated*" mental significance: the worries and fantasies, whether probable or far-fetched, that bob along a different current.

So Freud revised his model to factor in this sense of looming threat that we may feel but cannot pinpoint or avoid. As biology receded from his argument, however, he found it maddeningly difficult to explain what was left behind, calling anxiety both "a nodal point at which the most various and important questions [of our psychology] converge" and "a riddle whose solution would be bound to throw a flood of light on our whole mental existence."[60]

As he struggled to grasp what purpose anxiety serves, Freud in these middle years came to view it less as tension resulting from blocked energy than as a conundrum borne out of our stalled and unpredictable transition from biology to culture. Anxiety's excessive, almost unappeasable quality "upsets" the symbols we tend to use unthinkingly, making them unreliable guides to our emotions. (To the worried woman he treated, for example, the image of a funeral ultimately designated concern about her husband's cold.) As soon as one tackles anxiety from the perspective of individuals in language, however, there is no going back to a raw state of nature. "The 'danger' that triggers anxiety," as Charles Shepherdson puts it, assumes "an inescapably subjective dimension" that overrides the reality governing our survival as an organism or species.[61] If nothing else, the unique, sometimes tortuous paths of our worries will frustrate psychiatrists wanting to call anxiety a behavioral disorder, composed of seven subgroups, each of them treatable by drugs. Psychoanalysis insists, by contrast, that the unique, sometimes unconscious form that anxiety takes in each of us is more trenchant and varied.

———————

As he settled into the last phase of his work, Freud focused on understanding why aggression and guilt thrive unequally in our minds and culture. What struck him in particular was the "tormenting uneasiness" we experience if we're "prevented from carrying out certain actions."[62] At first blush, this reaction doesn't make sense. If we're unable to do what we want, then we might be frustrated, but we also should feel guilt-free and without remorse. Yet as Freud noted, based on clinical experience, the opposite often is true. Those who deny themselves pleasure may in fact feel *more* anxious than others who do not. This paradox ultimately was what sent his thinking down a fresh track, toward the uneasiness and unhappiness that even routine adjustments to society can entail.

If the ego is our "actual seat of anxiety," humiliated for infractions it often only imagines, the superego is a despotic, implacable source of our guilt. It may seem strange to think of this insight as the missing explanatory piece that eluded Freud's earlier accounts of anxiety, but the superego is itself a counterintuitive addition to psychoanalytic thinking.[63]

One aspect of us is normally so overdeveloped, Freud argued, that it not only enjoys tormenting us, but also is aggressively "on the watch" for opportunities to trap us externally—perhaps by inducing us to act in ways that are socially or professionally degrading.[64] Doubtless this judgment is more intense when the approval of others matters intensely, but the agent of our woes, Freud stressed, is not society or other people but an internalized variant of them distorted beyond recognition.

In its heyday, psychoanalysis had considerable authority and prestige in the United States and Europe and was, to many, synonymous with American psychiatry. If the extent to which Freudianism dominated the profession seems almost incredible today, it is partly because efforts at discrediting the work have been so emphatic and far-reaching that one can barely mention Freud's name without being derided as hopelessly uninformed and out-of-date.

Even so, it is worth recalling that as late as 1961 the *Atlantic Monthly* devoted a special issue to "Psychiatry in American Life," in which the editor could plausibly insist: "To an extent not paralleled elsewhere, psychoanalysis and psychiatry in general have influenced medicine, the arts and criticism, popular entertainment, advertising, the rearing of children, sociology, anthropology, legal thought and practice, humor, manners and mores, even organized religion."[65] "It is hardly necessary to document," a psychiatrist added casually two years later in *Daedalus*, "the extent to which psychoanalytic thought has pervaded every aspect of modern American life."[66]

Largely because of this emphasis, "descriptive diagnosis" of the kind neuropsychiatrists now favor was at the time "considered to be irrelevant or nearly so by the major thinkers in the field."[67] That Kraepelin's books gathered dust in academic and hospital libraries was because scholars and doctors thought his work rigid and simplistic. As Columbia University's Donald Klein put it in 2005, in a statement betraying annoyance at past condescension and pleasure at his colleagues' apparent vindication, "Psychoanalysts . . . say that the real thing is the internal conflicts. So to be interested in descriptive diagnosis was to be superficial and a little stupid."[68]

Actually, the situation was more complicated than that. For in the United States, unlike in Europe or South America, psychoanalysis entered the culture via the medical establishment, an outcome many still think a mixed blessing. Whether one could call American psychiatry "Freudian" for much of the twentieth century is a matter of serious dispute. As the hospitals, clinics, and mental asylums spurned lay analysts as quacks, they tried streamlining psychoanalysis through accreditation, while limiting expertise to medical doctors by allowing it to be taught only to interns.

Ironically, this bid to make psychoanalysis medically respectable undercut Freud's most counterintuitive arguments about sexuality, anxiety, and the unconscious. After he died in 1939, the claims made in his name, especially in the United States, bore little if any resemblance to his actual arguments, which many perceived as weird and anachronistic. The unintended consequence was that psychoanalysis began to merge, almost imperceptibly, with the neurological model from which Freud deliberately had broken at the end of the nineteenth century.[69]

In light of this fundamental redaction of his thinking, Freudians find it especially galling that the medical version of psychoanalysis—bearing so little resemblance to their own—ultimately was what galvanized neuropsychiatrists into believing the pendulum had swung too far. Long frustrated by professional condescension, neuropsychiatrists began to fight back, increasing tension between the two schools of American psychiatry. As we'll see in the next chapter, these tensions finally boiled over on the DSM-III task force.

The influential Group for the Advancement of Psychiatry certainly helped to turn up the heat. Initially nonpartisan and favoring a catholic psychosocial model, by 1955 the group was asserting that an "objective critical attitude" should orient the field.[70] It capitalized on the agenda set by the first DSM, appearing shortly before, in 1952, and created momentum that Robert Spitzer's DSM-III task force welcomed, then drew upon, when seeking rule-driven diagnoses of its own.

In 1952 scientists also announced a major breakthrough that not only refashioned American psychiatry but also helped sound a death knell for psychoanalysis: chlorpromazine, the first antipsychotic drug, had antidepressive effects. True, laboratories in Europe and the United States had worked intensively throughout the 1930s on the antihistaminic effects of several dimethylamines (raw material for many pharmaceutical products, as well as a key ingredient of soaps, dyes, and dehairing products); cruder experiments on alizarin (a dye from coal tar) even date to the 1860s. But everything changed in the 1950s. Scientists formed the Collegium Internationale Neuropsychopharmacologium (CINP), beginning with meetings convened by influential pharmaceutical houses such as Geigy, Ciba, Roche, Sandoz, and Rhône-Poulenc.

Hoping to capitalize on the latest research developments, these companies had reason to be upbeat. In July 1955 the U.S. Congress passed the Mental Health Study Act, which "provided the framework for large-scale donations to research," including $2 million annually for research on psychopharmacology.[71]

During these years, the use of chlorpromazine (Thorazine/Largactil) "spread like wildfire through American asylums," signaling a powerful new trend in the way doctors prescribed drugs and treated patients. Thorazine's manufacturer, Smith, Kline and French, made $75 million in 1955 alone, a vast sum at the time.[72] Fortune has smiled on pharmacology ever since. Corporations have fallen over one another to tap new markets, clinicians have expanded *DSM* categories to help fund the latest research, and the media have reported even relatively modest developments with breathless excitement.

As they regained momentum, neuropsychiatrists overseeing the second edition of the *DSM,* circa 1965, adopted almost wholesale diagnostic changes to the eighth edition of the *International Classification of Diseases* (*ICD-8*), the once-parallel system developed by the World Health Organization in Geneva. The WHO system reflected the emphases and nuances of European psychiatry and therefore was a good deal more accepting of psychoanalytic terms than its North American counterpart. The DSM task force made minor alterations, including adding more subtypes, but otherwise accepted the changes as necessary and valuable.

The revisions to *ICD-8* were bold, even cavalier, and had lasting consequences. Consulting few outside experts, a situation unimaginable a generation later, the person appointed to update the manual quietly eliminated the term *reaction* from many diagnostic labels. As a result, diagnoses like *schizophrenic reaction,* which in *DSM-I* had referred to sporadic psychiatric incidents, evolved almost overnight into *schizophrenia,* even if the person's symptoms were rare or not especially violent.[73] The same was true for terms like *paranoid reaction,* which the DSM-II task force determined henceforth would be known simply as *paranoia.*

When I asked Robert Spitzer about these revisions, he confirmed my suspicions: "*ICD-8* was written by one person, [Sir] Aubrey Lewis at the Maudsley [Institute of Psychiatry, London], and he didn't have the word 'reaction'" in the eighth edition, so *DSM-II* didn't either. "No," Spitzer added, "there was no discussion at all" on the DSM-II task force about the viability or consequence of adopting these changes. Turning phrases like "*schizophrenic reaction*" into simple nouns ("*schizophrenia*") may seem insignificant. But as Spitzer concedes, it was "a major shift" in approach, because it altered at a stroke the very meaning of illness for clinicians and patients.[74]

DSM-I had characterized illnesses by the number and intensity of their episodes, tending to see them as fueled by various traits, but the same ailments in *DSM-II* began to look, in Kraepelinian fashion, like permanent, even innate conditions. The dynamism and struggle of the patient's *reaction* also disappeared. Illnesses started to define patients rather than appearing as simply facets of their personality, and psychiatrists found it increasingly difficult to assess the full extent of their patients' unease.

These changes are starkest when one focuses on psychosis, but the difference between saying "You had an anxious *reaction*" and "You are suffering from anxiety" is equally far-reaching. Indeed, when one anticipates that the *DSM-III* would soon render this as, in effect, "You have social phobia" or even "You are a social phobe," the impact of the revisions begins to hit home. Once lying entirely outside the domain of psychiatrists, ordinary behaviors like shyness began to enter their reference manual as mental disorders that afflicted growing numbers of the population.

2

THE DIAGNOSTIC BATTLES:
EMOTIONS BECOME PATHOLOGIES

If you visit the Biometrics Department of the New York State Psychiatric Institute, as I did in the summer of 2005, you'll spot a charming cartoon of Dr. Robert Spitzer on one of his office walls. The handsome psychiatrist is pictured leaning over a neatly stacked house of cards. Half-winking to his audience, as if performing a magic trick for them, the maestro declares, "Now if we just remove this card . . . " As Spitzer takes one from the bottom tier, thereby removing part of its foundation, his figure breaks into a smile. The pleasure seems fitting because, for that one moment, the other cards defy gravity and stay in place.

It's easy to see why Dr. Spitzer would enjoy this conceit. The cartoon also has a gratifying kick that adds to its interest, for each of the cards is labeled "*DSM-III*," short for the third edition of the *Diagnostic and Statistical Manual of Mental Disorders*. To the uninitiated, the cartoon could seem trite or insignificant, as if merely a private joke. But *DSM-III* revolutionized the way psychiatrists and the public think about mental health, and Spitzer deserves much of the credit for that remarkable feat. He's one of the men responsible for turning shyness into an illness.

Robert L. Spitzer may not be well-known outside his field, but as the *New Yorker* put it in 2005, "he is, without question, one of the most influential psychiatrists of the twentieth century."[1] In 1974 Judd Marmor, then president-elect of the American Psychiatric Association (APA), asked him to chair a strategic task force, charged with the herculean job of updating the profession's manual of disorders. A spiral-bound paperback costing just three dollars and fifty cents, the previous edition had appeared a few years earlier, in 1968, selling mainly to large state mental institutions.[2] As it offered only cursory descriptions of almost two hundred illnesses, DSM-II was often derided as flawed and outdated. The entire field of psychiatry it represented badly needed a makeover.

American psychiatry was at the time in serious disarray. Several embarrassing, widely reported scandals had battered its reputation. One of the best-known, appearing in *Science,* concerned eight ordinary citizens whom investigators had persuaded to tell 12 different hospitals they kept hearing voices saying "empty," "hollow," and "thud." All but one of the volunteers was hospitalized, then discharged with schizophrenia "in remission."[3]

The implications of such carelessness were staggering, bearing an uncomfortable resemblance to the nightmare scenarios portrayed a decade earlier by Ken Kesey's *One Flew over the Cuckoo's Nest* and other cautionary tales. Another study, revealing similar discrepancies in judgment among young psychiatrists of all stripes, found they "were no more likely to agree with an examiner's diagnosis than would be expected by chance."[4]

These incidents were viewed as signs of something rotten in the state of American psychiatry. The hundred years' war between neuropsychiatrists and psychoanalysts had reached a level of acrimony possible only when fundamental differences in approach and philosophy seem insurmountable. With each side hunkered down, the skirmishes had begun to fester, disabling the profession as a whole and damaging its reputation.

As if the situation weren't grim enough, healthcare costs were spiraling out of control, causing alarm especially among managed-care companies. With its cautious, unhurried interest in mental conflicts—and commitment to a treatment plan shared only by the analyst and patient, with loose empirical guidelines and no obvious end in sight—psychoanalysis seemed to its opponents an increasingly costly and dispensable culprit.[5]

If something radical weren't done to stanch the discipline's internal problems and costs, many began to mutter, the entire field might collapse under the weight of its many conflicts. So Melvin Sabshin, then medical director of the APA and a man drawn to "evidence-based psychiatry," decided the DSM needed a fresh edition. "I wanted it to rely on data rather than opinion or ideology alone," he explained, so the field would be "better prepared to deal with the vicissitudes of economic pressures."[6] Another key factor was that the World Health Organization in Geneva was due to update its own diagnostic manual, the *International Classification of Diseases,* and wanted the North American and European models better aligned.[7]

Hoping his suggestion would end the fights and scandals, Sabshin pressed for a standardized "classification system that would reflect our current state of knowledge regarding mental disorders."[8] From the start, then, new disorders like social anxiety were seen as underreported maladies updating "our current state of knowledge," not strategic constructions that would end up completely redefining it.

Since any changes to the *DSM* were likely to favor the neuropsychiatrists, given their commitment to rapid, standardized results, Sabshin's decision was unavoidably political. So in hopes of placating the psychoanalytic group, he urged Marmor to appoint Spitzer, a friend and charismatic professor with expertise in both camps and thus every appearance of neutrality.

Spitzer had trained as an analyst after undergoing psychoanalysis as a child and adolescent. "My mother sent me to a psychoanalyst when I was 9 or 10," he told me, "because I'd slapped her when we were in an eye doctor's office, . . . but I didn't really have therapy until I was 15."[9] In light of this experience, it's curious that he then went on to train as a Reichian—apparently in secret, as his parents opposed his plan.[10] "I was intrigued by Wilhelm Reich's approach," he says, which at the time included way-out experiments with "orgastic potency" and a firm belief in extraterrestrials.[11] But Spitzer's research, also adopting Reich's model, didn't work out well. In 1952, he laughs, he wrote to the guru, earnestly explaining that he'd not gotten satisfactory results from his experiments. Reich responded, assuring him that the cause was doubtless fallout from the atomic bomb![12]

Reich's was a truly esoteric form of pseudo-psychoanalysis, as many grasped at the time; Spitzer "never felt comfortable with what [he] was doing" when he saw patients.[13] So he kept his interest in quantifying psychological matters, but did a 180-degree turn in how he viewed them and began honing an interest in diagnostic issues. Later still, after helping to update *DSM-II* in the late 1960s, he proved himself an able diplomat, negotiating a difficult truce over the fiercely contested status of homosexuality in the manual—a further reason Sabshin and Marmor wanted him leading the task force.[14]

Others were less kind about Spitzer's talent and the task that he was given. Allen Frances once said of his colleague, with a noticeable pat on the head, "He's kind of an idiot savant of diagnosis—in a good sense, in the sense that he never tires of it."[15] Donald Klein adds dismissively, "When Bob was appointed to the *DSM-III*, the job was of no consequence. In fact, one of the reasons Bob got the job was that it wasn't considered that important."[16]

Nevertheless, Marmor picked him as the man who would restore scientific credibility to the study of mental disorders. Whether—or how—Spitzer succeeded, since his group redefined ordinary behaviors like shyness, is a fascinating but largely untold story.

Over the next six years, the APA Task Force on Nomenclature and Statistics reviewed almost every tic and trait imaginable. The work was slow, difficult, and often contentious. Spitzer regularly labored 70 to 80 hours a week over the sprawling document, for his team of 15 set about codifying every aspect of phobia and anxiety, rendering them discrete illnesses.[17] They discarded many current theories, and mined large amounts of research for fresh insights.

Just keeping track of the many intricate debates that developed or stalled over each behavior was itself a formidable challenge, generating—long before email—hundreds of memos, notes, and letters. Given the nuggets of insight that had to be culled from six years of meetings, in ways that would do justice to the gravity of the work, it's a wonder the document was ever finished, much less published with one side's approval.

Embarrassed by *DSM-II*'s diagnostic "holes," the task force tried to fill or replace them with numbered "axes" and "subcategories," in the parlance of the field. Yet each of these spawned so many inclusive criteria and symptoms that the terms frequently buckled and merged. Undeterred, the task force "discovered" 112 new disorders and disease categories. It also split anxiety neurosis into seven new parts: agoraphobia, panic disorder, post-traumatic stress disorder (PTSD), obsessive compulsive disorder (OCD), generalized anxiety disorder, simple phobia, and social phobia.

So whereas *DSM-II*, the 1968 edition Spitzer helped update, had cited

180 categories of mental illness—including just one all-embracing form of "anxiety neurosis"—*DSM-IIIR* ("R" for "revision") eventually listed 292, and *DSM-IV*, appearing in 1994, over 350.[18] In just 26 years, that is, *the total number of mental disorders the general population might exhibit almost doubled*. As David Healy comments on this astonishing outcome, the revised parameters for depression alone resulted in "a *thousandfold* increase, despite the availability of treatments supposed to cure this terrible affliction."[19]

You could argue that psychiatry needed revamping and that only a fundamental shift in thinking would do. Spitzer's team and supporters in fact proudly claim they were correcting a false medical picture, in which certain maladies had escaped notice. Consequently, against substantial odds, and with the highest standards of rigor and integrity, they pushed through reforms that prevented thousands of people from suffering needlessly and the profession from languishing in confused mediocrity.

The story behind these changes is not, however, quite as smooth or noble as Spitzer and other commentators suggest. For one thing, psychiatrists in the 1950s and 1960s were highly attuned to their patients' problems. Then, as now, the drug companies were eager to tap vast new markets, and the media certainly were not slow to report their discoveries; if anything, they did so with great alacrity. From a statistical perspective, moreover, the escalation of illness categories was by any measure so extreme that even factoring in underreported problems couldn't possibly account for it. Today Spitzer cheerfully concedes that younger colleagues tease him for being someone who never saw a disorder he didn't like.[20] But with the risk of mislabeling so high, many readers will not find that humor very reassuring.

While Spitzer and his allies prefer to cast their actions in a winning light, others feared the victors would soon repress this notable (indeed, unfortunate) chapter of psychiatric history. As far back as June 1979, Roger Peele at the U.S. Department of Health, Education, and Welfare urged Spitzer, "Please write or have written a history of the development of DSM I, II, and III that will include all the warts"—a request that Spitzer has so far answered selectively.[21]

Even so, Theodore Millon, a consultant to the DSM-III task force, broke rank in admitting: "There was very little systematic research, and much of the research that existed was really a hodgepodge—scattered, inconsistent, and ambiguous. I think the majority of us recognized that the amount of good, solid science upon which we were making our decisions was pretty modest."[22]

Given the now-global influence of the *DSM* and the fact that psychiatrists still cannot agree on this key chapter of its history, it is time to present "all the warts," including what happened behind the scenes.

When they met to hammer out the details of each new and existing diagnosis, the results were often chaotic. David Shaffer, a British psychiatrist who worked on *DSM-III* and *DSM-IIIR,* gives a memorable snapshot, conveying less the concentrated energies of brilliant minds than the raucous class of a teacher whose unruly pupils won't stay quiet: "There would be these meetings of the so-called experts or advisers, and people would be standing and sitting and moving around. People would talk on top of each other. But Bob would be too busy typing notes to chair the meeting in an orderly way."[23] Another participant called the chaos "disquieting," adding, "Suddenly, these things would happen and there didn't seem to be much basis for it except that someone just decided all of a sudden to run with it."[24]

Many of the actual memos and letters combine gamesmanship with alarming amounts of carelessness and expediency. For starters, the hope that their own particular spin on anxiety, depression, or related illnesses might be accepted and thereafter invoked led some members of the task force to push too zealously for adoption. When Klein asked members of the Personality Disorders Subcommittee to review his proposal for "Emotionally Unstable Character Disorder," for example, he announced rather breezily, "You'll note that this syndrome has been repeatedly described by me," with drug and follow-up studies "attesting to the reality of this syndrome, which is more than can be said about a number of the syndromes in DSM III."[25] Spitzer's exasperated reply, the following week, tried to head Klein off, amusingly, by invoking Kraepelin's description of an "irritable temperament."[26]

In other eruptions, the psychiatrists traded barbs over jargon and diagnostic precision. Asked Spitzer of Klein at one particularly tense moment over the criteria for avoidant personality disorder, "Does the reference to 'hypersensitivity to rejection' get too close to Hysteroid Dysphoria for your personal comfort?"[27]

Given the stakes, a certain amount of jockeying was probably inevitable; even though they are trained to be impartial and somewhat detached, psychiatrists are as human as the patients they see. They may be adept at interpreting other people's behavior, but they sometimes are unaware of their own. Spitzer's difficulty in appeasing so many competing demands, many from close friends, at times became immense, and the strain began to show. Jean Endicott, his collaborator, explains: "He got very involved with issues, with ideas, and with questions. At times he was unaware of how people were responding to him or to the issue. He was surprised when he learned that someone was annoyed. He'd say, 'Why was he annoyed? What'd I do?'"[28]

And what about the psychiatrists' actual decisions? Shaffer is unusual in disputing their expertise; most would accept their track record in key areas. But perhaps owing to groupthink, inertia, or overreach, the results were often strikingly unimpressive, and at times downright alarming. Renee Garfinkel, an administrative officer at the American Psychological Association, later observed, "The poverty of thought that went into the decision-making process was frightening." According to her, when one leading psychiatrist was asked to define how he was using the term *masochistic* during a meeting about its possible inclusion as a personality disorder, he replied: "Oh, you know what I mean, a whiny individual . . . the Jewish-mother type."[29]

"I couldn't believe my [ears or] eyes," Leonore Walker, a Denver-based psychologist, remarked about a host of other discussions. "Here were professional people sitting around a computer, making decisions based on feelings or impressions, not facts." She added, "In some cases, the people revising DSM-III [were] making a mental illness out of adaptive behavior."[30]

Considering these objections, Irwin Marill and several colleagues in Bethesda and the D.C. area seem justified in lamenting "glaring deficiencies inherent in the conceptualization of the manual," calling its quality "spotty" and its judgments "often internally contradictory."[31] Of the proposed revisions to *DSM-III*, Robert Waugh declared: "I feel ashamed for psychiatry; I am fearful that we will be the laughing-stock of our scientific colleagues. . . . Please! There are enough things ludicrous in the field of psychiatry. Let's not invite being laughed at and scorned into oblivion."[32] Brooklyn-based N. S. Lehrman went further, saying the "pseudo-scientific veneer" coating the group's work displayed so much "amateurishness" and "pretentiousness" that the manual might better be known as "The Emperor's New Jockstrap."[33]

As these examples underscore, the challenge of conveying unanimity to the public was becoming more difficult, with relations within the wider profession increasingly strained. First, the fact that Spitzer had handpicked his team for its shared interest in diagnostic issues soon made abundantly clear to everyone else that it opposed all other schools of psychiatry, especially psychodynamic therapy and Freudian psychoanalysis. Second, Spitzer's earlier training as a psychoanalyst failed to mollify this group, which felt that key decisions about the profession were being made over its head. Further deals and compromises had to be struck, many at the eleventh hour, and few were satisfying to all parties. Third, there was the risk of error or simple inconsistency—no small or laughing matter when the new categories were so elaborate and the diagnosis of millions of patients would soon be at stake. No wonder Spitzer's daunting task spun out for six years. As he said to me rather ruefully, his marriage also collapsed at the time, owing partly to the strain. "There was," he concedes, "a lot going on."[34]

Spitzer argued strenuously that his task force was unbiased, because it was merely cataloging symptoms and thus in theory steered clear of contentious questions about their cause and treatment. Accordingly, he argued that the DSM-III work was not skewed toward any one approach, whether neuropsychiatric, psychoanalytic, or indeed social and environmental. On the face of it, the *DSM* certainly does not favor neuropsychiatric over psychodynamic frameworks, a key point I have no wish to downplay. But Spitzer's argument, as will emerge, was also partly a clever ruse to mask that the task force was in fact extremely mindful of etiology; indeed, it tipped the scales in neuropsychiatry's favor by excluding conditions (including *anxiety neurosis*) that other psychological perspectives such as psychoanalysis had recognized for decades. Nor was the task force disinterested in assigning symptoms to newly christened disorders, for each decision (including those to rename) involved not only research whose conclusions were often open-ended, but also acts of interpretation that drew heavily on the clinical trials of task force members and their friends.

In some cases, as we'll see, the trials involved but one patient whose behavior was reported anecdotally by the very member hoping to formalize his or her line of research. More often than not, however, the perspectives of several consultants had to align. Frequently they did not, because of fundamental disagreements about the traits and their underlying significance. Spitzer's team (or Spitzer alone) then decided what was "right and true."

As these decisions tended to exclude terminology and treatments that their predecessors had used for generations, psychoanalysts perceived that the fate of their profession lay unfairly with a few colleagues committed to eliminating all trace of their work. As Paul Fink, Chair of Psychiatry and Human Behavior at Philadelphia's Thomas Jefferson University, fumed in May 1978 to his colleague Lester Grinspoon: "I do not know who determined that this small group of people should try to reorganize psychiatric thinking in the United States, but I am somewhat concerned that they have such an arrogant view of their mission and are not willing to incorporate some of the things which we have learned over the past 70 years."[35]

"I think a lot of my success with *DSM*," Spitzer told me, "was being able to negotiate with different groups . . . And, you know, having an analytic training certainly helped me to deal with analytic people better—although it became a real conflict toward the end."[36] Some would say the reason for these battles was that the task force derailed almost all psychodynamic arguments about the mind, while shunting the profession to neurochemical arguments about the brain. In creating dozens of new illnesses and altering the wording of countless more, the updated manual certainly helped psychiatry to jump tracks. Almost overnight, shyness and many other routine moods and ailments became bona fide diseases.

Given the pressure on Spitzer to make the APA's large membership (forty-one thousand) agree to his group's recommendations, it may be unsurprising that a man surviving such conflict—including trying committees, tense correspondence, and sometimes-rancorous conventions—would, at moments of acute irony or stress, appreciate that he was presiding over a house of cards. Still, the image seems strangely apt in portraying the large-scale transformations that Spitzer and his colleagues managed to push through. While Spitzer's cartoon figure removes one card, he seems on paper to keep everything else in place, as if, miraculously, the sum of *DSM-III* is independent of its many parts.

If one sees the cartoon in this way, then Spitzer's wink conveys justified pride in what he and his colleagues accomplished: You can remove or redefine a single card or illness, the smile says, but psychiatry will stand firm. Yet Spitzer, like his audience, knows that gravity is stronger than willpower or magical thinking. After all, the house of cards will collapse seconds later.

Even from this angle, the cartoon's meaning enhances its charm. For in decorating the office of so influential a man, it serves as a brilliant corrective to hubris and a jovial demand for humility. Just when you think you have the brain licked or psychiatry sewed up, the knowing smile confirms, a problem will arise that alters the whole picture. This reading is in fact the one Spitzer prefers. As he made clear to me, Bruce Rounsaville's drawing of *DSM-III*'s creation is meant to "acknowledge its limitations," an admission that must sound astonishing to those once dazzled by Spitzer's interpretive confidence or infuriated by his railroading.[37]

Yet the third edition of *DSM* appeared in 1980, just a couple of years behind schedule. (One can imagine the smile from this perspective, too, as endorsing persistence and canny diplomacy.) At five hundred pages, it provided detailed descriptions of more than three hundred mental illnesses, a third of which (including social phobia) the task force itself discovered.

Several unflattering articles greeted its appearance, including a lampoon in *Harper's Magazine* ("The Encyclopedia of Insanity: A Psychiatric Handbook Lists a Madness for Everyone") and a lament by Peter Janulis in the *Archives of General Psychiatry* on the consequences of deleting "neurosis" from the *DSM*—a reasonable problem to raise and, for the discipline, an equally significant problem to solve.[38] Spitzer was not in the mood for concessions, and with two colleagues he responded with a poem that even *The Lancet*, supporting their approach, called "arrogant doggerel":[39]

> Peter [T. Janulis], oh Peter, your pain is so real,
> the word, *neurosis*, has great appeal.

> It tells you what the problem is not,
> > neither psychosis nor organic rot.
> How comforting it is for you to know
> > the cause of all mankind's woe.
> If only we could be so sure
> > that untangled conflict led to cure.
> But other theories now abound,
> > who's to tell which of them is sound?
> Bad mothering, of course, sure isn't good,
> > but consider these paths to "patienthood":
> Could bad cognitions be the hex,
> > instead of conflicts over sex?
> A transmitter lacking in your brain
> > may lead to lots of psychic pain.
> Had your neurosis *Bacillus* been found,
> > in *DSM-III* the term would abound.
> Have cheer, dear Peter, this isn't the end,
> > neurosis can still be your comforting friend.
> Use *DSM-III* for a diagnostic description,
> > and neurosis to help you with your prescription.[40]

Spitzer and his colleagues clearly thought they were being witty in mocking psychoanalysis while drawing attention to "bad cognitions" and "a transmitter lacking in your brain," but it would be difficult to find a more tone-deaf response to the widespread concerns of Janulis and others. Spitzer and the task force had purged, at a stroke, almost a century of thought.

Even so, the reply makes clear, Spitzer was blithe about the consequences. And though the hefty manual needed a lot more tweaking and updating, partly to keep pace with rapid developments in neuropsychiatry and pharmacology and partly because Spitzer wanted new illnesses added, his task force believed it had transformed the *DSM*—and, by extension, the profession it represented—into a pristine scientific entity.

The psychiatrists attending the final key meeting, at which six years' work came down to a single vote, gave Spitzer a standing ovation that left him speechless and teary-eyed. But to those on the losing side, the stampede toward neuropsychiatry had all but flattened the intense arguments flaring over the truth and accuracy of the new categories.

The outcome was especially galling to them, because the losses they endured—of authority, prestige, and the power to determine the future of their field—did not feel at the time like a fair defeat. Instead, the cards (house-like or not) were stacked against them from the start. As Healy observes, "The creation of DSM-III was the Trojan horse by which they effected entry into the citadel of psychoanalysis."[41] William Frosch, who later joined the task force, was even blunter: "Once people realized a lot of icons were being smashed, then everyone wanted a piece of the action."[42]

The fears psychoanalyst Otto Kernberg voiced at the time therefore seem justified. The neo-Kraepelinians were, he said, a group "whose ideas are very clear, very publicly known and [whose] guns are pointed at [psychoanalysis]."[43] In light of such acrimony, it is all the more remarkable that Spitzer and his colleagues recall this episode as stringent and fair.

Perhaps not realizing quite what he was conceding, Spitzer told me how the analysts might have foiled him. They could have drawn comparisons between the DSM emphases his colleagues supplied and those already accepted by European psychiatry, which "uses the term *neurosis*. It's in ICD. So when I said to the DSM-III [task force], 'We've got to get rid of the word *neurosis* because it has psychoanalytic meaning,' the answer to that would've been 'Not necessarily,' because of the international classification." Spitzer backtracked quickly after realizing what he'd said. The key difficulty with *neurosis,* he added, is that "it would [have been] hard to define what the boundaries of that category would be."[44] What the term should include, in other words, is as fraught as what it must exclude.

The task force faced this problem all the time. For instance, Spitzer and his committee members openly lamented the number of "issues" they "wrestled with" when trying to nail down the major criteria of social phobia, even admitting that their definition of the disorder's cut-off point was "open to multiple interpretations."[45] Supportive colleagues intent on retaining these and other terms in future issues of the DSM still fret that the disorders "appear not to have meaningful thresholds."[46]

If one canny analyst had pointed to the ICD system and asked Spitzer publicly to explain why the European model couldn't prevail, he admits it "would've been a tough argument" to counter. "I suppose the reason they use" terms like *neurosis,* he muses, referring to the Europeans, "is because of the history of Freud. I mean, Freud developed those categories."[47] Certainly, Freud did develop many new terms to describe his patients' behavior, and many of his followers applied the terms narrowly and reductively, especially in the 1940s and 1950s, trying to fix the behavior as a component of the patient's identity, in ways that ended up pathologizing them.

It is also true that Freud's work differs massively from the judgments of his midcentury practitioners. I doubt those arguing with Spitzer at the time ever heard him openly declare, "We've got to get rid of the word *neurosis* because it has psychoanalytic meaning."[48] Still, he did joke privately to Edward Sachar and Klein that, with regard to various psychoanalytic opponents and institutions, he was embarking on a "strategy of entrapment."[49] Ignoring them was no longer possible. At such moments, the games and strategies fall away, leaving in plain sight the stakes for Spitzer and his opponents.

The war over Freud was not the only controversy to emerge. Another was how the Task Force on Nomenclature and Statistics set about devising the new disorders. It sometimes pushed through reforms so hastily and vehemently that many observers found the process extremely disconcerting.

"During a forty-minute conversation" in Washington, Alix Spiegel observes, Spitzer and two other psychiatrists "decided that 'hysterical psychoses' should really be divided into two disorders. Short episodes of delusion and hallucination would be labeled 'brief reactive psychosis,' and the tendency to show up in an emergency room without authentic cause would be called 'factitious disorder.' 'Then Bob asked for a typewriter,' [Roger] Peele says. To Peele's surprise, Spitzer drafted the definitions on the spot. 'He banged out criteria sets for factitious disorder and for brief reactive psychosis, and it struck me that this was a productive fellow! He comes in to talk about an issue and walks away with diagnostic criteria for two different mental disorders!'"[50]

Not all maladies received such cursory attention; some generated much lengthier discussions. But Peele's retort about Spitzer's "productiveness" hints uneasily that the chairman's zeal could sometimes tip into unrestrained inventiveness.

While meticulousness was hardly the group's forte, countless other procedural questions marred its work. Just as there were no firm guidelines establishing how long discussion about each illness should last, so there were not enough people holding Spitzer accountable for the final wording. "He must have had some internal criteria," David Shaffer says. "But I don't always know what they were."[51]

Part of the problem, Paul Fink grasped, was that "all communications" concerning the task force and its working groups were "filtered through Bob Spitzer." By Fink's reckoning, Spitzer also scheduled too few meetings; by the time the annual ones came around, a lot of business and discussion "had been handled through correspondence which served to divide and conquer, leaving much of the final decision in Bob's hands, with the help of people like Don Klein who works in the same institution with him." A third and even more basic problem was that "the process by which the DSM III has been developed [was] highly prejudiced," since the task force was "from the very beginning, very much skewed toward a phenomenological and descriptive point of view, and [was] quite anti-psychodynamic."[52]

Spitzer wouldn't characterize the problems or biases in this way, but he agrees he "picked everybody that [he] was comfortable with," a statement referring to just over a dozen friends and "kindred spirits" drawn primarily to "diagnostic research and not to clinical practice."[53] By laying down so few guidelines, Sabshin and Marmor seemed carefully neutral in 1974, when things were getting under way, but their hands-off approach gave Spitzer carte blanche to proceed as he wished, with no checks or even an illusion of balance. In selecting only "kindred spirits," then, he either forgot or tried to ignore the other side of the equation—the psychodynamic colleagues who had dominated the profession for decades and doubted Spitzer's emphasis on diagnostic reliability.

The net effect was that key debates got bogged down over first principles. While the task force tried to redress psychiatric terminology, much of the actual discussion and correspondence swirled around more elemental conflicts, with a lopsided effect. According to Spitzer and his allies, the analysts—feeling threatened and under attack—became aggressive, envious, and obstructionist.[54] When word reached them that the task force planned to eliminate *neurosis* from *DSM-III*, they were "aghast," Klein admits, because they "thought . . . we were calling into question their livelihood." But in a real sense, the neuropsychiatrists were doing just that. To the analysts, moreover, *neurosis* wasn't just a "bread-and-butter term";[55] its elimination, although needless, was slyly motivated to undercut their standing. When they tried to reason with Spitzer, adding that his alternatives were rigid and simplistic, they found him capricious and unyielding. He has responded, to others and to me, that he proposed several compromises (the record confirms this, especially when a final showdown loomed) but was stonewalled or overwhelmed by alternatives too diffuse to succeed.

Spitzer became especially animated when revisiting this period with me, recalling the fight from almost three decades ago as if it had unfolded yesterday:

> You know, the analytic critique of *DSM-III* as it was developing was not, "We have another way of classifying." It's not like they said, "Here's our system for classifying." Their main complaint was that in the description of the disorders we left out psychodynamic factors.
>
> Now there's one interesting story about that. The American Psychoanalytic Association had a liaison committee that met with me. And the chair of their committee said, "You know, the problem is, we know so much more about these disorders than *DSM-III* puts in there." Well, what he meant was, we know the psychodynamic [side]. So I said, "Why don't you take one disorder and write it up the way you think, with the stuff we don't have in there?" So they gave it to Larry Rockland, who happened to be a friend of mine. He took OCD and he wrote up the psychodynamics. And it was embarrassing. I mean, he had included "anal conflicts" and stuff. So I said, "This just won't fly. This is not something we can use."[56]

Although Spitzer in fact responded differently at the time to his colleagues and opponents,[57] he does have a point. Notwithstanding recent attempts at remedying this problem,[58] psychodynamic approaches to diagnostics tend to flounder; they freight clinical treatment with a set of empirical expectations that psychoanalysis, in particular, sees as anathema. Freud explicitly refuted such expectations as ways of assessing how well treatment was proceeding. So Spitzer's invitation raised a fundamental question about apples and oranges that he surely knew he could win. (That doesn't mean that apples—in this case, neuropsychiatry—should prevail, just because on paper its approach seems more efficient and easy to codify.)

Nor is Lawrence Rockland's correspondence with Spitzer at all "embarrassing"; on the contrary, it comes across as smart and reasonable. "It seems to be part of the general argument throughout DSM III," he observed in early 1978, "that lists of symptoms are somehow more scientific and 'harder' facts than muddle-headed psychodynamic theorizing and fantasizing. I think that this is a very unfair characterization of psychological thinking." Instead, he wanted more attention paid to "the particular shades and varieties of intrapsychic conflict," which, as he underscored, "exists in all psychopathology and in all people." What this required, in practical terms, was "an attempt at a positive diagnosis of anxiety disorder based on a psychodynamic understanding of the patient, the patient's conflicts, and the psychosocial stresses operative which add up to a coherent picture of why the patient developed an anxiety neurosis at this time."[59]

Rockland's was far less of a cookie-cutter approach than Spitzer wanted, and had taken it upon himself to mandate. Even so, it seemed unfair to dismiss Rockland's suggestions; and Leo Madow, chair of the liaison committee, wrote to say so, in a letter sufficiently important to reproduce in full:

> Dear Bob:
>
> I am sure you can realize my deep concern when I spoke to you on the phone, and you indicated that your Committee had met and apparently was rescinding the modifications we had recommended and that had been incorporated in the revision you sent me.
>
> As you know, we have been trying for some time now to assist in making changes in the DSM III that we felt were a contribution from our present state of knowledge of psychodynamics. As mentioned above, Larry Rockland, one of our Committee members, had submitted material which at first had been apparently rejected, but then some of the material was incorporated, particularly under the category of "predisposing factors."
>
> When our Committee on DSM III met on Friday, December 16,

1977, in New York with Bill Frosch, this was reaffirmed. We were quite enthusiastic and made assignments for other categories to be re-written following the model of Larry Rockland. These included:

1. Disorders arising in childhood and adolescence;
2. Impulse disorders;
3. Personality disorders;
4. Psychosexual disorders;
5. Somatoform disorders.

When your phone call indicated that there was another change, apparently following a Task Force meeting, I must confess I felt quite defeated and wondered what could have happened.

I gather that this meeting did not include Bill Frosch, but that you had conveyed the information to him. One of my confusions, then, is that I had thought that Bill and Jack Frosch had been added as members of your Task Force. Was this action to rescind an action of the whole Task Force?

I am not sure how to proceed from here. We are still eager to submit material to you that we hope would be useful. In the past, you have indicated that you would welcome this material and had actually felt the lack of our participation. Now that we have evolved the machinery to develop contributions, it appears that we are being blocked in our efforts to recommend these changes. Is there any appeal mechanism?

Sincerely yours,
Leo Madow, M.D., Chairman
Ad Hoc Committee on DSM III
The American Psychoanalytic Association[60]

Whether Spitzer had "actually felt the lack of [the analysts'] participation" or Madow was just saying so to be diplomatic must remain in doubt, given Spitzer's published and off-the-cuff remarks on the subject. There was, alas, no mechanism for appealing. So when the revised system collapsed, Spitzer explained—giving no clues about his own conduct—"the analytic group really tried to defeat the whole thing. And there was a possibility that they might be successful."[61]

True, the analysts wanted to take the discussion back to square one, to hammer out first principles. But they also retorted in letters that they were set up to fail by false deadlines, inadequate lead time, lack of committee representation, and predetermined outcomes that were not shared with them. As two other members of the liaison committee observed, when the analysts and their allies in effect said, "Please let us have a sandbox to play in," the reply they most often received was, "Here we play baseball."[62]

To cap it all, the analysts believed they were being treated with disdain (the letters, alas, confirm this). Small wonder they felt manipulated, sabotaged, and ultimately betrayed. Even Spitzer concedes, with poorly concealed relish, "I came up with all kinds of ways of muting their concerns."[63]

Business wobbled along in this uneven way for months, with only the hardiest or most stubborn prepared to drag out the fight. As Spitzer pressed on with his mission, presumably taking minutes as he tapped away during meetings, discussion hovered over a topic that, in Spitzer's mind, was already settled: whether mental ailments were really medical disorders.

This issue turned out to be so fundamental that it dominated most of the arguments flaring on and off the task force. All related questions—including how the psychiatrists should classify suffering, apportion symptoms to each disorder, and even define thresholds for who is sick—came back to this bedrock problem. As Spitzer admits, diagnosis is at the heart of psychiatry, and thus the source of so much acrimony, because it "defines what is the reality."[64]

The first matter here is that the terms proposed, like *avoidant personality disorder* and *social phobia*, were not just descriptive, they were also prescriptive. Simply to include them in a "Diagnostic and Statistical Manual of Mental Disorders" was to convey that they are bona fide mental illnesses needing psychiatric attention. To rule out other terms, such as *anxiety neurosis*, was also to broadcast that these were outdated ways of labeling or thinking about illnesses.

To psychiatrists the word *disorder* implies a stronger biological connection than *neurosis*. This last term recedes far into the eighteenth century (the Glaswegian physician William Cullen first mentioned its usefulness in 1769), but it generally conveys eruptions of nervous energy that would class it as a psychological conflict, rather than (as Spitzer wanted) a medical condition.[65]

A second, related matter concerns the parameters for each diagnosis, including when a psychiatrist should indicate that a patient is ill. As the DSM-III task force stressed "nomenclature and statistics," it signaled the importance of getting these matters straight. Even so, the guidelines it adopted were far from being so. "A diagnosis should be made if the criteria for that diagnosis are met," one memo advised in a claim both facile and maddeningly circular, for the group had cast itself as both judge and jury.[66]

"The initial task force memorandum," comments Mitchell Wilson, "clearly stated a desire to erect a high threshold for making a psychiatric diagnosis, but with the addition of new diagnostic categories, the threshold for making a diagnosis was lowered. As DSM-III went through its various modifications," he explains, summarizing crucial letters and procedural turns, "it became more inclusive."[67] To appalled onlookers promised scientific rigor, Spitzer set the bar for inclusion far too low.

"We didn't want anybody to feel that their diagnostic concepts were being excluded," Spitzer explained in another interview, magnificently ignoring the psychodynamic colleagues who felt exactly that. So "we took the attitude that we would include anything that seemed reasonable, that we could make some attempt to operationalize."[68] Given the task force's low standards and vaulting ambition, it's difficult to say what would not be included.

One can appreciate why the number of new illnesses skyrocketed, but what in theory constituted a new disease? When asked about this, Spitzer responded, rather vaguely, "How logical it was . . . Whether it fit in. The main thing was that it had to make sense. It had to be logical." He continued, "For most of the categories, it was just the best thinking of people who seemed to have expertise in the area."[69] In other words, his friends would approach him and say they had conducted trials with promising results that fit his vision for the *DSM*. Bingo! Another disorder was added to the list.

But Spitzer wasn't giving the fullest account of his rationale, which was more elaborate and certainly more manipulative. To his allies, for instance, he would periodically explain, sotto voce, that "the only way to block" his enemies, and so win the "bloody battle" over terms like *neurosis,* "was to offer an alternative" that made him feel he was forging a "peace treaty" comparable to that emerging between Egypt and Israel.[70]

"I was convinced I was dynamite," he couldn't help bragging, even if Northwestern University's Jules Masserman, considerably less impressed, called his ploys "a self-righteous propaganda campaign."[71] At other times, Spitzer apparently resembled "a magician." At least that's what Allan Stone, then president of the APA, once said to him. "When I would appear in front of the committee," Spitzer proudly relays, "I could just get my way by sweet talking and whatnot."[72]

So politics often clouded the science—in this case, the politics stemming from a hundred years' war—and overwhelmed the many improvements, big and small, that *DSM-III* made over *DSM-II,* including the later edition's greatly increased clinical reliability and more systematic research. Regrettably, the perspective offered by Spitzer veers disconcertingly from that of a faceless bureaucrat and impersonal scientist to that of a radiant prophet or entertaining maestro, presiding once more over a wobbly house of cards.

If all of these deliberations begin to seem inspired by Lewis Carroll's looking-glass world, we aren't alone in thinking so. After publishing three influential essays on psychiatric diagnosis in the mid-1970s, Alvan Feinstein, Yale Professor of Medicine and Epidemiology, presented a paper containing this intriguing hint: "Be sure to heed the Queen's advice to Alice in Wonderland: Consider everything." It wasn't by any means Feinstein's weightiest suggestion. "Concentrate on raw evidence and on [the] standardization of elements," he cautioned, and "avoid arbitrary demarcations." Yet "as you struggle with the magnitude and complexity of this enormous challenge," he couldn't resist adding, "don't get too depressed."[73]

Appearing roughly midway through Spitzer's term as task force chair, when things were starting to slip, Feinstein's advice was so well timed that when Jacques Quen recommended his work, after an evening's discussion with Spitzer, the chairman responded with alacrity, vowing to contact Feinstein immediately and adding, with almost a spring in his step, "Keep us on our toes."[74]

In Carroll's topsy-turvy world, the Queen is better known for ordering capricious executions than for promoting encyclopedic knowledge ("Off with their heads!" is doubtless more memorable than her peculiar variant of "Know thyself"). Yet if the Queen's advice seems a curious addition to Feinstein's otherwise sober analysis, Spitzer himself began a lengthy treatise on "Classification and Nosology in Psychiatry," two years earlier, with an epigraph from Carroll's sequel, *Through the Looking Glass*:

> "What's the use of their having names," the Gnat said, "if they won't answer to them?"
>
> "No use to *them*," said Alice, "but it's useful to the people that name them, I suppose. If not, why do things have names at all?"[75]

The article that follows is rather dry, making Carroll seem merely an appetizer to whet our hunger for the stolid main course. But the epigraph is strangely apt. For in all of Carroll's works, philosophical games about names, meaning, and nonsense play a significant role, as they did on the task force. Consider Masserman's jibe about its playing "antics with semantics" and Lehrman's crueler observations that its "pseudo-scientific veneer" led to such Carrollian wordplay as "continuingly unstable personality." Tongue in cheek, Lehrman called these personality disorders "stably unstable," before deadpanning, "I do not recall ever having seen a patient with a 'continuingly unstable personality.' I have seen many adolescents without goals."[76]

When John Frosch, a late addition to the DSM-III task force, announced his resignation in 1978, moreover, he explained that all the bickering and guesswork had given him "an Alice in Wonderland feeling."[77] And as one burrows through the group's vast correspondence, trying to make sense of its arcane, sometimes hilarious discussions, it's not difficult to see why. One can also share Frosch's disbelief and Lehrman's exasperation—indeed, feel that one is, like Alice, either tumbling down rabbit holes or hotly pursuing a mad hare that is about to dart into a new psychiatric Wonderland.

Frosch had reason to feel such vertigo, for Spitzer had encouraged him to join the task force at a particularly turbulent point in its history. In his and Ronald Bayer's truncated and slightly whitewashed "history of the controversy," Spitzer calls Frosch and his nephew "a perfect choice" for the group, as both were analysts who nonetheless "accepted the descriptive, criteria-based approach to diagnosis." For this very reason, though, they soon found themselves in "an unenviable position."[78]

The analysts who observed such business with their faces pressed against the glass expected John Frosch to fight at least some of their battles, yet his heterodoxy on the task force was not, Spitzer concedes, "always a welcome addition." Indeed, "they themselves believed," he writes of both Frosches, in alternating amazement and stunningly evasive attribution, "that, at times, their suggestions met with an unreasonable animus."[79] That is one way of explaining why John Frosch resigned after two fruitless years on the task force, and why William, replacing him, called the pervasive anti-Freudian hostility tantamount to icon smashing.

John Frosch participated in several meetings and urged the task force to compromise on one symbolic matter—not to delete *neurosis* from DSM-III. But the proposal came to nothing and appears to have been met with stony silence. After that, he rarely contributed to the correspondence and in his resignation letter calls himself a "fainéant" (idling) member of the group. The final sentence of his opening paragraph trails off into bewildered or frustrated silence: "I respect the efforts and the energy of the participants but I cannot help wondering at times ———."[80] Hinting at self-censorship, his dash makes it seem as if he's biting his knuckles to hold back a flood of irritation.

Regarding John Frosch's replacement, Spitzer admitted to me candidly that Bill was "pretty much a token figure."[81] Although they were clearly unwanted guests, the Frosches were given a belated place at the table because the psychoanalytic community was up in arms about its lack of representation. It is not difficult to see why. The task force had in fact met and corresponded for almost *four years* before it even occurred to an onlooker, Herbert Pardes (then Chair of Psychiatry at the University of Colorado Medical Center), that its membership and perspective were skewed entirely toward one approach: neuropsychiatry. "The resultant friction," Pardes warned, is "potentially divisive and likely to cause considerable strife within the psychiatric community."[82]

Spitzer later characterized this moment as the psychoanalytic community's getting "very uptight." One might thus conclude that if Pardes had said nothing, even more than halfway through the task force's term, Spitzer would have carried on typing, keeping things just as they were.[83]

Although their invitations were clearly symbolic, then, the Frosches were meant to be cosmetic placaters, giving outraged analysts at least the illusion that things were fair and inclusive. Alice held the same illusion in Wonderland, before realizing that the Queen's verdict was a foregone conclusion.

We have seen glaring discrepancies between how the task force was meant to work and how, in fact, its members tilted the issues to suit their perspective. But it's worth looking in more detail at the disparities between theory and practice, because doing so gets us to the heart of a debate in psychiatry about how one defines—to say nothing of explains or endeavors to treat—mental illness.

"I don't subscribe to any particular aetiology," Spitzer insisted, referring to different schools of thought on the causes of psychiatric illness. "As far as I'm concerned I'm totally neutral."[84] But Spitzer's claim to disinterestedness looks almost comical beside correspondence explaining how he staged debates to predetermine their outcome, gloated over his obstructionist or "entrapment" strategies to allies, then torpedoed or sidelined countless other proposals, many of them psychodynamic, because they didn't fit his belief that *DSM-III* should be atheoretical—meaning that it should list only the symptoms of each illness and thus look agnostic about their probable causes.

Even without this contrary evidence, the phrase "truth and reliability in diagnosis," ricocheting frequently from one letter to the next, sounded increasingly like a call to arms.[85] Certainly, it spurred a demand that the working groups under Spitzer's supervision standardize the traits and boundaries they gave each disorder, and thereby in theory stamp out awkward disparities in judgment.

Besides Emil Kraepelin, who gave it a model for classifying diseases from the nineteenth century, the task force had another, less distant precedent: colleagues in Washington University's psychiatry department who, under the guidance of Eli Robins and Samuel Guze, set out to define mental disorders in "descriptive, explicit, and rule-driven" ways.[86] The St. Louis group wanted to devise firm criteria for each illness and undertook field trials that would measure, in strict, quantifiable ways, where the cutoff point for each disorder should fall.

The beauty of such work is that it gives the impression of being very clear and exacting. It describes every facet of an illness in rapid, surefire strokes, making the overall medical picture seem so meticulously drawn as to be indisputable. One article on diagnostic criteria, coauthored in 1972 by John Feighner, Robins, Guze, and others, became so famous that it was soon known as listing simply the "Feighner criteria." Its authors were, however, adamant that every symptom had to be "chronic," a benchmark that disappears from the DSM-III correspondence.

Consider Feighner's criteria for *anxiety neurosis*. "For a diagnosis" to be made, his team insisted, "A through D are required," and the symptoms of A alone are logged with striking precision: "A. The following manifestations must be present: (1) Age of onset prior to 40. (2) Chronic nervousness with recurrent anxiety attacks manifested by apprehension, fearfulness, or sense of impending doom, with at least four of the following symptoms present during the majority of attacks: (a) dyspnea [shortness of breath], (b) palpitations, (c) chest pain or discomfort, (d) choking or smothering sensation, (e) dizziness, and (f) paresthesias [tingling]." In specifying how often these severe attacks must recur for a diagnosis to hold, paragraph B states unambiguously, "There must have been at least six anxiety attacks, each separated by at least a week from the others."[87]

Feighner's team warned that its "criteria [were] not intended as final for any illness," and added, with refreshing candor, "Unfortunately, consistent and reliable laboratory findings have not yet been demonstrated in the more common psychiatric disorders," like anxiety neurosis.[88] Even with this proviso, which Spitzer and many other psychiatrists conceded to be almost inevitable, the Feighner criteria became a beacon for one side of the profession. They set a new standard for measuring chronic maladies that patients and doctors once thought too subjective and unpredictable to bear such scrutiny.

The St. Louis group unnerved the wider psychodynamic community, however, because its assessment of mental illness gave a rigid, one-dimensional account of symptoms. In essence, it amounted to a cookie-cutter approach to psychiatry. The notion that one could slot each person into diagnostic molds ruled out other factors, such as the dynamic nature of illness, which the Washington University group mistakenly tended to take at face value. For psychodynamic clinicians, by contrast, illnesses are not uniform because their symptoms are inherently *unreliable* guides to patient distress: they tend to mask as much as they reveal. The point is to unearth what is *behind* the symptom, not to take the latter as an end or a complete picture in itself.

Still, Bayer and Spitzer were right to observe that "with its intellectual roots in St. Louis instead of Vienna, and with its intellectual inspiration derived from Kraepelin, not Freud, the task force was viewed from the outset as unsympathetic to the interests of those whose theory and practice derived from the psychoanalytic tradition."[89] Kraepelin's doctrinaire approach to mental illness greatly influenced those at Washington University; and though Spitzer has played down his debt to the German, his colleague Gerald Klerman not only christened the task force "neo-Kraepelinian," but also later caused a ruckus when declaring, during a major debate about *DSM-III*, "The problem of [diagnostic] reliability [has] been solved."[90] Even Spitzer now winces at this unfortunate boast, telling me it was "regretful, because the problem of reliability *hasn't* been solved at all."[91] Nevertheless, concerning German psychiatry, Spitzer hoped to substitute reliability for validity, and repeated Griesinger (Kraepelin's forebear) almost verbatim when asserting another crucial, polarizing statement: "A mental (psychiatric) disorder is a medical disorder."[92]

Of course, phrasing so provocative and tendentious failed to settle this crucial debate, and Spitzer's colleagues balked. While his definition extended a much longer one harking back to the nineteenth century, his allies actually found Spitzer's revisions too open-ended.

According to Klein, for instance, the idea that a "disorder or illness" might somehow "reflect social deviance or discomfort" wrongly eclipsed "that subclass of *biological dysfunction* that in a given society entitles the person to the exemptions inherent in the sick role." The enormity of Klein's intervention isn't difficult to grasp. If psychiatrists didn't specify whether an illness is chiefly biological or psychological, society might discount the symptoms, and patients couldn't say the impairment stemmed from factors beyond their control—for instance, chemical imbalances in the brain. As Klein declared starkly, "If a dysfunction produces very limited manifest disability then society is less likely to award the sick role, since the person should be capable of carrying out the usual social demands."[93]

Put another way, unless one says that anxiety and depression are chronic afflictions deriving entirely from biological problems, various subcategories in the *DSM* (such as "social phobia") might be dismissed as trifling problems that don't belong there. For one thing, medical insurance wouldn't cover them.

When word got out that Spitzer's team was trying to redefine mental disorders, angry letters denounced the move. Howard Berk and Hector Jaso, members of the liaison committee, resorted to sarcasm: "In the process of simplification and restriction we see that the proposed nomenclature displays a generous measure of linguistic and conceptual sterility."[94] Even a few of Spitzer's allies pleaded for restraint. Paul Chodoff called the definition needlessly "complicated and cumbersome," and added, weakly, "I wonder if we have to say that everything we are classifying is a mental illness."[95]

Of all the skeptics, Richard Schwartz at the Cleveland Clinic put the issue best: "My quarrel with DSM-III," he declared, "is that for many of the disorders listed therein, the social consensus that they *are* true diseases and should be managed by the psychiatric profession is lacking." The task force had resorted to classifying as illnesses "abnormalities of thought, emotion, or behavior" that "lie outside the domain of psychiatry."[96]

Spitzer's allies were upset because they had tried to dance around this particular minefield, opting for a less contentious model of mental illness. As Henry Pinsker stated in an early memo from June 1975, "Our Task Force has been unanimous that *mental disorder* should be defined narrowly, and that people should not be called mentally ill simply because they are different or unhappy."[97] To credit every psychological disorder with an underlying medical origin struck the Spitzer group as not only a massive and unnecessary shift in thinking, but also a betrayal of first principles.

Unsurprisingly, qualms began to crystallize around the increasingly rigid use of Kraepelin. As Madow muttered semiprivately to Lester Grinspoon, "I hope that we were able to indicate our feelings that this document will not enhance the image of American psychiatry but rather appears to be a neo-Kraepelinian approach which indicates the level of our knowledge of the field to be at a point much less developed than it really is."[98]

In his defense, Spitzer was concerned that diagnostic terms such as *neurosis* would be "used in two very different ways by different groups within our profession."[99] This worry sounds quite reasonable until you consider that similar ambiguities riddled *DSM-III*. As Spitzer wanted the manual to list only symptoms, the conflict over *neurosis* should never have arisen. But since he had sided with the neuropsychiatrists over the fate of this term, reminding his task force members of "our long-standing opposition to the inclusion of neurosis in the *DSM-III* classification," he could hardly claim to be impartial.[100] Transparently, his task force was trying to ban terminology associated with psychoanalysis, as Spitzer admitted to me. Jaso and Berk pointed this fact out to him at the time, when lambasting the group's "large-scale, arbitrary extirpation of established concepts." They complained, "The *DSM-III* gets rid of the castles of Neurosis and replaces it with a diagnostic Levittown."[101]

Once again, then, advancing a theory of mental illness and trying to crush one's enemies became inseparable. Each theoretical claim also spawned a litany of conceptual and procedural questions that beset the task force for years. Even among Spitzer's "kindred spirits" no one could guarantee that psychiatrists would interpret every sign of illness the same way ("interrater reliability," in the lingo of the field). Spitzer's group could list all the telltale signs of a particular disorder and hope these were sufficiently complete to rule out misdiagnoses ("false positives").[102] But there was still the thorny issue of who would assess a patient's distress and dysfunction, and stipulate that he or she was suffering from generalized anxiety, say, rather than avoidant personality disorder.

In practice, *DSM-III* made it unnecessary to choose. When in doubt, psychiatrists could simply list both. Still, as the task force had staked its reputation on diagnostic clarity and reliability, it needed to set a clear example. And as these judgments varied wildly among the field's leading experts, what hope was there of producing flawless consensus in the wider culture?

———

In theory, the process was supposed to work this way: After completing the field trials, which likely would generate a wide range of patient responses, the psychiatrists would shrink them to fit an abstract concept like "social phobia." Devising the criteria for such terms was of course a major act of interpretation in itself, involving clinical and sometimes moral judgment, as well as speculation. As George Vaillant put it, "*DSM-III* represents a bold series of choices based on guess, taste, prejudice, and hope."[103] Once the diagnostic term appeared with its associated criteria in the *DSM,* psychiatrists ideally would interpret signs of it in just the same way, by focusing on how many criteria a patient met—something a short (forty-five-minute, cross-sectional) interview apparently would establish.

In practice, however, and as further evidence of circular reasoning, the examining psychiatrist would seek only corroborating signs of prescribed traits and syndromes. One begins to see why the committee's criteria for selecting and recoding behavioral traits became so important, and so political. Irwin Marill and his Bethesda colleagues observed that the idea that "persons could 'objectively' be classified as 'average' [or not] by some 'average' psychiatrist . . . promulgates a pseudo-objectivity which simply substitutes the subjectivity of the *observer* for the subjectivity of the *patient.*"[104]

Spitzer's colleagues countered that they would diagnose only disorders causing patients acute distress, dysfunction, deviance, and danger (the so-called 4Ds characterizing abnormal behavior, to which their discussions initially adhered quite firmly).[105] But *DSM-III* flouted this principle repeatedly, partly because in including so many new disorders it inevitably lowered their diagnostic threshold, and because it ignored the extent to which its procedures still relied on subjective interpretation and bias. As Marill and his coworkers insisted, the manual "ignores what we all know: namely, that a stimulus which is exciting and pleasurable for one person, may be indifferent to a second, and horrifying or depressing to a third."[106]

To put it differently, the very attempt to bypass human judgment and produce a rule-driven account of a disorder's effects would almost certainly overlook profound differences in not only degree, but also kind. It would likely run together disparate kinds of behavior that only the psychiatrist naming the disorder would recognize had anything in common. "That's a big problem," Spitzer acknowledged to me, and "it still is a big problem."[107]

Beyond matters of bias and interpretation, when the task force tried to apportion symptoms to each disorder, it found an illness like introverted personality disorder initially aligned with Axis II personality disorders. As the debate intensified, however, the same trait acquired the qualities of an anxiety disorder, which the task force had resolved should appear in Axis I, and so on.

Other protracted discussions spun out for months over ambiguous and dubious terms, such as *oppositional defiant disorder, psychosexual relationship capacity disorder, labile personality, malingering, chronic undifferentiated unhappiness, chronic complaint disorder,* and, most relevant here, *withdrawn, sensitive,* and *introverted personality disorder,* which will be part of the focus of Chapter 3.[108]

Among the "associated features" of chronic undifferentiated unhappiness, according to Steven E. Hyler, is that "the person with this disorder will often present a very sad face. The corners of his mouth will usually be lower than the center, the shoulders are usually hunched, [and] the gait is slow." But it was in describing the signs of chronic complaint disorder that Hyler really found his stride:

> The essential feature [of] this disorder is the person's persistent and consistent complaining in such a manner that it is obvious to even the unskilled observer. To be included in this category are persons who heretofore were known by the synonyms: "kvetch," "scootch," "noodge," and just plain "neurotic."
>
> An episode of acute complaining is usually elicited by the question: "How are you?" The pathognemonic response is, "Don't ask." The response complaints are of a general nature and include such diverse topics as the weather, the energy crisis, taxes, or the previous evening's track results. . . .
>
> Associated features in this disorder include an outlook on life which is characterized as pessimistic. . . . The complaints themself [*sic*] are usually presented in a high pitched whining fashion which is especially noxious to the listener. . . .
>
> There also appears to be an ethnic association with this disorder in that it is found predominantly in persons of Eastern-European ancestry. In these cases, the pathognemonic expression becomes, "Oy vay, don't ask."[109]

Perhaps unsurprisingly, the task force had to reject these and related proposals because it could not decide on their validity or distinct criteria. Often it simply adopted new categories to accommodate them, like "V:

Codes for Conditions Not Attributable to a Mental Disorder That Are a Focus of Attention or Treatment." (Three examples: "V62.30: Academic Problem," "V61.10 Marital Problem," and "V62.81: Other Interpersonal Problem," whose symptoms include "difficulties with co-workers, or with romantic partners.")[110] Perhaps it shouldn't surprise us, then, that one member joked that serving on the task force had been enough to induce the very pathologies it sought to classify: "I have had a 309.28 [adjustment disorder]," he declared, "over *DSM III*."[111]

The task force also made it possible for a patient's symptoms to count several times and thus to qualify as multiple, simultaneous illnesses ("comorbid factors" in the new lingo, due to its "multiaxial approach"), something "that happens nowhere else in medicine" (distinct illnesses may of course overlap). It was a situation earlier editions of the *DSM* had ruled out from concern about double jeopardy.[112] Even so, when it comes to diagnosing patients, psychiatrists generally stick with the terms and criteria they memorized in medical school.[113] How likely was it, then, that they would monitor the appendix and disease criteria of each *DSM* edition, in hopes of keeping up with the task forces' increasingly arcane distinctions?

One thing is clear: The proliferation of categories between *DSM-II* and *DSM-III* should have raised eyebrows among mathematical purists and even diehard neuropsychiatrists. The latters' response seems, in hindsight, almost supine. It was left to two professors of social work, Stuart Kirk and Herb Kutchins, to show that Spitzer and his colleagues offered only "the illusory precision of statistical accuracy." *DSM-III*, they wrote, had set the range of kappas too high (above 0.7 or even 0.8, rather than, as would be normal, a range from 0.4 to 0.6). Kappas are "an index of reliability that corrects for chance agreement," and thus a major factor in all *DSM* calculations. Spitzer's setting them too high skewed the math by greatly increasing the number of patients meeting the new criteria.[114] When one adds such statistical problems to the conceptual ones here detailed, the results become chaotic. As Kutchins and Kirk put it in their follow-up study, *Making Us Crazy*, "By simply altering slightly the wording of a criterion, the duration for which a symptom must be experienced in order to satisfy a criterion, or the number of criteria used to establish a diagnosis, the prevalence rates in the United States will rise and fall as erratically as the stock market."[115]

Spitzer's rejoinder is in some respects surprising, given his ardent defense of *DSM-III:* "We've been accused of exaggerating how much reliability improved [in the third edition], which I think is not true. . . . If you ask clinicians now how reliable is the *DSM* or how much it's improved, I don't know what they'd say, but it's a modest improvement. It depends on the settings." These are best, he concedes, when the population of those afflicted is high, as in Anxiety Disorders clinics, but "it's very modest" if one tries calculating prevalence among even related groups, such as those attending outpatient clinics.[116]

David Barlow, codirector of SUNY-Albany's Center for Stress and Anxiety Disorders, in fact alerted Spitzer to this general problem in July 1985, warning: "The other difficulty we see with returning GAD [Generalized Anxiety Disorder] to the type of broad residual category that it occupies in DSM-III was the extremely low KAPPA that we achieved with that definition."[117] The admission is very significant, because it indicates the prevalence rates were low even among Barlow's clinical patients, a population that by Spitzer's reckoning should yield higher-than-average results.

Many would therefore discount the inclusion of that population, insisting they are not statistically representative. Barlow's statement also makes clear that the diagnostic criteria in *DSM-III* were at odds with the clinical reality and needed to be fixed, either by reducing the numbers said to suffer from GAD, which would shrink the magnitude of the disorder, or by relaxing the criteria used to gauge the suffering associated with it, which would maintain or even increase the disorder's apparent severity. With the solution pointing logically to the need to lower the disorder's prevalence, as the clinical population should always drive the criteria (not the reverse), one wonders with Kutchins and Kirk why Spitzer, already warned about the "extremely low KAPPA" result, ended up setting the range too high.

Summing up the consequences of these allegedly scientific revisions, Healy writes: "Today's classification systems make it possible to have many different illnesses at the same time—something that happens nowhere else in medicine. It would seem inevitable that there must be a collapse back toward larger disease categories at some point."[118] The collapse may seem inevitable, but instead of reaching that conclusion or questioning the logic spawning the categories in the first place, neuropsychiatrists today fiercely defend them by pointing to the vast numbers of North Americans they have identified as suffering from the afflictions catalogued. In light of this and other documented sleights of hand, David Faust and Richard Miner seem justified in asking whether *DSM-III* shouldn't be dubbed "the empiricist's new clothes."[119]

"To be meaningful," Marill and his colleagues aptly forewarned in June 1977, psychiatric terminology "should not be changed casually or capriciously . . .; otherwise fads of conceptualization may seriously interfere with the steady evolution of our science. We cannot be sure what we are talking about," they cautioned, "if someone is constantly pulling the words out from under us."[120]

3

A DECISIVE VICTORY:
SHYNESS BECOMES AN ILLNESS

Robert Spitzer's task force obviously thought it was perfecting American psychiatry by representing mental disorders in such a clear-cut way. Its critics charged that the group was opening up vast, complex issues it was ill equipped to resolve. Even now, Spitzer has few regrets and insists the task force was right to undertake such sweeping changes. But the incidents leading to social phobia's inclusion in *DSM-III* betray so much guesswork that the splitting of anxiety into seven distinct illnesses seems more the result of accident than of careful design or scientific deliberation.

According to David Healy, the term *social phobia* began circulating unclaimed among British psychiatrists in the late 1960s.[1] So while Pierre Janet actually coined the term in 1903 (as *des phobies sociales ou des phobies de la société*), neither the American nor the British psychiatric communities noticed, pursued, or adopted it until Isaac Marks and Michael Gelder in 1966 published a review sketching several different kinds of panic they witnessed in patients. According to both psychiatrists, a small number of patients (10 male, 15 female) became anxious primarily when required to participate in social situations.[2] Rather than shunning particular objects like spiders or snakes, they tried whenever possible to avoid eating in public, preferring their office to the staff canteen. Signs of their distress included "fears of blushing in public, . . . [of] going to dances or parties," and "shaking when the center of attention."[3]

Sometimes, Marks and Gelder conceded, the distinction between these patients and agoraphobics was "rather arbitrary." They would, for instance, label "a patient who feared walking on the street for fear of seeming ridiculous to other people" as socially anxious, not agoraphobic, because of the patient's embarrassment. Yet the type of anxiety that prevailed was not, they admitted, always clear or easily defined.

As DSM-II had referred only to "anxiety neurosis," none of these subtleties could be formal distinctions. Marks and Gelder neither lamented that fact nor advocated breaking up the overarching, diagnostic term. On the contrary, they concluded that "behaviorist and psychoanalytic views favor unitary explanations of phobias, and attempts to subdivide the[m] have proved fruitless."[4] Four years later, in a report scholars say was instrumental in ensuring the inclusion of social phobia in DSM-III,[5] Marks restated his position more firmly: "Evidence is lacking that [social phobia] is a coherent group." He warned, "We need to know more about social phobics before definitely classifying them on their own."[6]

Spitzer's group welcomed the review as evidence that the phobia existed, and apparently adopted it wholesale in 1980 as justification for listing the phobia as a distinct illness.[7] But as knowledge of social phobia remained largely unchanged throughout the 1970s, the group had ignored Marks's final proviso. It also had glided over two of his and Gelder's major conclusions: the number of patients affected is proportionately small, and anxiety's various facets are so entwined that it is a mistake to split them up.

Of the few reports on social phobia that *did* appear between the 1966 review and the 1980 publication of DSM-III, moreover, two sided with Marks in voicing serious doubts that social phobia was a distinct syndrome. In 1969, Eliot Slater and Martin Roth signaled clearly in *Clinical Psychiatry* that "on the present evidence there is no very clear line of demarcation" between those with social anxiety and those with agoraphobia, a position almost identical to R. P. Snaith's lengthy report on the two types of anxiety, appearing the previous year.[8]

Given all the hoopla around social phobia in the 1990s, you might think Marks and Gelder would want credit for reviving the term and writing one of its foundational documents—a review that follow-up articles cited so many times it soon wielded an almost talismanic authority. On the contrary, when asked about the phenomenon he had witnessed, Marks, a soft-spoken South African, shrugged. He still insists that modest levels of anxiety accompany most, if not all, social situations; that recognition of this type of anxiety as a minor ailment recedes far into history; and that the 1990s bid to turn "social phobia" into a neglected pandemic is nothing short of an "advertising ploy."[9]

Healy, a charismatic Dubliner now based in northern Wales, was similarly wry when asked about the urgency his American colleagues have attached to social phobia. After the Marks and Gelder review came out, he noted, it "took a further ten years before a small number of groups got around to following up this lead and providing initial estimates of the frequency of the disorder and its characteristic features."[10] Yet even with these studies, the evidence for proceeding was so slim that Healy, a scrupulous researcher and historian whose book *The Antidepressant Era* contains almost 40 pages of notes, decided not to reference them.

These are, one might think, rather scant beginnings for a problem so "crippling" and woefully "neglected" it would soon earn the tag "disorder of the decade."[11] According to Healy's summary of the follow-up studies, moreover, the type of social anxiety unearthed remained "uncommon, almost rare"[12]—adjectives echoing *DSM-III,* which posed a few problems for those ratcheting up the drama in later years.[13] Still, after a number of false starts, Spitzer's task force canonized the term two decades later, in *DSM-III.* As Healy puts it laconically, the few studies that pursued Marks and Gelder's observations had done "enough to provide a set of inclusion and exclusion criteria by which [social phobia] could be diagnosed, and this led to its incorporation into *DSM-III* in 1980."[14]

It is tempting to assume that these studies were comprehensive, objective, and uninfluenced by the drug companies funding them. But it would be unwise to generalize. The "inclusion and exclusion criteria" the task force adopted (Chapter 2) often were not scrupulously defined. Spitzer and his colleagues "took the attitude that [they] would include anything that seemed reasonable, that [they] could make some attempt to operationalize."[15]

What about the field trials Spitzer would sometimes invoke? To quell criticism, he once stated grandly, "The Task Force believes that the DSM-III classification should not include the concept of neurosis or neurotic disorders, and in fact, the Field Trials have been rather successfully carried out without those categories."[16] But N. S. Lehrman retorted by calling attention to the "79% not answering Spitzer's survey," a figure that makes a mockery of Spitzer's pronouncement.[17] And when Donald Klein argued with him over the amount of social anxiety a person with avoidant personality disorder could experience, Spitzer snapped, "These changes [to the operational criteria] were made based upon an intensive case study of one that I personally conducted."[18]

Perhaps the most damning evidence of all comes from Marks himself. When I asked him about the motivation for renaming various disorders, he relayed what had happened at one crucial conference on panic disorder. According to Marks, the Boston conference "began with the chief executive of Upjohn saying unashamedly, 'Look, there are three reasons why Upjohn is here taking an interest in these diagnoses. The first is money. The second is money. And the third is money' . . . They were quite upfront about it," he marveled. "And they were exceedingly successful at it for at least the first six years."[19]

Nor was it really a secret that Upjohn had paid for the conference because it hoped the experts attending would endorse Xanax (alprazolam), its drug, as the preferred treatment for panic disorder. Some demurred. Details about panic *disorder* were sketchy at best, as distinct from panic itself, which few could mistake and everyone attending was committed to treating. As Marks explained to Spitzer at the time: "The presence of panic per se is not the hallmark of any particular anxiety syndrome. . . . There is thus . . . little point in separating panic syndromes from anxiety syndromes."[20]

As the differences here are not trivial, you would think those seeking to clarify them would want all available input and expertise. Yet as Marks says of a strategy that soon became a pattern marking the approval of other disorders, "The consensus was arranged by leaving out the dissenters." Those, like him, who wouldn't toe the line were quietly dropped from future meetings.

"I remember being in the loo at the Boston conference," he recalls, "having a pee at the same time as Bob Spitzer, and he said to me, 'Isaac, you're not going to win. Panic [disorder] is in. That's it.'" Marks adds ruefully, "Never mind about the pros and cons intellectually," characterizing Spitzer's obstinate rejection of facts that didn't fit his vision for the disorder and, indeed, for psychiatry overall. "'Don't confuse me with the data. It's in.'"[21] Despite his vast expertise, including a pioneering study of phobias and the founding document on social phobia, Marks never received an invitation to the crucial follow-up meeting on panic disorder.

When I questioned Spitzer about this incident, he asked rather nervously, "What did he say?" He was quick to downplay Marks's concerns. That Upjohn paid for the conference "was a mistake on our parts," Spitzer conceded regretfully. "We should never have done that. But they had no influence on any criteria or the name. So this thing that we were influenced by pharmaceutical companies is just, I say, is just absurd. . . . They never made any attempt to say, 'We would like you to define [panic disorder] more broadly' or anything. It never happened."

Even without addressing Marks's point about the broader pattern of leaving out dissenters, Spitzer felt obliged to add: "They [Upjohn] *were* delighted that we had the category panic disorder, because they felt they had a drug for it." And when I later steered the interview toward the future approval of other disorders in the *DSM,* he conceded quite matter-of-factly that such an outcome was partly "a function of 'Do you have a treatment?' If you have a treatment, you're more interested in getting the category in [the *DSM*]. If you have no treatment for it, there's not as much pressure to put the thing in."

Spitzer characterized the approval of panic disorder as follows: "Along comes Don Klein and says there's this thing called 'panic disorder.' Okay, so if we're going to recognize panic disorder, clearly the *DSM-II* needs a broader category, so we need a name for that other part."[22] The inclusion of other illnesses, like social phobia, was easier and smoother after panic disorder won approval. Indeed, with the charm for which he is well known, Spitzer has since conceded of his manual, in semijocular fashion, "You could make fun of it as a Chinese menu."[23] Certainly, one could (and several have), but the way Healy summarizes the updating of psychiatry's bible makes clear that he, too, is far from sanguine about the results:

> Spitzer and a number of the others involved in drafting DSM-III were keen to get rid of the older term *anxiety neurosis,* because of its Freudian connotations. There was agreement that [Donald] Klein's panic disorder should be included, partly because a clear set of inclusion and exclusion criteria could be set out for it but also because its inclusion chipped away at the anxiety neurosis

monolith. Agoraphobia with and without concurrent panic disorder was also included, as was social phobia. However, it was clear that there was more to the anxiety disorders than simply panic disorders, agoraphobia, and social phobia. Floundering somewhat, members of the anxiety disorders subcommittee stumbled on the notion of generalized anxiety disorder (GAD), and consigned the greater part of the rest of the anxiety disorders to this category.[24]

Whether deliberately or inadvertently, Healy's use of passive voice veils how the task force made such consequential decisions. In addition to last-minute bargaining (hence the assortment of undercooked entries) and prejudice against Freudianism, the committee's decisions reflect more of the opportunism, fuzzy math, and wild speculation that we've already seen in abundance.

Spitzer's version of this momentous transformation differs only slightly from Healy's, and is scarcely less troublesome in its implications. He does, however, insist that the creation of social phobia came after generalized anxiety disorder, not before: "We came up with that name [GAD] after we had *anxiety neurosis* in *DSM-II,* and if you had panic then there had to be something that was left over. So that became Generalized Anxiety Disorder. And then there was the discussion about social phobias. [But] . . . then, the common notion of phobias was simple phobias. And then people said, 'Well, but some phobias are more generalized.' And that became generalized phobia. And later that became social phobia. And now, with *DSM-IV,* it's social anxiety disorder, which is a better word than social phobia."

When I pressed Spitzer on this matter, asking him when the task force decided to distinguish social phobia from specific phobia, and why, he continued even more vaguely: "Well, I think, you know, with specific phobia there are things that scare people and they avoid them: heights, tunnels, snakes, dogs, things like that. And then people said, 'Well, some people avoid *people,* so let's call that "social phobia."' I mean, 'Let's call that "generalized phobia" [which became social phobia].'"[25]

One of several big problems here is that the *DSM* does *not* define social phobia strictly as avoidance of people. If it did, the manual would pathologize misanthropy, which would raise a host of other issues.[26] According to other framers of the disorder, however, social phobia is very different from either reclusion or people-hating. Nor does it resemble a conventional phobia, because the phobic object ("society") is not only vast in scope but also an inconsistent source of concern to those afflicted (the opinions of bosses, colleagues, and large numbers of strangers seem to matter greatly, whereas those of friends and loved ones apparently do not). So the *DSM* likens the phobia to undue fear of and embarrassment about other people's *judgments,* real or imagined, which is altogether different than "avoid[ing] people," and certainly much harder to quantify.

None of these changes, in Spitzer's summary, sound especially scientific or systematic, but they were partly a consequence of the people he'd selected and of the research they had undertaken. Doubtless, a key reason Klein's definition of panic disorder made it into *DSM-III* was that Klein served with Spitzer on the task force, as well as the Anxiety and Dissociative Disorders Committee and the Personality Disorders Committee.

Spitzer calls the double bind of expertise an "interesting" dilemma, without connecting it to the *DSM*'s burgeoning categories: "Researchers always give maximal prevalence for the disorders that they have a particular interest in. In other words, if you're really interested in panic disorder, you're going to tend to say it's very common. You never hear an expert say, 'My disorder is very rare.' Never. They always tend to see it as more common."[27]

This explanation not only sounds credible, but also helps account for the hyping of mild problems and the frenzied conversion of them into new disorders. But one can't help wondering whether a task force with a different constituency would have adopted an alternative model of anxiety, perhaps with no generalized or socially phobic component at all. Klein later called the neurosis controversy "a minor capitulation to psychoanalytic nostalgia," for instance, long after the terms themselves had lost all psychoanalytic meaning.[28] He also declared, as suitable criteria for panic disorder and social phobia: "If a patient has social phobias and then in the context of social appraisal also has unexpected panic attacks, they deserve two separate diagnoses. I feel the same way about a patient with panic disorder who also avoided restaurants because of fear that he may drop some food on his necktie and look ridiculous. I don't think the cure for these complex situations is in the construction of hierarchies, but rather in multiple diagnoses."[29]

Klein's hostility to psychoanalysis did not abate in the spring of 1978, when Spitzer's Advisory Committee on Personality Disorders began considering whether "Introverted Personality Disorder" (IPD) should appear in *DSM-III*. Nor, intriguingly, did he and Spitzer see eye to eye on this topic. More than a key chapter in the story of how shyness became an illness, the episode also illustrates how Spitzer's committees tacitly sanctioned "diagnostic bracket creep," a phrase Peter Kramer coined to indicate that the goalposts defining social phobia and the like are constantly shifting, not fixed.[30]

Although personality disorders are normally different from anxiety disorders, both can cause significant distress and impairment, and sometimes run on parallel tracks. There was, however, so much substantive overlap among social phobia, introverted personality disorder, and avoidant personality disorder (APD) that their symptoms, like their fate, became almost inseparable.

When the advisory committee let it be known that it planned to include introverted personality disorder in *DSM-III* and wanted feedback on where to set its boundaries, Spitzer received a larger-than-usual amount of mail, including exasperated letters from analysts pleading for restraint. "It is a gross disservice to the valuable and well-functioning introverts in our society," a "greatly concerned" Naomi Quenk wrote him from Albuquerque, "to have a pathological label attached to their normal and healthy attitude. It is discouraging that the psychiatric community has seen fit to encourage the extraverted bias characteristic of our society. . . . I therefore urge you to reconsider this change in the nomenclature, as its retention in the presently planned form may only serve to create pathology where none is warranted."[31]

At least two other analysts urging Spitzer to reconsider insisted the diagnosis would also pathologize *them*. "In many ways my own personality fits into the characterization of the new disorder," Massachusetts-based Otto Allen Will noted philosophically, while Ralph Crowley in New York City was more adamant: "I do not disagree with being labeled Introverted

Personality, but Disorder, No! And in bringing in the personal, I mean to speak for all others of my kind."[32]

Mindful of such opposition and never one to cower before Spitzer, Klein sent him a memo about introversion that was terser than usual, with two short sentences: "I hate to say it but I think that [yet another dissenter] is right. It's a lousy term and will lead to endless confusion." Less than a month later, he explained why: "I am not concerned about the [term's] surplus meaning suggesting a relationship with schizophrenia here as much as I am about the surplus meaning connecting the term to Jung's ideas, and the idea that this is in some fashion the opposite of being extroverted. Also, the complaint that the term 'schizoid' is related to schizophrenia seems hardly justified when under 'complications' you point out that there may well be a relationship between this disorder and schizophrenia."[33]

The discussion therefore forked at this point. On one side were analysts appalled that the committee could appropriate a neutral term Carl Jung had amplified (but not coined) without prejudice in the 1910s, and about which analysts had since written volumes. On the other side were Klein and several neuropsychiatrists, also troubled, but not by the judgment they would pass on normal behavior, or the confusion they could cause between introversion and schizophrenia. As Klein put it, Spitzer had "point[ed] out that there may well be a relationship" between them, and merely posing such unsubstantiated connections seemed enough to convince them the chairman was right. What concerned them was that the term was hazy and came with too much psychoanalytic baggage.

Spitzer's initial response, characteristically, was to concede some ground to each side, then dig in his heels before finally turning on his detractors. Signs of this pattern recur so often in the *DSM* correspondence that it would seem Spitzer's concessions were meant to blind all but his closest colleagues to his real intentions: to keep such diagnoses in the manual, whenever possible.

The *DSM-III* advisory committees frequently decided, on the basis of often-tenuous evidence, that there was reason to create new anxiety and personality disorders.[34] With introverted personality, however, Spitzer could at least say that earlier editions of the *DSM* had established precedents. His problem was that the precedents had completely different criteria and appeared under another name. But that didn't stop him from saying he was merely adjusting an existing illness.

DSM-I and *DSM-II* included "Schizoid Personality" among a dozen personality disturbances (including "Antisocial," "Inadequate," "Passive-Aggressive," and "Emotionally Unstable"), and both editions made clear that the behavior was so extreme it was but a whisker from "actual psychosis." In *DSM-I*, the disorder's traits are listed, with characteristic brevity, as "(1) avoidance of close relations with others, (2) inability to express directly hostility or even ordinary aggressive feelings, and (3) autistic thinking." The edition added that such patients, when children, are "usually quiet, shy, obedient, sensitive and retiring."[35]

DSM-II amplified this perspective—and, in doing so, deleted the numbered distinctions—by representing the personality disorder, like all others of its kind, as a "*behavior pattern* [that] manifests shyness, over-sensitivity, seclusiveness, avoidance of close or competitive relationships, and often eccentricity." To avoid any ambiguity, the 1968 edition restated that such "autistic thinking" had to be so chronic it might lead a patient to "react to disturbing experiences and conflicts with apparent detachment."[36] Nowhere in either edition was there even a hint that acute introversion could represent a stand-alone diagnosis. Nor did either edition distinguish, as *DSM-III* would, between "schizoid" and "schizotypal" disorders, representing respectively mild and more severe stopping-off points on the way to full-blown psychosis.

One reason there is such a distinct shift in emphasis between *DSM-III* and the earlier editions is that Spitzer would write to a plethora of experts, many of them allies and friends, asking whether they would like to modify and perhaps update existing categories to include various kinds of behavior he and colleagues claimed to have witnessed. One such letter survives, about a different disorder:

> Dear Colleague:
>
> I would like to invite you to a working meeting to discuss the advisability of including a category in the revision of DSM-III for premenstrual-related dysphoric symptoms. The meeting will be co-sponsored by the Center for the Study of Affective Disorders of

the NIMH [National Institute of Mental Health]. . . . If the group decides that having such a category is advisable, then most of our time will be spent in developing diagnostic criteria for the category, and agreeing on its name and how it would fit into the rest of the classification.[37]

Note how the phrase "premenstrual-related dysphoric symptoms" begs the question, stopping just a fraction short of Spitzer's preferred name for the problem: "Premenstrual Dysphoric Disorder," or PMDD. In such cases, too, Spitzer invariably would hint that the symptoms—and the wider phenomenon—had outgrown the existing category. The tactic was loaded, in other words, but no one on the task force appeared to notice or mind.

In the case of introverted personality disorder, however, the sheer volume of outraged letters Spitzer received forced him to acknowledge, in replies, that each author was but "one of many who have objected to our use of the categories of [IPD] and Introverted Disorder of Childhood in DSM-III." Even so, he continued to one of the objectors, it should be clear: "What we have in mind refers only to the pathological extreme of the personality variable which *you* describe as *introversion*. Our problem has been that we have found no alternative term that would be suitable for this purpose. The term 'schizoid' historically suggests Schizophrenia. The term 'asocial' suggests antisocial, and in fact is an inclusion term in the *International Classification of Diseases* for Antisocial Personality Disorder—therefore precluding our use of it in a different context."[38]

Although Spitzer's phrasing may seem like hair-splitting, by insisting his addressee was referring to "introversion" while *he* was referring mostly to "schizoid" behavior that, if pressed, he might be willing to call "introverted," the chairman was walking a tightrope between adjusting earlier disorders and fabricating brand-new ones. While this led to immense confusion among the uninitiated, as well as tremendous contortions in his own thought and rhetoric, Spitzer adopted the strategy many times, with great success.

With Mary McCaulley, director of Gainesville's Center for Applications of Psychological Type, Spitzer had to tread carefully; McCaulley, in particular, had a wealth of compelling evidence that flatly contradicted his argument. He wanted to avoid worsening prejudice against introspection, he assured her, and was eager to find a solution to this minor difficulty, even if that meant adding a caveat to the DSM, insisting diagnosis should be limited to "the pathological extreme of this dimension of personality."[39]

Yet as Thomas Kirsch, president of the Jung Institute in San Francisco, shrewdly anticipated, if the disclaimer appeared in small print, "it is our feeling that [*introversion*] would become a standard diagnostic term."[40] Kirsch's concern turned out to be justified; it was realized almost to the letter when Spitzer and a few supportive colleagues pushed to include "Premenstrual Dysphoric Disorder"—which, against the objections of many and the resignations of a few, ended up with its own diagnostic code (300.90 Unspecified Mental Disorder [Late Luteal Phase Dysphoric Disorder]), despite its location in just the appendix of DSM-IIIR and DSM-IV.[41]

Spitzer would ask his detractors if they could come up with a better term, which turned the tables, ignored that they'd objected to *all* aspects of a term's inclusion and in this case were responding to his definition of introversion (not pushing their own). Finally, they weren't there to solve a problem he had created by modifying existing terminology.

What Spitzer would not acknowledge was that his committee was barking up the wrong tree: introversion had no place in a manual of mental disorders. And so, with disarming speed, he turned his limited concession into an attack, telling McCaulley: "I do believe that you are not correct in saying that DSM-III has no category for the extremes of extraversion. I believe that Manic Disorder and Chronic Hypomanic Disorder do describe extreme forms of extraversion. It is true that the term 'extraversion' is not used because the disorder also has a disturbance of mood." Given the guesswork involved, his parting shot to McCaulley displays breathtaking chutzpah: "If nature were more symmetrical, we would have a more symmetrical classification."[42] As we'll see, the committee's ruminations on this subject were so vague and chaotic that to presume it was mirroring nature is amazingly arrogant.

In her cautionary letter to Spitzer, McCaulley insisted that introversion "is a normal attitude of normal people." The eight years of work she and her colleagues had completed at the center applied the Myers-Briggs Type Indicator in psychology to a database of more than seventy-five thousand cases. "We can therefore estimate the percent of introverts in different populations."[43] The figures she lists are fascinating and impressive; and given Spitzer's primary interest in biometrics, one would think he'd have taken them more seriously.

The percentage of introversion McCaulley's group detected among eleventh- and twelfth-grade Americans was 37 for boys and 31 for girls. As those in her sample matured in years, extending to more than twelve thousand men and almost sixteen thousand women at college, the numbers shot up to 51 percent and 43 percent, respectively. If one can extrapolate that introversion is more common in adolescent men than women—a perspective the psychiatric literature on social anxiety certainly endorses—things almost balance out at graduate school, where a remarkable *50 percent of men and 48 percent of women call themselves introverted.*

Of course, the DSM did not take these figures for introversion and call them evidence of social anxiety disorder. That would amount to saying half the population suffered from just one psychiatric disease—and DSM-IIIR, over which Spitzer also presided, would go on to include 291 others. The point is rather that Spitzer's team was blurring the distinction between a widespread characteristic and a far more restricted personality disorder, in ways that bolstered the latter's standing by encroaching on a benign behavioral trait.

McCaulley's next caution to Spitzer was suitably wry: "It is ironic to me that DSM III is being developed by two fields, psychiatry and psychology, where introverts appear to be in the majority. . . . On a more general level," she went on, "I do not think every human being needs to be classified under DSM III. We have enough trouble correctly categorizing our patients."[44]

McCaulley probably didn't know this, but many analysts had voiced almost identical concerns. Otto Will remarked, "I myself would not treat a person because he was 'introverted.' He might come to my attention if he complained of great loneliness or found that he had some difficulty which interfered with his relating to other people—but again, I would treat him for something more specific than a collection of attributes labeled as introversion."[45] Spitzer's reply to him, just a week before he wrote to McCaulley, was more insistent about the need for a caveat: "We do plan" to stipulate the difference between routine and pathological introversion "in the next draft," he told Will. "I hope that this is a satisfactory solution to a very sticky problem."[46]

To his own partisans Spitzer was arch and even sarcastic about the carping he'd received. "There are more Jungians in this country than I had realized," he began an April 12, 1978, memo to the advisory committee. The extent of the problem he outlined—and the terms of the vote he requested to remedy it—are sufficiently germane to reproduce in full. "It seems to me," Spitzer continued,

> that both for political and scientific purposes, we had best find an alternative term to "introverted" both for the Childhood Disorder and the Personality Disorder.
>
> I suggest that we consider "withdrawn" or "withdrawing," or "isolated." My *Webster's New Collegiate Dictionary* defines *withdrawn* as "socially detached and unresponsive: introverted." *Isolated* is defined as "being alone: solitary."
>
> As far as the Childhood Disorder is concerned, "withdrawing" would have the advantage of continuity with the DSM-II category of Withdrawing Reaction.
>
> Please let me have your vote on this crucial matter. Prepare a response that has:
>
> To: Dr. Spitzer
> From: Dr. So-and-So.
> I favor: (check one)
>
> _____ A. Introverted Disorder of Childhood and Introverted Personality Disorder, no matter how many Jungians there are in the country.
>
> _____ B. Withdrawing Disorder of Childhood and Withdrawing Personality Disorder.
>
> _____ C. Withdrawing Disorder of Childhood and Isolated Personality Disorder.

_____ D. Some other (Note: "Asocial" cannot be used because it is an inclusion term for Antisocial Personality Disorder, and "schizoid" cannot be used because it suggests Schizophrenia and would be hard to differentiate from our current Schizotypal.)[47]

Of the four votes Spitzer kept in his records, one was for B and two were for C. A fourth member voted for A *or* D, but the psychiatrist added a firm "NO!" to B and a "No" followed by an "OK" to each part of C.

What was Spitzer to make of this muddled response? Certainly, the vote was not remotely clear or conclusive. Of the various comments attached, the first person voting for C stipulated: "'Withdrawing' for the adult group would get confused with 'Avoidant P[ersonality],' which withdraws actively." The second person casting C as his vote (the ten-person committee was all-male) aptly warned, in intriguing metaphors, "The distinction between personality and personality disorder is becoming a minefield. It cannot be a border." And the psychiatrist giving a rather schizophrenic vote to behavior Spitzer's team would *almost* call "schizoid" (A *or* D, but *not* B, and only half of C) joked that he was "'Dr. So-and-so' but not 'So-so.'"

_____

Although there is, alas, no written record of the sense Spitzer tried to make of this response, not everyone was so casual about calling introversion an illness. The next day, Ann Chappell in San Francisco fired off an exasperated letter, calling the whole issue "very perplexing" and admitting she was struggling to "form an appropriate response." Here was the problem as she saw it—disclosing more troublesome details about Spitzer's one-sided research and manipulative procedure:

Your committee is using the term erroneously based on only one or two sources. The bibliography of introversion, on the other hand, contains literally an entire library of many, many volumes. They all disagree with *any* pathologic use of the term, such as your committee is doing. *Your instructions were for us to forward only the material that agrees with your use of the term.* It is impossible, Bob. The incredible weight of evidence says you are dead wrong in using the term for a pathologic diagnosis. Jungians literally invented the term and through the years have continued the development and use of the term and concept in the nonpathologic sense.[48]

Chappell was right about the committee's misuse of the term and egregiously limited research of its history, but Jungians did not invent the term. They drew on the key role it had played in British Romanticism, a point revealing a very different chapter in the history of shyness and introspection.[49] It is true that the noun *introvert* dates more recently to the 1880s and that Jung deserves the credit—if credit is due—for using it, circa 1912, to designate a distinct psychological type.

Spitzer does not seem to have shared Chappell's and similar correspondence with his committee. Instead, as a slew of letters arrived daily, each either vehemently opposed to the changes or stating a more moderate perspective completely at odds with those taken by other colleagues, Spitzer—backed into a corner by his initial enthusiasm for Introverted Personality Disorder—seemed to be gauging which way the wind was blowing. The day after Chappell expressed her exasperation, for instance, John Lion began a supportive letter from the University of Maryland's Institute of Psychiatry and Human Behavior with a wisecrack about Jungians: "Have [they] not been reading professional journals? Where have they been during the development of *DSM-III*?" Given the analysts' frustrations, cited in the previous chapter, these are questions they would be only too glad to ask and Spitzer would prefer not to answer.

"It seems to me," Lion went on, "that we are grappling with the problem of the Schizoid Personality without wishing to use the term because of its proximity to schizophrenia." He was spot-on, for expanding the existing term would end up casting the extreme edge of introversion as a mild form of psychosis. So if Spitzer and the committee were concerned about using "schizoid" in this way, he concluded gingerly, "I would suggest . . . we utilize the term 'Avoidant,'" since being alone, being withdrawn, and not wishing to form social relationships are "basically synonymous." True, he conceded, the avoidant personality differs from the introverted one in key respects, but "I do not believe that this [difference] is phenomenologically accurate. It might be better to call an Avoidant Personality simply 'shy' and to drop the term altogether."[50]

It isn't easy to parse Lion's logic. He begins by saying "schizoid" is acceptable, suggests "avoidant" as a possible alternative, then concludes that, best of all, they might ditch the latter in favor of calling such patients simply "shy." As we try navigating this muddled thinking, however, we can at least see why the Jungians in San Francisco balked at including "Introverted Personality Disorder" in DSM-III, regardless of Spitzer's suggested addendum. As the letters show, the experts couldn't even begin to assess mild or chronic introversion in vaguely comparable ways. What hope was there, then, that psychiatrists nationally and globally would do so? When specialists like Lion could propose such dissimilar options with scarcely a thought about their radical implications, there was every reason to fear widespread misdiagnoses and to wish Spitzer had not raised this ambiguous subject.

Donald Klein certainly thought so. In April 1978, just a couple of months after the debacle began, he sent Spitzer an aggressive memo titled "The Introversion Disaster." "Please note," he began, responding to Spitzer's earlier comment about the number of Jungians in the country, "that under no circumstances can I be considered [one], yet I thought that this label was ill-advised. I don't like 'withdrawing,'" he went on, "because it sounds reactive as in drawing away from something. That sounds very much like somebody being gun-shy or avoidant, and I don't think that's the connotation we want. 'Withdrawn,' on the other hand, sounds more like a state of being and, therefore, somewhat more acceptable."[51]

That these and other terms could enter the world's most influential manual of mental disorders on the basis that they were "somewhat more acceptable" than others is not exactly reassuring. Nor is it clear why *saying* a mood, trait, or behavior sounds like "a state of being" therefore *makes* it so.

Perhaps unbeknownst to Klein, however, Spitzer had penned a letter the day before "TO ALL THOSE WHO HAVE EXPRESSED THEIR CONCERN ABOUT THE INCLUSION OF INTROVERTED PERSONALITY DISORDERS: . . . In view of the widespread concern that to do this would distort the meaning of the term 'introversion' as used by many in our profession," he assured them, with a mild sting at the end of this last clause, "we have decided to find an alternative term for these two disorders [Schizoid Personality Disorder and Childhood Disorder]."[52]

The compromise, then, was simply to default to expanding the existing term *Schizoid*. Spitzer clearly had ruled out representing the term as it was in *DSM-II* (a state approaching autism) or eliminating it from the manual entirely. All that remained, then, was to agree on a term other than "introverted" to describe behavior that all the participants had recognized—and had been told all along—was "introversion."

As Klein had been so irksome throughout this exchange, Spitzer was in no mood to acknowledge him by calling the disorder "withdrawn." Allen Frances's timing was impeccable, then, when he chimed in that although "schizoid may have started as a lousy cliché, . . . it remains the best of this lot since it most clearly implies that the patient withdraws, isolates and introverts without deep regret for the loss of close relationships and that he has no capacity to do otherwise, whereas the avoidant longs to but is too frightened."[53]

You can see the canny diplomacy by which Frances touched on each of the contentious terms—"withdraws, isolates and introverts"—before quietly bypassing them all. Klein was not formally giving up on his own tack, but he did accept Frances's point, implicitly conceding much ground to him when telling Spitzer, "You have to differentiate between schizoid people who are out of it and avoidant people who would like to be into it but are too shy."[54]

Psychiatrists insisting on the scientific rigor of the *DSM* might be surprised that its intricate discussions could boil down to such distinctions. But Klein would not stop there. He complained that the term "avoidant personality" had been "unduly broadened"; agreed with Theodore (Ted) Millon that those with "introverted personality are[n't] preoccupied with internal mental processes . . . they just don't have much going on";[55] and threw down the gauntlet to Spitzer: "Apparently you and I don't see eye to eye about this. What is the process whereby this gets resolved?"[56] It's an intriguing question, echoing that of Leo Madow four months earlier.[57] Sadly, Spitzer did not answer it on the record. In reality, since few figures could serve as a higher point of appeal, one of the men would have to back down.

The debate about IPD stumbled on for several months, but came to a head in the summer of 1978. Shortly after the Jungians offered their own parting salvo—they would accept "Pathological Self-Preoccupation," with "Restricted Personality" and "Constrained Personality Structure" as backups, just in case[58]—Millon started to chafe at their influence and fumed about the "puzzling . . . flap" *they* had managed to cause over terminology. "The fact that the Jungians feel that it is their special language and would be dismayed by its use in this setting is a rather shocking reason to drop . . . the word 'introversion,'" he opined, especially as the latter "has long since past [*sic*] being one of their special items; it's common parlance among all reasonably educated laymen." Millon's last point conveniently ignored that the *committee* had encouraged the changes and was supposed to be using "introverted" in extreme cases only, in a realm quite distinct from ordinary usage.

What alternative was feasible, however, that didn't concede much, if anything, to the Jungians? Millon flung out three possibilities: "May I suggest such labels as: 'unsocial,' 'detached,' and 'solitary,'" he offered, though none of them went anywhere.[59]

Roger MacKinnon had begun to fret that the identifying criteria the committee had floated—"'self-absorbed,' 'absentminded,' and 'detached from their environment' ('not with it' or 'in a fog')"—were "unprecise [*sic*] and not descriptive." A better example of self-absorption, he declared, befitting the kind of "preoccupation with internal mental processes" they had affirmed, was of a man "laying his keys or glasses down someplace, and then not being able to recall where he had put them."[60]

Exactly how the example points to chronic pathology, not simple absentmindedness, isn't clear. Incredibly, all the other phrases MacKinnon flagged as imprecise, such as "not with it" and "in a fog," appear verbatim in *DSM-III*. Perhaps owing to his example, the manual also warns: "Excessive daydreaming is often present."[61] What constitutes an appropriate amount of daydreaming remains anyone's guess.

One may not know whether to laugh or cry, then, when hearing Steven Hyler (another committee member and the proponent of "chronic complaint disorder") cheerfully aver, "I don't believe that as many psychiatrists will be confusing Schizophrenia with Schizoid Personality as we fantasize."[62] The real fear that outside experts had voiced—that introversion might begin to resemble a pathology one could equate with psychosis—apparently was just an illusion.

Still, if Hyler could reassure himself and his colleagues about such major diagnostic confusion, the problem of naming the disorder persisted. Robert Arnstein was not formally on the committee, but as he served on the task force he offered five alternatives and then, just as promptly, undercut the viability of them all: "I thought of 'Hermitic,' but that sounds a little too much like vacuum-sealed. 'Solitary' might work or 'loner,' but the latter is too slangy. A resort to *Webster's* . . . suggests 'reclusive' as a synonym for 'withdrawn.' 'Misanthropic' is a nice word," he concluded vaguely, "but it probably suggests more active animosity than is involved in the Introverted Disorders."[63]

Arnstein's closing point obviously begged the question troubling the committee from the start, but no one seemed to mind. The discussion had turned into a frantic hunt through the dictionary and thesaurus, not the adoption of clear-cut profiles that research trials and scientific studies had laid out.

Meanwhile, other noises surfaced from beyond the committee: Joseph Finney complained that the very bid to pathologize introversion reflects a "cultural prejudice in our diagnostic classification system" since, he remarked, "ours happens to be an extroverted culture, and so we tend to stigmatize introverts." "The opposite is true in Japan," he noted, "where introverts are regarded as normal and extroverts are regarded as abnormal."[64]

By the time Ivan Elder and Carlos Santiago wrote to Spitzer,[65] independently complaining of class bias and "psychiatric name-calling," Spitzer clearly had had enough. "You are quite correct about the middle-class orientation sneaking into the examples for Axis V," he responded tartly. "Perhaps we should include the example of the ghetto woman providing a high school education for all eleven of her children as an instance of Superior [*sic*]. Do you have any suggestions?"[66] Spitzer left it to his assistant, Janet Forman, to inform yet another troubled correspondent about the ultimate fate of IPD. Perhaps appropriately, the letter signals that—at least in the matter of terminology—Klein had not won, that Spitzer ultimately had retained the upper hand:

Dear Dr. [James] Hall,

Thank you for your letter of November 28th. I'm sorry you never received our letter about the name of Introverted Personality Disorder. We have changed the name of this disorder to Schizoid Personality Disorder, and will not be using the world "introverted" in this category.

Thank you for your interest.

Sincerely,
Janet B. W. Forman, MSW
DSM-III Project Coordinator[67]

The "change," then, was to give an existing term in *DSM-II* ("Schizoid") entirely new meaning, so it would refer to introversion in all but name. The debate may have been rancorous and have stalled several times, but Spitzer had accomplished his initial objective. In doing so, however, he had done much more than alienate large numbers of analysts and psychiatrists not serving on the committee; he had also sacrificed logic and rigor on the altar of expediency. The committee either had overlooked or had ceased to mind that its final decision flatly contradicted Spitzer's own earlier warning, in his April 12 memo to "Drs. So-and-So," that "*'schizoid' cannot be used* because it suggests Schizophrenia and would be hard to differentiate from our current Schizotypal."[68]

Psychiatrists meeting with patients for the first time were thus encouraged to look for an "absence of warm, tender feelings for others," especially in those having "close friendships with no more than one or two persons, including family members," and those "working in jobs that involve little or no contact with others, or living in skid-row sections of cities."[69] *DSM-I* and *DSM-II* had included no such language, yet *DSM-IIIR* actually expanded it to include the person who "neither desires nor enjoys close friendships, including being part of a family."[70] And if that struck the psychiatrist in question as unusually broad (after all, many patients seek counsel for problems with their nearest but *not* dearest), an additional sentence in *DSM-III* presumably made the parameters infinitely clearer: "Individuals with this disorder are usually humorless or dull . . ."[71]

The decision to call introverted behavior a mild form of psychosis was instrumental in reshaping the anxiety disorders, too. For as the boundaries of each personality and anxiety disorder expanded to accommodate a growing list of symptoms, the overlap among illnesses multiplied accordingly. Concerned onlookers and even a few task force members began to fret that each illness was rapidly losing its distinctiveness.

As Spitzer's task force had pushed for a "multiaxial evaluation" of disorders, it nudged psychiatrists to focus on the interface between two or more areas of psychiatry rather than insisting that they pinpoint the illness exclusively in one.

DSM-I and *DSM-II* had made it impossible to factor in common traits, which frustrated many by making them put illnesses into sometimes falsely discrete boxes. But *DSM-III* went so far in the other direction that the edition made it increasingly tempting *not* to rule out other factors, for fear of missing undetectable symptoms and thus underdiagnosing the patient. Personality and anxiety disorders were, in short, no longer mutually exclusive categories; the multiaxial approach turned them into complementary traits.[72]

As the task force favored more, not fewer, areas of overlap, its revised philosophy tended to quell concerns that it was getting carried away. Still, even the most ardent supporters of the multiaxial approach couldn't ignore that as the disorders moved closer, sharing more and more traits, they became increasingly difficult to distinguish. Where, for instance, did schizoid personality disorder end and social phobia begin?

The question became especially urgent—and difficult to resolve—when the Advisory Committee on Personality Disorders decided to introduce a brand-new illness, "avoidant personality disorder" (or APD), of which there is no hint in *DSM-II*. None of the leading experts on the committee could say precisely what it was or how it differed from social phobia and schizoid personality disorder. And when Lion took the easy way out, insisting with a scandalous lack of rigor that being alone, being withdrawn, and not wishing to form social relationships were "basically synonymous," his claim dug the members a deeper hole.[73] How could the committee form three distinct illnesses out of behavior that was, by his reckoning, essentially all the same? Why, indeed, did it need to?

Klein insisted one *could* distinguish meaningfully between "people who are out of it and . . . people who would like to be into it but are too shy."[74] Still, as both men basically agreed that patients with APD were simply "shy" and that the trait encompassed both schizoid personality disorder and social phobia, the cutoff points for each illness had become, as one committee member conceded, a "minefield," not a "borderline."[75]

Spitzer's defenders insist the committee was diligent in snaring neglected disorders. Because they wanted no one to suffer in silence from unacknowledged psychiatric problems, they decided to place these disorders on a continuum.[76] Rather like the American housewives Betty Friedan diagnosed in 1963, people with APD, SPD, or SP apparently were battling, before *DSM-III* noticed them, a "Problem That Has No Name."[77]

One needn't agree with Friedan to see the shared logic. If you think about social phobia, avoidance, or even shyness in this way, it makes sense to view the underlying problem, as Friedan did, as "a strange . . . sense of dissatisfaction, a yearning that . . . [has lain] buried, unspoken, for many years."[78] As Michael Liebowitz remarks of social phobics, "It's not like these folks didn't exist before. It's that they'd be seen for conditions . . . viewed more as contributing factors. So . . . the pieces [were] always kind of there—but nobody sort of tied them all together."[79]

To want to end such suffering is appropriate and even honorable. One must still ask, Was the distress really ignored and untreated beforehand? And did psychiatrists on the task force limit their role to identifying chronic symptoms that affected a small number of people, or get carried away and exaggerate the severity and frequency of those symptoms, to the point where they were arranging terms to fit predetermined molds, expanding disorders to increase prevalence, and even targeting populations that previously hadn't considered themselves at all unwell?

The answers to these questions vary dramatically, depending on whom you ask and about which disorder. "There are all kinds of elements you *could* call social phobia," David Healy told me, including whether you prefer using a bank's ATM card to using a teller. "But when it reaches the point where you *won't* go into the bank, even if the card won't work, that's obviously different." The problem, according to him, is that the DSM working groups didn't *limit* their discussion to such patients. They wanted also to incorporate less severe cases that "could be made to meet the criteria."[80] One can see his point, for when "being alone: solitary" is considered one sign of a mental disorder, rather than a source of simple "dissatisfaction," it leaves the door to psychiatric illness widely ajar.[81]

Avoidant Personality Disorder, in particular, raised a fascinating conundrum. As the committee had run out of distinguishing symptoms, it had to set the bar even lower than usual. The adjective "avoidant" raised a host of philosophical questions, not least about what the patient was shunning, and why. Looking back on their own decisions and those of others, Liebowitz and Richard Heimberg are among those who say Spitzer's team was trying to reach only the acutely withdrawn. Yet whenever the DSM-III committee specified the avoidance, it inevitably looked as if it was stigmatizing anything that didn't reach its own rather muddled standard of participation.

One need only consult the snarling letters Spitzer and Klein fired back and forth over the years to appreciate the irony of their setting a benchmark for sociable collaboration. The standard for gauging avoidance was so nebulous that the slide into bias and even prejudice was almost inevitable—and the impression of overkill largely impossible to shake.

When assessing people with "introverted personalities," for instance, Millon averred: "I would like to see us make more reference to their characteristic behavioral apathy, their lack of vitality, their deficits in . . . spontaniety [sic], their inability to display enthusiasm or experience pleasure, their minimal introspectiveness and awareness of self, as well as their imperviousness to the subtleties of everyday social life. I think our description and our diagnostic criteria would be strengthened if we included these personality dimensions that clearly signify the disorder."[82]

To concerned onlookers who threw up their hands at such criteria, the presence of personal bias and social prejudice was too blatant to ignore. After Millon's interest in targeting people who are "minimal[ly] introspective" or "impervious . . . to the subtleties of everyday life," for instance, any claim that the committee or wider task force was still holding to the "4D's" (significant distress, dysfunction, deviance, and danger) begins to seem incredible.[83]

A deeper irony is that Millon's concern about introverted patients' "*minimal* introspecti[on]" flatly contradicted those trying to gauge the pathology of people whom others on the committee thought *too* introspective. Behavior the committee would target as pathological would thus logically be conduct Millon would reward. Even if we can ignore that startling inconsistency, when "impervious[ness] . . . to the subtleties of everyday social life" and "being alone: solitary" become criteria for psychiatric illnesses, we are surely in deep trouble.

Nor did the proposed criteria end there. Roger MacKinnon called these people "the opposite of adventuresome," complaining that they "will always travel the same route . . . [and] very frequently have not learned to drive a car, or would suffer the inconvenience of public transportation in a situation where a private automobile is available."[84] While it's difficult to believe these could be considered criteria for a psychiatric disorder, it's harder to see how a person using public transportation would better exhibit "avoidant" personality than would a counterpart opting to use his or her own car.

Klein, however, thought it a mistake that APD's operational criteria centered on "interpersonal rejection";[85] this time he wouldn't back down, restating a couple of months later that the avoidant "are angry at themselves because they have failed. The avoidant personality is not a blame-avoiding type."[86]

It would be difficult not to say the same about Klein himself, but his curious use of psychological language didn't help him outmaneuver Spitzer. When the latter opened the matter for discussion, Millon privately replied, "Nix to Don's view on the matter," before acknowledging, "I do feel somewhat narcissistically wounded by not having been mentioned on the 'multiaxial' committee."[87]

Meanwhile, the diplomacy Allen Frances had shown over schizoid personality disorder looked more like vacillation when he tried to nail down the characteristics of APD. "Some avoidant personalities are most motivated by hypersensitivity to rejection," he opined; "others by fears of failure, others (I think) by fears of loss of control."[88] He seemed to favor keeping avoidant and schizoid personality disorders separate, even if, as Klein observed, no one had really specified what the "avoidant personality is steering clear from" in the first place.[89]

Should APD merge with SPD and SP, then, or strike out on its own as a separate disorder? Perhaps inevitably, the question resulted in more dithering, with Lion saying APD "should be deleted," or, failing that, "the introverted personality criteria [should] be incorporated under the term 'avoidant.' Otherwise, the two seem so similar that no one can tell the difference except the people who generated the phrases."[90]

If only even this last belief were true! But with Frances waffling and Spitzer looking vulnerable again, Klein was unwilling to lose another fight. He pushed so strongly for APD that he declared its parameters should be expanded further: "I . . . think it might make sense to broaden the variety of affects in situations that the avoidant personality is steering clear from." Don't look for consistency on this matter, though, for as we saw earlier, Klein would complain three months later, after he'd gotten his way, that the term "avoidant personality" had been "unduly broadened."[91]

Despite these inconsistencies, it is crucial to ask, What *was* such a patient really avoiding? Regrettably, the *DSM* is as vague as the psychiatrists coining the term. Persons with APD "may have one or two close friends," the manual asserts, and be "distressed by their lack of ability to relate comfortably to others and suffer from low self-esteem."[92] Who is to gauge what "relat[ing] comfortably to others" amounts to and when levels of self-esteem are too low or high? And when did the number of one's friends determine one's sanity or mental distress?

Rather than acknowledge that APD overlaps so patently with social phobia as to make itself redundant, the task force went on the offensive, leaving psychiatrists enough wiggle room, if they wanted it, for a dual diagnosis. "Social Phobia," the manual advised, "may be a complication of this disorder."[93]

Today Spitzer is prepared to concede that between generalized social anxiety disorder and avoidant personality disorder there is almost "total overlap."[94] The minutes of the *DSM-IIIR* Anxiety Disorders meeting on October 4–5, 1984, confirm that he pushed for this result: "Let's allow joint diagnosis of social phobia and avoidant PD." Frances had implied earlier in the meeting that social phobia be reclassified ("If it resembles a state condition, [I] don't have a problem about calling it an Axis I disorder"), but Klerman demurred, insisting they "don't have the data to move avoidant people up to Axis I," so Spitzer's proposal was a compromise. At one point in the meeting, however, Spitzer proposed reclassifying social phobia as a personality disorder on this basis: "If it goes on forever, it's personality."[95]

Liebowitz is still adamant that social phobia remains a "neglected disorder," but he too acknowledges that "it doesn't make sense to have these two separate categories—social phobia and avoidant personality." For "they lived sort of parallel lives" in *DSM*, he adds, half-chuckling, before pointing out, "*DSM-IV* still has avoidant personality. It's actually *more* overlapping with social anxiety than it was in pre-definitions. [Now] it's all interpersonal fears. But I believe it's sort of redundant with social anxiety."[96]

So why does the *DSM* still list these as separate disorders, with one a potential complication of the other? Regarding avoidant personality disorder's overlap with cognate or identical terms, *DSM-IV* actually states, "If an individual has personality features that meet criteria for one or more Personality Disorders in addition to Avoidant Personality Disorder, all can be diagnosed."[97]

Despite all the wrangling over terms, Spitzer's allies knew that *DSM-III* would be a watershed for American psychiatry. But Spitzer himself was not entirely satisfied with the edition, wanting new problems added and existing ones refined. For starters, "social phobia" conjured austere visions of misanthropy, not routine images of bashfulness and stage fright. For another, although the manual implies otherwise, the disorder *was* too close to avoidant personality, and Spitzer found the overlap embarrassing.

Having touted his own scientific rigor and that of his colleagues, Spitzer knew he was vulnerable. So, with the full support of the APA administration, he formed and later chaired a new task force with a set of working groups, which spent the next seven years tweaking the work of its predecessors and quietly erasing some of the compromises Spitzer had struck with his psychoanalytic rivals.

Although *social phobia* officially entered the psychiatric stage in *DSM-III*, the new Committee on Anxiety Disorders and reconstituted task force soon massively expanded its parameters. Unlike avoidant and schizoid personality disorders, which underwent a similar transformation, social phobia acquired a new name. Once again, the official explanation for these changes differs noticeably from what happened behind the scenes.

When a group of experts on social phobia decided to publish an explanatory letter in the influential *Archives of General Psychiatry*, they called it "Social Phobia or Social Anxiety Disorder: What's in a Name?" After glancing backward at the earlier discussions, they set about answering their own question: "Social phobia was originally described as a fear of specific social situations, such as public speaking, eating in front of others, or using public restrooms. It was described as infrequent and rarely associated with meaningful impairment. Initial indifference to social phobia led one of us [Liebowitz, working with another team] to call it 'the neglected anxiety disorder.' Two decades later, those of us who work with social phobia recognize it as a chronic and highly prevalent disorder often associated with serious impairment. However, this message has yet to be widely embraced."[98]

As *Psychology Today* had dubbed the illness "disorder of the decade" seven years earlier, and an avalanche of media and scholarly articles had since insisted on the phobia's gravity, the psychiatrists would seem to be overstating their case. In 1999, the year before their letter appeared, SmithKline Beecham spent tens of millions of dollars running an aggressive publicity campaign about social phobia that resulted in "1.1 billion media impressions"[99]—hardly a sign that the message about social phobia had "yet to be widely embraced."

Even so, the psychiatrists averred, social phobia "often goes unrecognized" by colleagues and the public—and its very name "may contribute to this problem," apparently because its history "suggest[s] that the disorder is unimportant." To Liebowitz and the coauthors of the "What's in a Name?" letter, the solution was for the wider psychiatric community to adopt the "alternative name, *social anxiety disorder,* which appropriately connotes a more pervasive and impairing disorder than is implied by the label *social phobia* or its limited and outdated description in DSM-III." Rather than viewing the two names as interchangeable, moreover, the authors "recommend[ed] taking this initiative one step further by making *social anxiety disorder* the primary name."[100]

It is difficult to know where to begin with this letter. For starters, its principal author served on the DSM-IIIR Anxiety Disorders Committee before chairing the crucial—and, by comparison, quite small (six-person)—DSM-IV Anxiety Disorders Work Group, itself instrumental in proposing the malady's alternative name. Of the letter writers, Liebowitz was the sole person serving also on the DSM-IV task force. The letter says this last group

"gave social phobia the alternative name," but fails to mention Liebowitz's key role in the process, leaving the impression that the letter writers
are following the lead of other experts, not sanctioning their principal author's earlier initiative.

Even more significant is the faulty reasoning pervading the letter. As
phobias in psychiatric literature are a distinct subset of disorders, altering
the name *social phobia* to *social anxiety disorder* would signal the problem
is "more pervasive" by rendering its terminology more elastic, but it
wouldn't at all suggest that the disorder is "more . . . impairing." On the
contrary, the more patient-friendly term inevitably would catch a great
deal more in its expanded net.

When the authors also conclude, without elaborating, that the alternative name, *social anxiety disorder,* has "no history to suggest that the disorder is unimportant," they could only mean the qualifier appearing in *DSM-
III* under "Prevalence": "The disorder is apparently relatively rare."[101]
While such caution about a new disorder seems reasonable, "apparently"
and "relatively" gave everyone considerable latitude that later committees,
with Liebowitz, were quick to appreciate.

During the seven years in which Spitzer's new task force revised and
greatly expanded *DSM-III*, there is every indication the Anxiety Disorders
Committee took social phobia very seriously, even as it rendered the phobia increasingly routine and unexceptional. When the committee, which
included Spitzer, met in March 1986 to reassess how well the *DSM-III* categories worked together, Liebowitz told him: "I think under Criteria A
[for social phobia], you could say as a result of this fear patients may have
difficulty with speaking or auditioning, eating, drinking or writing in public or in social activities [such] as dating, actual conversations, going to
parties."[102]

Spitzer followed suit and the revised manual opened the floodgates, declaring: "Social Phobia involving fear of public speaking and Social Phobia
involving a generalized fear of most social situations are *common*."[103]
True, the manual still carried the proviso, "Social Phobia with the circumscribed symptoms of fear of eating in public, writing in public, or using
public lavatories is relatively rare," which hardly looks like "better differ-
entiat[ion]" from the criterion in the earlier edition.[104] Liebowitz's com-

mittee had won half the battle, and by using another hazy qualifier, "relatively," his DSM-IV Anxiety Disorders Work Group soon managed to alter the second half of the equation, too.[105]

Increasing the prevalence and ordinariness of social phobia's general characteristics was by no means all that *DSM-IIIR* accomplished. When the revised manual appeared in 1987, the disorder also had carefully modified features. While *DSM-III* had defined social phobia as "a persistent, *irrational* fear of, and compelling desire to avoid, situations in which [we're] exposed to scrutiny by others,"[106] seven years later the description had morphed into "a persistent fear of *one* or more situations (the social phobic situations) in which the person is exposed to *possible* scrutiny by others *and fears that he or she may do something or act in a way that will be humiliating or embarrassing.*"[107] By silently deleting the proviso that these fears be "irrational" and multiple, the second task force made the diagnosis so mild and casual that it could actually include, as an example of "social phobic situations," a fear of sounding foolish.

Even more important, the scrutiny did not need to occur; simply *anticipating* it was enough to identify the disorder. And as diagnosis no longer required the presence of the phobic object ("society"), the problem was swiftly recast as one of fear rather than strictly avoidance, which also required a lower burden of proof.

By radically shifting the disorder's goalposts to include routine embarrassment and fears of being stymied when asked questions in social settings, *DSM-IIIR* was instrumental in turning an "apparently relatively rare" problem into one that could afflict almost everyone on the planet. Perhaps it shouldn't surprise us, then, that by 2000 the *Harvard Review of Psychiatry* was calling social phobia "the third-most-common psychiatric disorder, behind only major depressive disorder and alcohol dependence."[108]

When I mentioned to Liebowitz that some people think he and his colleagues have medicalized routine problems like public speaking anxiety, he replied: "You know, you've gotta be careful not to trivialize that, because people are really suffering, are tormented, and would rather, you know, think about giving up careers than give speeches. Perhaps they're suicidal . . . it's a pretty serious condition." Still, he does admit that "people who have just public speaking anxiety—it's not 100% clear that they need a chronic treatment like Paxil or the others, and something on an as-needed basis may do well enough, and beta-blockers do seem to help. . . ."

So, is fear of public speaking truly an anxiety *disorder*? "I've got an open mind about it," Liebowitz concludes. "You know, I'm the one who actually proposed the subtypes [of social phobia]. Most people sort of like the dimensional model and want to *blur* those distinctions: I think there really is a difference between pure public speaking anxiety and social anxiety. But that doesn't tell us one way or the other about how to classify them . . . or whether it makes sense to keep them distinct."[109]

When the bar for mental disorders is set so low, almost any emotion can be listed as a disorder in the *DSM*. Yet many psychiatrists not only vigorously defend the changes, but also take exception to having their judgment questioned. When for instance Shankar Vedantam in 2001 published an excellent, balanced piece in the *Washington Post,* addressing several experts who feared that the redefinition and marketing of mental illness had gone too far, he quoted Murray Stein, one of the above letter writers, responding rather tartly: "The idea that this is cosmetic psychopharmacology I find offensive."[110]

Stein does at least acknowledge that SSRIs or "selective serotonin-reuptake inhibitors" (a type of antidepressant) can have dramatic side effects, but he doesn't concede the scale of the problem or admit the lengths to which the drug companies have gone to shield it from the public. Sounding only marginally less defensive, he adds, "I know there's lots of concern about, 'Are we medicalizing normative things and is the pharmaceutical industry trying to put SSRIs in the water.'" He concludes, "'The people I see talking about that have not seen these patients.'"[111]

Healy has, and he is deeply skeptical that we are facing a pandemic of social anxiety disorder. "It's all about, 'If we don't treat this problem then these people won't work. They'll become alcoholic, perhaps, and need a drink to go out of the house,' and things like that. And there *are* people for whom that's true—but at a rate of, perhaps, 20 per million," which is far less than the figures touted in the favored literature.[112] Many therapists and psychoanalysts have shared with me the pros and cons of antidepressants and antianxiety medication; and when patients become fully aware of the risks, as Stein and others perhaps fear, many not only rue how quickly they were lulled into believing the drugs were a solution to their problems, but also seek every available safe means of ending that risk as quickly as possible.

Stein has staked his career on the need for drugs to treat reticence and social phobia; he is renowned for asking rhetorically in *The Lancet*, "Might there be a brand of 'shyness' serious enough to warrant medical attention? There is. It is 'social phobia.'"[113] Consequently, I'm unlikely to persuade him to rethink his position.

I *am* concerned about the rigor of a study his team conducted in 1994, which helped determine where psychiatrists should set the benchmarks for the disorder. Stein's article became so influential that it is quoted and cross-referenced in almost all the early literature on social phobia. Yet it drew from a single study—a random telephone survey of 526 urban Canadians. Nor is Stein's conclusion especially impressive: His team concedes, predictably, that "social anxiety is common in the community, but precise delineation of the prevalence of 'social phobia' depends heavily on where the diagnostic threshold is set."[114] In other words, shyness is an illness if you make the criteria sufficiently inclusive; it's a run-of-the-mill trait if you don't.

Where does that leave Stein's team? Their survey concluded that the frequency with which participants experienced social phobia ranged from 1.9 percent to 18.7 percent, depending on where the team set the threshold.[115] That sounds sufficiently open-ended to make the study valueless, but the authors and the drug companies didn't see it that way. Not surprisingly, the latter seized on the upper figure and published it frequently in brochures and ads (without of course reporting the lower figure). In doing so, they fostered the illusion that shyness had reached epidemic proportions in North America and thus, by extension, in many other parts of the world.

The article doesn't enumerate the questions Stein's team asked or at what point in the day they did so, but those queries are likely to bear a strong resemblance to the "Liebowitz Social Anxiety Scale," which became a foundational questionnaire adapted by the drug companies when promoting Paxil and Zoloft as antishyness pills. The activities Liebowitz lists include "calling someone you do not know very well," "urinating in a public bathroom," "taking a test," "trying to pick up someone," and "resisting a high-pressure salesperson."[116]

There is no knowing whether the shy would put the psychiatric callers in that salesperson category. But when the fourth edition of the *DSM* appeared the same year as Stein's article, social phobia had its more inclusive name, "social anxiety disorder." Simply renaming the illness and lowering its "diagnostic threshold," as Stein's team encouraged, made the percentage of Americans seemingly afflicted leap almost overnight from less than four people in every hundred to almost one person in five.[117] As the team explained, "By altering the threshold for interference with lifestyle or subjective distress or by restricting diagnosis to particular social situations, the rate was seen to vary by up to tenfold."[118] The only people who grasped the full implications of these dubious results were the researchers, who appeared to have unearthed the clinical bonanza of a "neglected disorder," and pharmaceutical giants like SmithKline Beecham, which sensed a vast new audience for its unimpressive antidepressant, Paxil.

Within a few years, this company—touting the same percentages—was running massive promotional campaigns for both the problem and its apparent remedy. Ads, brochures, and carefully placed video information packages appeared across Europe, North and South America, the Middle East, and parts of Asia.

Social anxiety disorder was now a global phenomenon.

4

DIRECT TO CONSUMER:
NOW SELL THE DISEASE!

Before you sell a drug, you have to sell the disease. And never was this truer than for social anxiety disorder, which by the 1990s encompassed shyness, fear of urinating in a public lavatory, and concern about saying the wrong thing.[1]

The moment the American Psychiatric Association grouped these fears, calling them elements of a troubling, underreported problem, it not only defined a new segment of the population as ill but also cast their woes in an entirely different form. A signal therefore went out that researchers, mental health professionals, and the drug companies should unearth fresh remedies. These had to fit the APA's newfound biological emphases, adopted almost wholesale from nineteenth-century models of pathology. Psychiatry also freed itself to partner with pharmacology (and so treat social phobia mostly with drugs) by dismissing psychoanalysis as costly and ineffective.[2]

What Robert Spitzer's task forces began, in terms of redefining mental disorders, the pharmaceutical companies soon completed. For by splitting anxious and phobic reactions into seven new disorders, the *DSM* at a stroke had greatly expanded the market of potential clients. The task forces had also given social phobia a more patient-friendly name and helpfully lowered its diagnostic threshold. The numbers of patients potentially affected skyrocketed (Murray Stein put the upper ceiling at almost one in five),[3] but the pharmaceutical giants decided even more needed to be done.

As the trade journal *PR News* announced quite candidly, the British firm

SmithKline Beecham resolved to "position social anxiety disorder" as "a severe medical condition."[4] The company's internal memos confirm that it was going all-out on this front, representing Paxil (paroxetine hydrochloride) as the sole means of treating a "highly debilitating" illness.[5] "Efforts [were] concentrated," a confidential report confirmed in 1998, on SmithKline's having "the first SSRI approved for social phobia/social anxiety disorder, an anxiety disorder with enormous potential."[6]

To reach this goal, the company needed to raise the malady's profile, so it ratcheted up the plight of the socially anxious and stressed the maximum number said to be afflicted.[7] "What these companies do," notes Isaac Marks, "is say, 'Gee, here's this undertreated, underrecognized problem, and we really want to show you how common this disorder is in the community, and all these poor people are suffering when they could benefit from our drugs.' . . . It's an advertising ploy, and this has been done for other conditions too. And so suddenly, they say, 'Social anxiety is all the rage. Look what we've been missing.'"[8] "If anything, Paxil was worse than the other SSRIs" in terms of side effects, adds David Healy, "but the company took a very, uh, deliberate line that they were going to go after this end of the market."[9]

"Every marketer's dream," Barry Brand told *Advertising Age,* "is to find an unidentified or unknown market and develop it. That's what we were able to do with social anxiety disorder."[10] As product director for Paxil (Seroxat in Britain), the aptly named Brand had reason to crow. Although the drug he championed hit the U.S. market in 1993,[11] quite late in the game and thus at a considerable disadvantage to its main competitors (Prozac and Zoloft), his aggressive policies soon turned it into one of a few blockbuster drugs, so named because their annual sales exceed $1 billion. In 2001 alone, with 25 million new prescriptions written for the drug, Paxil's sales in the United States increased by a massive 18 percent from the year before.[12] With yearly revenues exceeding $2 billion nationally, the drug had swiftly outpaced its competitors. It became America's best-selling antidepressant, with more than five thousand Americans beginning a fresh course of treatment with it every day.[13] Nor are its sales insignificant in other countries. In Japan, to consider just one other example, sales of Paxil "reached ¥12 billion ($96.5 million) in 2001, its first full year on the market," and rose sharply in subsequent years.[14]

These days Paxil racks up annual sales of $2.7 billion worldwide.[15] And while this may sound like a simple success story, it worked, as Brand admits, by pushing social anxiety disorder so aggressively that the public learned to think about mental health and unease in entirely new ways. Although the APA task forces set this process in motion, the drug companies were quick to seize the baton. Together, they turned a rare disorder into a full-blown epidemic afflicting millions, making Paxil and social anxiety disorder household names.

These strategies may seem new, but they had strong precedents. As an example, in 1961 Merck decided to market depression by buying and distributing fifty thousand copies of Frank Ayd's study, *Recognizing the Depressed Patient*. The company was especially pleased that Ayd, writing for a general readership, called depression a problem afflicting more than inpatients in asylums. Merck quickly sensed a vast new market for amitriptyline, the first of a new class of antidepressants it patented. Through its marketing efforts it sold not only the drug, but also a more expanded idea of depression.[16]

Merck's actions set a new norm for drug-company marketing. A barrage of excited media articles had greeted a generation of slightly earlier pills—especially tranquilizers like the muscle relaxants Miltown (meprobamate) and Meprospan, the antidepressant Nardil (phenelzine), and sedatives like Librium and Valium (diazepam)—making clear that Americans in the 1950s were predisposed to pharmacology and its promised relief. In his *Social History of the Minor Tranquilizers*, Mickey Smith culls from the period's mass-media articles an astonishing range of euphemisms for these pills: "Wonder Drug" (*Time*, 1954); "Aspirin for the Soul" (*Changing Times*, 1956); "Happiness Pills" (*Newsweek*, 1956); "Mental Laxatives" (*Nation*, 1956); "Don't-Give-A-Damn Pills" (*Time*, 1956); "Peace of Mind Drugs" (*Today's Health*, 1957); and even "Turkish Bath in a Tablet" (*Reader's Digest*, 1962), all the way to "Bottled Well-Being" (*Time*, 1980).[17]

While Anne Caldwell called 1950s pharmacology "the empire *Psychotropia!* A world power,"[18] Morton Mintz was so appalled by the country's frivolous enthusiasm that he outlined in *The Therapeutic Nightmare* (1965) a marketing ploy that is now standard fare:

1. Public wants drug news.
2. Reporters look for drug stories.
3. Drug industry plants stories, often withholding vital facts.
4. Patient, aroused by promises of relief, pressures physician to prescribe new drug.
5. Physician accedes.[19]

While specialist advertisements at the time struck a more sober tone, they nonetheless insisted that tranquilizing anxious patients was the best way of turning them into happy, smiling people. One revealing ad from 1960, promoting Meprospan, even gave this transformation a mininarrative, with six accompanying photographs. The first portrays a physician listening "to a tense, nervous patient discuss her emotional problems." After taking one 400-mg capsule at breakfast, however, the patient "enjoy[s] sustained tranquilization all day." The copy adds that "she stays calm" on the drug, "even under the pressure of busy, crowded supermarket shopping." Indeed, as she saunters down the supermarket aisle, selecting items for her cart, she looks like a newly minted Stepford wife. After taking another 400-mg dose in the evening, she is "relaxed, alert, attentive . . . able to listen carefully to PTA proposals."

Taking 800 mg of Meprospan each day, a substantial dose, apparently causes no side effects, withdrawal symptoms, or risk of addiction. Likewise, the ad expresses no qualms about abulia—a form of emotional blunting that overmedication frequently causes. What happened, then, to the woman's "emotional problems," sketched in the first photograph? The ad implies that drug-induced tranquilization simply made them disappear.

Rather than describing such anxiety, other ads from the 1960s seem almost designed to induce it before holding out the apparent remedy. Like posters for bad B-movies, they feature frantic actresses caught in psychedelic spider webs and doctors calming overwrought housewives who torture their handkerchiefs or clutch their pearls.

The last of these has a surprisingly expansive psychological account of "depression and associated anxiety." It adds, unusually, that the drug in question works best when combined with psychotherapy or psychoanalysis. "In neurotic depressive reactions," its manufacturers advise,

The physician listens to a tense, nervous patient discuss her emotional problems. To help her, he prescribes Meprospan® (400 mg.), the only continuous-release form of meprobamate.

The patient takes one Meprospan-400 capsule at breakfast. She has been suffering from recurring states of anxiety which have no organic etiology.

She stays calm while on Meprospan, even under the pressure of busy, crowded supermarket shopping. And she is not likely to experience any autonomic side reactions, sleepiness or other discomfort.

She takes another capsule of Meprospan-400 with her evening meal. She has enjoyed sustained tranquilization all day—and has had no between-dose letdowns. Now she can enjoy sustained tranquilization all through the night.

Relaxed, alert, attentive . . . she is able to listen carefully to P.T.A. proposals. For Meprospan does not affect either her mental or her physical efficiency.

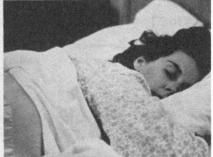

Peacefully asleep . . . she rests, undisturbed by nervousness or tension. (Samples and literature on Meprospan available from Wallace Laboratories, Cranbury, N. J.)

How to stay relaxed, alert, and attentive on a tranquilizer (Meprospan, *Archives of General Psychiatry* 3, December 1960)

'sees no way out'

... the patient who is caught up in the intricate web of her own worries and problems... MILTOWN brings the composure that leads to a new outlook on life.

Miltown*

MEPROBAMATE   *REGD. TRADEMARK OF CARTER PRODUCTS INC.

the safe sedative that relaxes both body and mind

TABLETS	400 mg.	Bottle of 50
		Bottle of 250
CAPSULES	200 mg.	Bottle of 50
		Bottle of 250
CAPSULES	400 mg.	Bottle of 50
		Bottle of 250

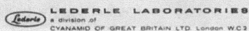

LEDERLE LABORATORIES

Lederle a division of
CYANAMID OF GREAT BRITAIN LTD. London W.C.2

When there's no apparent exit (Miltown, *Journal of Mental Science* 106, October 1960)

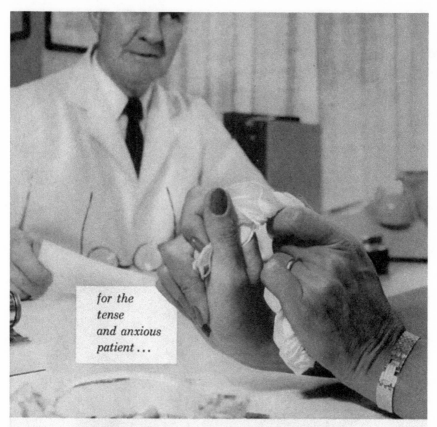

for the
tense
and anxious
patient ...

the only sustained-release tranquilizer
that does not cause autonomic side reactions

- SAFE, CONTINUOUS RELIEF of anxiety and tension for 12 hours with just one capsule—without causing autonomic side reactions and without impairing mental acuity, motor control or normal behavior.

- ECONOMICAL for the patient—daily cost is only a dime or so more than for barbiturates.

Meprospan®400

400 mg. meprobamate (Miltown®) sustained-release capsules

Usual dosage: One capsule at breakfast lasts all day; one capsule with evening meal lasts all night.
Available: *Meprospan-400*, each blue-topped capsule contains 400 mg. Miltown (meprobamate). *Meprospan-200*, each yellow-topped capsule contains 200 mg. Miltown (meprobamate). Both potencies in bottles of 30.

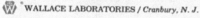 WALLACE LABORATORIES / *Cranbury, N. J.*

CWE-4292

Reassurance for the tense and anxious (Meprospan, *American Journal of Psychiatry* 117, June 1961)

To relieve symptoms
of depression
and associated anxiety

helps release normal aggression
In neurotic depressive reactions, 'Deprol' helps
relieve oppressive despondency and reduce self-
hostility. Psychotherapy can then more readily
guide the patient's aggressions into more normal
and acceptable channels.

helps calm related anxiety
'Deprol' is particularly useful in reducing the
anxiety associated with depression and thereby
promoting restful sleep.

helps relieve depressive rumination
'Deprol' can often relieve depressive rumination
and help the patient function better in home, social and business environments while more lasting
gains are being sought through psychotherapy.

Deprol

meprobamate 400 mg. + benactyzine hydrochloride 1 mg.

WALLACE LABORATORIES / Cranbury, N. J.

Helping to release normal aggression and to calm related anxiety (Deprol, *American Journal of Psychiatry* 121, June 1965)

"'Deprol' helps relieve oppressive despondency and reduce self-hostility. Psychotherapy can then more readily guide the patient's aggressions into more normal and acceptable channels." While assuring readers that therapy promotes "better" functioning, the copy implies that a pill is not itself a cure for every anxious ill.

Chapter 5 goes into more depth about links among anxiety, aggression, and "self-hostility," but the Deprol ad is significant because it's the only one in this cluster to appear after Congress passed the 1962 advertising amendment to the Food, Drug, and Cosmetic Act. That was approved in part from serious concern that these and other ads had become too manipulative and one-sided for public and professional use. The ads cited scientific assertions out of context, oversold their effects, and, above all, gave trained and lay audiences no information about side effects, including the potentially lethal risk of overmedication.

Concern ran so high in the late 1960s and early 1970s that various Senate committees and subcommittees continued meeting to review pharmaceutical advertising. One ad causing particular concern was for Serentil (mesoridazine). Clearly trying to target outpatients and the "worried well" rather than, say, doctors treating inpatients in asylums, Sandoz marketed the pill "for the anxiety that comes from not fitting in." With the remedy carefully echoing the word *serenity,* Serentil's beneficiaries would thus be numerous but unexceptional: "The newcomer in town who *can't* make friends. The organization man who *can't* adjust to altered status within his company. The woman who *can't* get along with her new daughter-in-law. The executive who *can't* accept retirement."

By today's standards, the copy sounds rather tame. But in 1971, the Subcommittee on Intergovernmental Relations to Study the Safety and Effectiveness of New Drugs deemed the ad a troubling example of overreach. Since mesoridazine is a powerful phenothiazine (a chemical ingredient of numerous psychiatric drugs and pesticides), the subcommittee felt it was "inappropriate for use for the problems of everyday living."[20] Already obliged to publish a correction with revised copy, Sandoz promptly withdrew the ad.

Such instances of congressional involvement in pharmaceutical advertising may shock readers used to the FDA's current approach to these corporations. As Beth Hawkins reports, the agency in 1997 "relaxed its rules on pharmaceutical advertising to let the pharmaceutical industry bypass healthcare providers to market its wares 'direct-to-consumer' (DTC in marketing shorthand)." With what effect? "In 1996," she continues, "drug companies spent $595 million on advertising. Within a year, spending rose to $843 million. By 2000, the amount had shot up to nearly $2.5 billion."[21] Today that figure is considerably higher. Health journalists Ray Moynihan and Alan Cassels put the total for all drug-related marketing at $25 billion, with $3 billion spent annually on direct-to-consumer advertising alone.[22] That's almost $10 million a day.

The same companies also effectively sponsor the FDA on a pay-for-play basis, which gives them a cozy relationship with those overseeing their products. Government watchdogs call this "capture": The regulatory

For the anxiety that comes from not fitting in

The newcomer in town who can't make friends. The organization man who can't adjust to altered status within his company. The woman who can't get along with her new daughter-in-law. The executive who can't accept retirement.

These common adjustment problems of our society are frequently intolerable for the disordered personality, who often responds with excessive anxiety.

Serentil is suggested for this type of patient. Not simply because its tranquilizing action can ease anxiety and tension, but because it benefits personality disorders in general. And because it has not been found habituating.

Serentil®
(mesoridazine)

(Serentil, *Medical World News,* December 11, 1970)

agency ends up so close to the industry monitored that it ends up tooth-less. As David Healy warns of the FDA, "The regulators . . . depend for ad-vice on experts who increasingly claim independence on the basis that they have consultancies with *all* the [drug] companies."[23] A spring 2006 re-port in the *Washington Post* underscored that every expert working on the DSM criteria for depression and schizophrenia had financial ties to the pharmaceutical industry, and more than half of those working on the re-maining disorders had similarly compromising ties.[24] So while American psychiatry has developed an almost insurmountable conflict of interest with the drug companies, the FDA, a small, overworked agency, has grown so close to the latter that it has become lax about granting fresh licenses for existing drugs.[25]

Congressional attention certainly didn't resolve this problem in the 1970s, but it had a swift effect on the drug industry's cavalier ads. By the time the Warner company pitched the following for Nardil three years later, its marketing department alternated hyperbole with a reasonably full account of the drug's clinical and medical effects. "This man is an island," it declares, altering Donne's most famous line to portray the anxious soli-tude of a man wringing his hands. "He is a phobic patient, living alone with his fear and anxiety. Nardil, a proven MAO [monoamine oxidase] in-hibitor, will help bring him back to the mainland of society."[26]

The obvious message here—massively intensified in later ads—is that groups vanquish loneliness, while solitude is intrinsically troubling. A recluse or misanthrope would doubtless invert such claims, representing solitude as a much-needed reprieve from the competition, malice, and big-otry that groups often incite. But when loners seem *intrinsically* to be suf-fering from psychiatric disorders (in this case, avoidant personality disor-der, later formalized by *DSM-III*), their perspectives become harder to trust. If they are already mentally ill in the eyes of psychiatrists, then sadly we are less likely to heed their words and more inclined to side with the ex-perts in saying they need help.

As the examples make clear, the drug companies represent depression and anxiety with shrewd attention to our weaknesses and concerns. So while mental illness is not a fabrication (a claim that in this context is worth underlining),[27] the way marketing and other venues define illness greatly influences how our culture and mass media gauge its impact and severity.

He is a phobic patient, living alone with his fear and anxiety. Nardil, a proven MAO inhibitor, will help bring him back to the mainland of society.

The evidence of Nardil's effectiveness in phobic states is increasing with usage. One patient, 26 years of age, had suffered from phobic anxiety for over ten years; a number of treatments had failed to alleviate his condition. "Phenelzine was started in doses of 15 mg. t.d.s., and within two weeks there has been a complete change in his behaviour. He looked relaxed, did not complain, talked freely and was able to go to the town, which he had not been able to do for over twelve months"[1].

In 1970, the Practitioner published its first major review of psychotropic drugs for three years; Nardil was selected as the most valuable drug for combination therapy in the treatment of phobic states.

"And patients with atypical depression, particularly those in whom phobic anxiety symptoms are prominent, will respond dramatically and almost specifically to the combination of an MAO inhibitor, such as phenelzine, with chlordiazepoxide or diazepam"[2]. Nardil is supplied as tablets containing 15 mg. phenelzine as the dihydrogen sulphate.

1 *Brit. J. Psychiat.*, 117, 237, 1970.
2 *Practit.*, 205, 307, 1970.

NARDIL

Full information available on request. William R. Warner & Co. Ltd., Eastleigh, Hants.
Telephone Eastleigh 3131

An insular man brought back to the mainland of society (Nardil, *British Journal of Psychiatry* 122, May 1973)

Virility helps overcome the chains of depression (Seroxat/Paxil)

Effortless exuberance: "It's me" (Seroxat/Paxil)

Rapturous sociability: "Your *life* is waiting" (Paxil)

With visual and rhetorical cues both crude and subtle, the ads also make clear that our models of illness—like our cultural aspirations—have changed dramatically over time.

These days we're more likely to want emotional and professional balance on our own terms than to fret so blatantly about fitting in. (Susie Scott, who writes about shyness and society, calls this "standardized ways of being unique.")[28] So even post-1999 ads for social anxiety disorder, which psychiatrists view as closest to manifesting acute concern about peer evaluation, tend to frame such concerns with this desire for balance in mind. Like so many other Paxil ads, attractive models visually underscore the desired *outcome*—"balance," happiness, and self-confidence. They downplay the experienced or merely feared *source* of difficulty, which the ads describe marginally, in tiny print, at the bottom of each page. In ways that counteract Warner's marketing strategy for its 1973 Nardil ad, these Slovakian, Arabic, and North American ads for Paxil play up virile strength, effortless exuberance ("It's me"), and rapturous sociability ("Your *life* is waiting"). "Come join us" or envy us, the figures invite and cajole. Ending social anxiety seems to be a lifestyle choice after all.

The variables of marketing—like the models of disease they portray—obviously change, but the fundamentals of identifying, or generating, audiences for one's product are more constant. The story of how SmithKline Beechman (now GlaxoSmithKline, after a merger with Glaxo Wellcome in 2000)[29] marketed paroxetine for social anxiety disorder fits this pattern so closely that it is strikingly predictable: First push the disease, then promote the drug that will treat or cure it. Still, the story of Paxil's success could easily have taken a quite different turn.

When SmithKline finished developing the drug, it faced a number of hurdles. For one thing, Eli Lilly's Prozac had been around since 1987, attracting phenomenal media coverage, patient loyalty, and doctor support. Pfizer too had beaten SmithKline to the punch, releasing Zoloft in 1992 and touting it as a milder alternative to Prozac. Paxil risked appearing as merely a me-too variant of the new class of antidepressants soon known as "selective serotonin-reuptake inhibitors," or SSRIs, in a market fast reaching saturation. So SmithKline did what any corporation with deep pockets would do. It hired an exclusive Madison Avenue public relations firm, Cohn and Wolfe, a company with expertise in handling pharmaceutical products. Together they launched an aggressive marketing campaign to create a new market for its product.

Just one of the many challenges facing Cohn and Wolfe, as an internal memo explained, was "generating excitement about a drug that was introduced seven years ago."[30] Another was that Paxil, first developed back in the 1970s, had a spotty record and at the outset produced troubling side effects—chiefly dependency issues and withdrawal symptoms—within a very short period of time.[31] Further, the earliest clinical trials for paroxetine made painfully clear that the drug was actually *less* effective than older antidepressants, a point the Danish University Antidepressant Group soon confirmed in a large study.[32] SmithKline was so unimpressed by the drug's potential that it considered shelving paroxetine.[33]

Given the high stakes for public health, it is remarkable that these and other cautionary findings got only a fraction of the airtime they deserved. In 2002, moreover, rigorous studies reviewed the *same figures* the drug companies had presented to the FDA to secure approval for the drugs, and found that Paxil, Prozac, Zoloft, and other SSRIs show negligible improvement over placebos (sugar pills).[34] With results so poor, the researchers concluded that these drugs should never have been approved to treat depression or anxiety.

Studies appearing since confirm these doubts, signaling that as many as 25 percent of patients taking Paxil experience *severe* problems when trying to end treatment. Far greater numbers suffer nasty side effects during treatment, with many researchers putting the figure for those experiencing sexual side effects like loss of libido and anorgasmia from *any* SSRI at a staggering 70 percent.[35] Even so, these effects may be the least of the concerns: we must now add much more severe problems like renal failure, susceptibility to strokes and coma, blood clotting, pregnancy complications (including serious birth defects), and increased risk of self-mutilation and suicide.[36]

In the case of Paxil/Seroxat, these risks were dramatic enough to prompt inquiries on both sides of the Atlantic, including a belated, full-scale FDA review in this country, a battle in the courts over whether the drug was habit forming (a battle in which, unusually, the FDA decided to get involved, thereby compromising the separation of powers), and an investigation on Britain's current affairs program *Panorama,* to which the public responded with a flood of concerned calls and emails.[37]

"When the British regulators got to see all these studies in June 2003," Healy reports, "they concluded that, combined, they pointed to a 1.5 to 3.2 times greater risk of suicidality on Paxil than on placebo."[38] In the spring of 2004 *The Lancet,* the prestigious British medical journal, published an article with clinical test data revealing problems with prescribing Paxil and other SSRIs to children. (*The Lancet* later named this article the scientific paper of the year.)[39] After several well-publicized lawsuits, SmithKline was forced to add a black-box health warning about the risk of prescribing the drug,[40] though just a few weeks later it was caught distributing memos advising its sales representatives *not* to discuss the suicide-related risk of Paxil/Seroxat with doctors.[41]

Worse still, there is no doubt the company knew about these problems right at the start—that is, "long before Paxil came to the market."[42] Its first press release for Paxil called the drug "safe and well-tolerated," touting the results of three studies allegedly proving it was "significantly more effective than placebo in treating social anxiety disorder." (How Smith-Kline defines "significantly" remains anyone's guess.) Other key statements trumpet largely meaningless pronouncements, including that "69 percent of patients treated with *Paxil* (20 to 50 mg daily) *responded to treatment* (compared to only 29 percent of patients given placebo) at week 12."[43] Although the company invites us to assume that those responses were positive, the nature and quality of the responses are not specified. The company also neglects to mention how many patients participated in the trial and how many dropped out because they had already begun experiencing side effects. Its own archives indicate, however, that dependency and withdrawal issues began affecting participants after just a few weeks.[44]

As these companies still are not required to publish findings that do not support their interests—even, remarkably, for the FDA—one has to calculate them by a process of elimination, in this case the alarmingly high *31 percentage* of patients that goes unreported: almost three in ten participants. The pharmaceutical industry is notorious for recasting severe problems like suicide ideation as "emotional lability" (mild-to-notable mood swings), which makes a drug's side effects seem less worrying and dangerous.[45] Finally, the FDA assesses this information purely on a comparative basis with placebo. This standard for judging efficacy is substantially lower than gauging whether the drug outperforms existing treatments. Nor is the FDA immune to conflicts of interest. "During a later consideration of Paxil," writes Healy, "[Tom] Laughren of the FDA denied detailed knowledge of the significance of a healthy volunteer study on Paxil showing problematic side effects, on the basis that he had inherited this file from Martin Brecher," a previous consultant at the FDA who had left to work directly for two pharmaceutical companies, first Janssen then AstraZeneca.[46]

How does SmithKline view these concerns? A classified report from 1998, with a foreword by Paul N. Jenner, director and vice president of neuroscience and worldwide strategic product development, gives us a crucial window into its thinking and actions.

The year before Paxil received FDA approval, the company decided to use "highly skilled sales and marketing efforts" to tilt the issues. Its efforts included "managing the discontinuation" problem by touting negligible clinical results and minimizing well-documented side effects and withdrawal symptoms.[47] Stress the drug's "flexibility and control," the report advised, and spin the problem of "sexual dysfunction" by "put[ting] the issue in context."[48] SmithKline also zealously controlled its own terminology and company rhetoric: "Highlight the benign nature of discontinuation symptoms, rather than quibble about their incidence."[49] Even so, "terminology such as 'withdrawal symptoms' should be avoided," the authors advised, "as it implies dependence."[50]

Given the seriousness of these side effects, it's shocking to see how aggressively the company dismissed the "flaws and failings" and "three main attacking points" of one of its main rivals, in ways that painfully reveal SmithKline's own hand: "Lilly has created these instruments to suit its own purposes," the report avers. "It is impossible to draw any meaningful conclusions from the[ir] study."[51] The writers then ridicule the policy of their competitors, who clearly play by the same rulebook: "a commercial smokescreen by Lilly" and "clearly a marketing ploy . . . and a sign of desperation in the fight for market share."[52]

Regarding when patients should end treatment, SmithKline's memo privately concedes: "The issue . . . has been almost entirely driven by marketing and is often based on misinterpreted or carefully selected data."[53] That might be news to pregnant mothers who had been assured it was safe to continue taking the drug into their final trimester, or to patients with kidney and blood-clotting problems whose doctors prescribed the drug to quell their anxiety and shyness.

Yet because *DSM-III* had so dramatically expanded the pharmaceutical market for anxiety disorders, SmithKline's executives enthused, "The opportunity . . . is enormous—around 90 million adults in North America and Europe are affected at any one time." Despite the drug's poor showing in clinical trials, the company sought to "add new anxiety disorders (e.g., social anxiety disorder/social phobia, GAD, PTSD) to the label which reinforce [its] positioning as first choice antidepressant for depression and depression with anxiety," the better "to own the . . . market segment."[54]

In March 1999 SmithKline Beecham received the first FDA license to treat social anxiety disorder. As things could have taken a quite different course, it's worth keeping that alternative scenario in mind as we assess how the drug was advertised and promoted.

Keenly aware of Prozac's skyrocketing sales, the robust demand for antidepressants, and the newly expanded market for anxiety disorders, SmithKline neither abandoned Paxil nor sought to account for its poor results. In a move of either bravado or cynicism, it called the drug "safe and well-tolerated" on the basis of a few limited results it was prepared to publish at the time. By going on the offensive, moreover, the company pushed the idea that the drug was the only *selective* serotonin-reuptake inhibitor,[55] calling it "Paxil CR" (for "controlled release" at the neuronal level), as if it targeted the brain's receptor cells more intelligently than either Prozac or Zoloft. The results in fact suggested nothing of the sort.[56]

Owing in part to existing fears that Prozac blanketed these cells indiscriminately, SmithKline's strategy paid off. Deciding not to present Paxil entirely as an antidepressant, the company used Cohn and Wolfe to style the drug mostly as an anxiolytic, or remedy for anxiety, and later still as a panacea for acute shyness. Although this strategy logically undermined the idea that Paxil was a *selective* drug (SmithKline was soon targeting it for "a spectrum of" problems—including generalized anxiety, panic, major depression, obsessive compulsive, and premenstrual dysphoric disorders), Cohn and Wolfe were such experts at pitching and recasting healthcare products that few noticed or seemed to mind the startling discrepancy.

"We're not only tapped into the latest trends," Cohn and Wolfe promotional literature boasts; "we set them."[57] With a list of clients including Taco Bell, Hilton Hotels, Visa, and many household brands, the statement is no idle boast. Indeed, by its own admission, the firm's healthcare division does a lot more than market drugs; by hyping modest results as breakthroughs and "manag[ing] crises" by burying equivocal and negative results, it also knows how to influence the FDA, EMEA (European Medicines Agency), and other regulatory bodies. "But it is often the work we do cul-

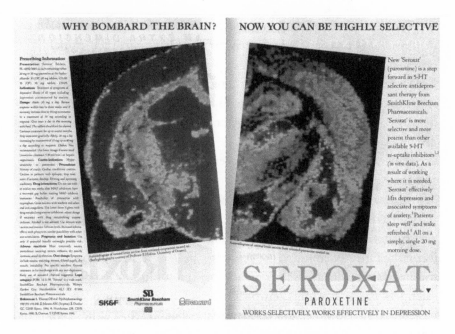

WHY BOMBARD THE BRAIN?   NOW YOU CAN BE HIGHLY SELECTIVE

SERO⨯AT.
PAROXETINE
WORKS SELECTIVELY, WORKS EFFECTIVELY IN DEPRESSION

(Seroxat/Paxil, *British Journal of Psychiatry* 159, October 1991)

tivating the marketplace prior to approval," the company asserts, "that demonstrates the true power of our communication efforts."[58] Social anxiety disorder was, and remains, a fascinating case in point.

Soon after the FDA gave SmithKline a green light to treat social anxiety, Cohn and Wolfe couched the first stages of its campaign as a generous bid to raise public awareness about the disease. The initial goal, as *PR News* helpfully broadcast, was less to promote Paxil than "to educate reporters, consumers, and, in some cases, physicians, in an effort to encourage diagnosis and treatment."[59] The 1998 memo from SmithKline, quoted earlier, was even blunter: The company needed to reeducate the public about its notions of mental illness and health, as "patients with social anxiety disorder often share the common public misperception that what they experience is severe shyness."[60] Nothing less than a total transformation in the perception of shyness would do. The title of at least one media article caught the drift: "You're Not Shy, You're Sick."[61]

As an opening strategem, then, Cohn and Wolfe plastered bus shelters across the nation with posters featuring the eye-catching slogan, "Imagine

Being Allergic to People." Accompanying this clever headline was a picture of an attractive yet forlorn man staring morosely into a teacup. "You blush, sweat, shake—even find it hard to breathe," the man seems to say. "That's what social anxiety disorder feels like."

One might wonder whether people suffering from an acute problem would need a PR company telling them what they or their loved ones are feeling. At whom, then, was the "awareness campaign" really aimed? The already afflicted, whom Cohn and Wolfe hoped would view their distress in a more severe light? Or the healthy but worried, who could be persuaded that run-of-the-mill concerns like public-speaking fears or reluctance to eat alone in public preceded something far more serious—a "crippling" mental illness now given an impressive new acronym?[62] Both constituencies were told that while their anxieties had psychological effects, a serotonin deficiency in their brains was most likely responsible. As one 2001 advertisement declared: "Paxil . . . works to correct the chemical imbalance believed to cause the disorder. . . . Most people who experience side effects on Paxil are not bothered enough to stop taking Paxil. . . . Talk to your doctor about non-habit-forming Paxil today."[63]

Once you begin talking about a deficiency or imbalance in anything to do with health, Moynihan and Cassels note astutely, the need to correct the problem becomes more than legitimate; it is also an *obligation*. Indeed, those failing to "take an *active interest* in their health," whether by seeking remedies or simply by "knowing their figures" for such matters as cholesterol, begin to seem too ill or lacking in self-respect to care about themselves.[64] Ingeniously, then, the diagnostic cycle begins to repeat itself without the aid of marketing. Ask for information if you're worried; not doing so may mean you're too unwell to grasp the full extent of your problems, in which case worried friends and relatives should rush you to the nearest doctor, psychiatrist, or emergency room.

By equating social anxiety with an allergy to other people, Cohn and Wolfe had greatly embellished what even their most loyal consultants were prepared to affirm. Yet such tactics pale beside those used to mask the campaign's sponsors and financial beneficiaries. For the posters made no reference to Paxil or SmithKline. They referred only to a group called the Anxiety Disorders Association of America, whose two other nonprofit members include the American Psychiatric Association and Freedom

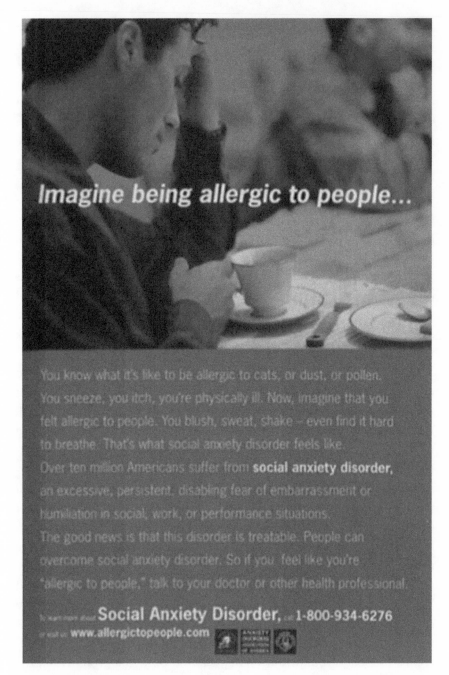

(Cohn and Wolfe, 1999)

new
hope
for
people with
social
anxiety
disorder

PAXIL
PAROXETINE HCl

(Paxil, 1999)

From Fear (FFF). Anyone seeing the posters would assume this "coalition" was a grass-roots alliance of independent agencies, developed in turn by patients wanting remedies for their suffering. Remedies that might include, but needn't be limited to, medications.

Not so. Until recently, Cohn and Wolfe handled all the group's media inquiries. FFF, several investigative reporters discovered, was an advocacy group that SmithKline quietly sponsored and financed behind the scenes.[65]

These tactics didn't seem to trouble the drug company or its shareholders. Wall Street shrewdly predicted a huge new market to combat shyness, and SmithKline Beecham, earning impressive sales shortly after FDA approval, saw steep rises in its share price. Cohn and Wolfe also had reason to brag: its "prelaunch initiative" ensured that 96 percent of media coverage delivered the key message, "Paxil is the first and only FDA-approved medication for the treatment of social anxiety disorder."[66]

Many smaller newspapers ran the company's press releases unedited. Indeed, Cohn and Wolfe's aggressive campaign was so successful that it not only generated "1.1 billion media impressions" in the first crucial year of

FDA approval (400 million in the first month alone), but also won it an award from the Public Relations Society of America. The prize givers were especially pleased to see "public awareness of SAD and other disorders" raised so diligently.[67]

With its awareness campaign under way, Cohn and Wolfe could turn to building a constituency of patients who would present themselves for medication. To this end, it had several strategies up its sleeve, as its own memo made clear:

- Educate the public via interviews with patients, physicians, and third-party groups.
- Avoid positioning Paxil as a "lifestyle drug," but [rather] as a safe and effective treatment for a severe, debilitating medical condition.
- Raise awareness [of] other indications for Paxil, while focusing on Social Anxiety Disorder.

The company's "action plan" comprised three more bullet points, with the first doubtless garnering the verdict, "mission accomplished":

- Partner with Social Anxiety Disorder Coalition to generate credibility for "severe, debilitating condition" message.
- Work through Coalition and physicians to identify patients to speak in telephone press briefing, satellite media tour, and online chats.
- Conduct aggressive media outreach with VNR/b-roll [Video News Release/documentary-style footage], press kit, graphics, radio news release, mat release [ready-made news story], and spokesperson network.[68]

In surveying this sequence of objectives and strategies, with its "aggressive . . . outreach" briefings and fervent bid "to generate credibility," one could be forgiven for thinking it resembled the outline of a military campaign. Certainly, it cost almost as much as one.

True to its word, the firm distributed "video news releases" nationwide to television stations, whose wide-eyed health reports dutifully declared that the shy and reclusive might be suffering from a "severe, debilitating condition." SmithKline also spent $30 million for an onslaught of even more television and media ads, featuring attractive, self-assured models—often, though not exclusively, female—who affirmed with perfect smiles

(Paxil, *American Journal of Psychiatry* 157, July 2000)

(Paxil)

that they had regained their emotional (and, presumably, neurochemical) "balance." One woman beams: "*I can see my future . . . I can taste success . . . I can feel peace . . . I can touch my life.*" Insisting Paxil has "proven efficacy that spans a spectrum of disorders," Cohn and Wolfe gave the ads memorable tag lines. In addition to the expectant ("Your life is waiting"), it offered the winningly affirmative ("I can") and the hopelessly corny ("Hello, my name is . . . me").

Although Cohn and Wolfe strove to portray Paxil as "a safe and effective treatment for a severe, debilitating medical condition," its second wave of

(Paxil, *American Journal of Psychiatry* 161, June 2004)

ads needed to appeal to such a vast constituency that the company quickly blurred the line between acute anxiety and common unhappiness.[69] Not surprisingly, then, the ads give the impression that this "debilitating . . . condition" was really about lifestyle choices and "balance" (a recurring word, but a shifting ideal). For instance, "Julie, outdoor enthusiast," betrays no hint of anxiety from her rural idyll; she radiates confidence as she smiles directly at the viewer from just outside her tent. "Start her on something she can stay with," the copy exhorts, something that will help like-minded patients (who surface in related ads as grinning outdoorsy types in soft focus and want "living without interruptions," including presumably those from drug-related side effects).

When Cohn and Wolfe included men in its marketing campaign, it tended to represent them in working environments, where Paxil might help them gain optimum job performance. They are depicted either clinching an important deal ("Paxil: Show them they can") or, just as emotionally charged, lamenting that they had failed to do so. One such ad from 1999 depicts a young businessman in three stages of office-related

Clinching an important deal (Paxil, *American Journal of Psychiatry* 156, August 1999)

despair and shame. Backlit, as if by an invisible sun, are the following words in bold: *"Show them they can. Paxil—Paroxetine HCl. Relieve the anxiety. Reveal the person."*

The PR firm also needed media stories to create buzz about the disorder. "Are you or someone you know suffering from symptoms of social anxiety disorder . . . ?" one of countless near-identical articles asked readers, in a *Spotlight on Health*. "If so, you are among the estimated 10 million Americans who have this debilitating disorder." Reproducing almost verbatim SmithKline's own press release and the upper ceiling of Stein's inconclusive phone survey, this article (and others) spread rapidly on the web and in a multitude of printed venues. According to the anonymous author, "An awareness campaign about social anxiety disorder conducted over the last two years has motivated people to seek professional help or, at the very least, made them feel less alone, according to a survey of callers to a toll-free phone line sponsored as part of the campaign by a group of patient and professional mental health organizations."

We already know who constituted these organizations and how they funded the campaign. The article then quotes Mary Guardino, executive

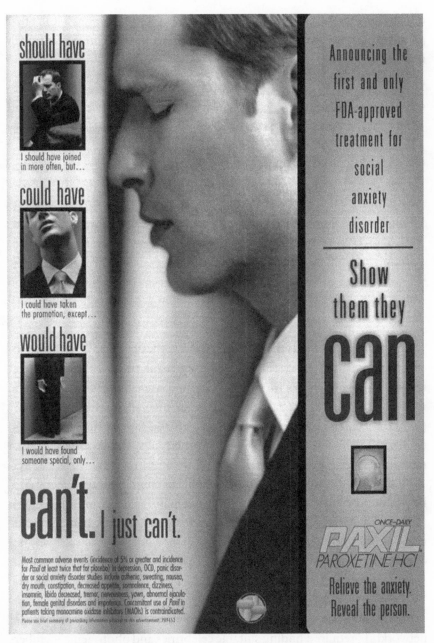

Three stages of office-related despair and shame (Paxil, *American Journal of Psychiatry* 156, October 1999)

director of Freedom From Fear, saying: "It is very gratifying to learn that people who saw the campaign and called to receive more information felt it improved their understanding of this disabling condition, and were prompted to seek professional support." The survey asserts:

- Two out of three (61%) of those surveyed [960 callers] said they had heard about social anxiety disorder compared with 38% who said they had not.
- Four in five (81%) said they found the social anxiety disorder campaign made them feel they were not alone in suffering social anxiety disorder symptoms.
- Three out of four (78%) said the campaign improved their understanding of social anxiety disorder; a similar number (75%) said it helped them identify what they were feeling.
- Three in five (60%) said it motivated them to seek additional information about the disorder and 44% said it motivated them to seek professional help.[70]

The more one rereads these claims, the less they really say. As direct-to-consumer (DTC) pharmaceutical marketing regularly exhorts viewers and readers to "ask their doctor about" one of a multitude of products, the final results are not especially surprising. Further, as SmithKline not only paid for this massive awareness campaign but also funded the organization earmarked to analyze its results, we must take all such percentages with a rather large pinch of salt.

Highlighting as much as anything that life in contemporary America can be profoundly lonely and isolating, the percentages do, however, confirm the relief that can result from giving suffering a scientific name or acronym. This support may be especially consoling when it implies a biological or genetic condition for which the patient is not to blame. Hence, in part, the success of the National Mental Health Awareness Campaign's posters: "It's not your fault."[71]

Cohn and Wolfe's "aggressive media outreach" with "spokesperson network[s]" required finding suitable celebrities and photogenic members of advocacy groups like FFF to put a face on the disease. In so doing, the firm gained valuable airtime without appearing to pitch a product and, best of all, without needing to balance the picture by enumerating Paxil's

(National Mental Health Awareness Campaign, 2001)

litany of harmful side effects. As the stories—seemingly spontaneous—would stress recovery from the ordeal of shyness, they would uphold and naturalize the disorder. By generating comparisons ("I've felt that, too"), such stories would win the recovering patients or celebrities so much sympathy and publicity that anyone doubting the magnitude of their suffering (that is, anyone mentioning what they were being paid to describe it) would seem heartless, uninformed, or both.

Public relations companies know that celebrities are especially useful in raising awareness of a medical or psychiatric problem, because they wield "an intangible sort of magic" for the public, which can greatly increase publicity and sales.[72] Already figures of admiration and trust, they diminish any remaining stigma attached to such problems. So, as before, these stories and ads repeatedly underscored a link between the condition and the drug.[73]

Indeed, this loop became so patent that when Ricky Williams, running back for the Miami Dolphins, announced to Oprah and several million of her viewers that he suffered from crippling shyness, he added rather sheepishly that he had recognized his condition only after watching a TV commercial about the disorder. Such a statement seems almost surreal when one considers that SmithKline, already spending a cool $30 million on these ads, paid Williams an undisclosed sum for his statement, too. Yet these moments of sponsored reverse affirmation—by celebrities, patients, and even paid consultants—epitomize social phobia's history as a clinical category. "I've always been a shy person," Williams declared, a statement dutifully repeated by the *New York Times,* the *Los Angeles Times,* and other media.[74] Apparently he was shy only about revealing that he'd been hired to raise public awareness about social anxiety disorder.

"No therapeutic category is more accepting of condition branding than the field of anxiety and depression," states Vince Parry, an industry insider. One reason, he says, is that mental "illness is rarely based on measurable physical symptoms and, therefore, [is] open to conceptual definition."[75] Neuropsychiatrists and pharmacologists, like those serving on the DSM task forces, would doubtless disagree, insisting their diagnostic criteria derive from hard facts and science. But the marketing of illness and its scientific foundations—already a precarious union—finally came apart in the 1990s, and since then the gap has only widened.

One learns a lot when insiders share their best tips with fellow marketers. According to Parry, "There are three principal strategies for fostering the creation of a condition and aligning it with a product:

- elevating the importance of an existing condition;
- redefining an existing condition to reduce a stigma;
- developing a new condition to build recognition for an unmet market need."[76]

Based on what we've seen, this advice is eerily familiar.

The list of fake or exaggerated conditions for which medical remedies have been launched is dismayingly long. So too, of course, is the history of quacks and swindlers conning the public with bogus antidotes for largely imaginary ailments. It's one thing when these misunderstandings stem from gossip, with merely local effects; it's quite another when the disease mongering is systematic and recurring on a massive scale, orchestrated by expensive marketing campaigns whose truth and legality often rest on the parsing of a single adjective or verb.

One of the easiest ways to overstate the gravity of a medical condition, Parry finds, is to dazzle patients with acronyms. He cites Pfizer's Viagra for ED (erectile dysfunction) and SmithKline's Zantac for GERD (gastro-esophageal reflux disease). In the case of GERD, the public previously assumed that over-the-counter remedies would be adequate in tackling heartburn, so a barrage of PR and advertising had to convince them otherwise. Almost identical strategies were devised to promote IBS (irritable bowel syndrome), ADHD (attention deficit hyperactivity disorder), PMDD (premenstrual dysphoric disorder), and a host of other doubtful terms and conditions the drug companies have spent millions trying to press into our daily vocabulary.[77]

SmithKline's "Social Phobia Inventory," a "reliable tool" for doctors and patients, abbreviates to "SPIN." Apparently unaware of this pun, the company adds: "SPIN is a well-tested . . . screen . . . for the symptoms of social anxiety disorder and thereby assists patients and doctors in identifying the disorder." Like many other self-administered quizzes, the test is extremely open-ended, urging potential customers to respond, on a scale of 1 to 4, to statements that seem far from typifying an acute psychiatric disorder:

- Being criticized scares me a lot.
- I avoid going to parties.
- Talking to strangers scares me.
- I avoid speaking to anyone in authority.
- Trembling or shaking in front of others is distressing to me.[78]

The drug companies don't create these guidelines in isolation. They borrow heavily from specialists in anxiety disorders, like John R. Marshall, whose aptly subtitled book *Social Phobia: From Shyness to Stage Fright* ("New Help for Millions of Sufferers") similarly emphasizes public speaking, dealing with authority figures, social gatherings, and other forms of largely job-related embarrassment. Although he warns, "There is no absolute score that indicates social phobia," he does concede, open-endedly, "Patients in a treatment study for social phobia had pretreatment scores on this scale ranging from 19 to 56."[79]

When Michelle Cottle, a journalist at the *New Republic*, encountered

Marshall's quizzes, she thought them so ludicrous that she decided to conduct an unscientific poll of her own: "I asked some of my coworkers at *TNR* to take a short diagnostic test developed by" Marshall. "Of the 23 . . . staffers to complete the survey (the rest were presumably too timid)," Cottle adds wryly, "a sizeable majority scored above 19. Based on these results, I've recommended that the magazine's benefits manager explore the possibility of getting a group discount on Paxil."[80]

The vagueness of these quizzes and their associated criteria might well invite disbelief and jocularity, but a huge number of self-help manuals take them very seriously, as do the many advocacy groups and organizations that sprang up after *DSM-III* appeared (doubtless because their rationale and business partly depend on them). At the Shyness Institute, founded in 1994 by two psychology professors at Stanford University, research focuses on "improv[ing] treatment methods for shyness and social anxiety disorder/social phobia," as well as "the role of affect/emotion in the phenomenon."[81] There's a similar "Shyness Research Institute" at Indiana University Southeast, and the "Public Speaking–Social Anxiety Center of New York" offers a range of workshops "for the chutzpah-challenged."[82]

Comparable classes at Manhattan's Learning Annex range in their topics from "Are You Shy? Is It Holding You Back?" to "Dating Strategies for Shy New York Singles."[83] Meanwhile, the Adult Anxiety Clinic at Temple University straddles the practical and theoretical sides of this divide. Its director, Richard Heimberg, grew interested in the issue after studying 75 college men with dating anxiety.[84] Must one really inflate such fears into disorders, however, to give them credibility?

While many universities are lending a hand to formalize the study of social anxiety and shyness, the drug companies frequently sponsor patient support and advocacy groups behind the scenes—as we saw when SmithKline funded Freedom From Fear to generate sales, buzz, and legitimacy for Paxil. Moynihan and Cassels report in *Selling Sickness:* "A global survey from Britain estimated that *two-thirds* of all patient advocacy groups and health charities now rely on funding from drug companies or device manufacturers. The most prolific, according to the survey results, is Johnson and Johnson and number two is Pfizer. While creating the appearance of corporate generosity, such sponsorship can bring many benefits to the sponsor as well as the recipient. Chief among them is that patient groups are a way to help shape public opinion about the conditions [the] products are designed to treat."[85]

The corporations adopting these practices have not suddenly become charities. The costs of funding these groups (like the costs of "free" samples and giveaways to doctors and psychiatrists) always return to the patient, whether as price hikes or as raised co-payments to healthcare providers. When challenged about these policies, the companies insist they are doing a public service by raising awareness of a hidden or underreported problem—a position many psychiatrists (also on the companies' payroll) are happy to endorse.

Support groups don't of course represent all patients, many of whom endure chronic symptoms—some exacerbated by the drugs themselves, as we'll soon see. Although these groups put a face on each illness and often challenge those questioning its legitimacy, they rarely disclose their funding. Nor do they volunteer that firms like Cohn and Wolfe handpick the patients for media appearances, based on their looks, then coach them to hone the clarity and force of their message. One of these messages, SmithKline's 1998 memo affirmed, is that "patients with social anxiety disorder often share [a] common public misperception that what they experience is extreme shyness."[86]

As we piece together this complex puzzle, the overall picture becomes disturbingly clear. By giving "social phobia" the more patient-friendly name "social anxiety" and by greatly expanding its parameters to cast the problem as one of fear, not avoidance, the DSM task forces significantly lowered the bar for the FDA and drug manufacturers. Euphoric about their massive new markets, which they rushed to cultivate with "carefully selected data," the drug makers then fudged key distinctions between routine fears and chronic disorders to make them seem identical.

When Pfizer tried to capture part of the shyness market in 2003 for its antidepressant Zoloft, for instance, it ran an ingenious campaign asking simply of a beautiful woman with downcast eyes, "Is she just shy? Or is it Social Anxiety Disorder?" Except for their content, the questions might be part of an ad campaign for cosmetics, Memorex, or a pricey shampoo.

(Zoloft, *American Journal of Psychiatry* 160, August 2003)

Such banality is the point. The phrase *social anxiety disorder* was so commonplace by 2003 that this last ad didn't bother to gloss it. Apparently, the public no longer needed to know it was suffering in vast numbers from a "debilitating medical condition." The PR firms and marketing departments, bludgeoning us repeatedly with this constant refrain, had already done their job.

5

REBOUND SYNDROME:
WHEN DRUG TREATMENTS FAIL

Robert Spitzer's task forces paved the way for the drug companies, creating seven new anxiety disorders that supposedly required medical attention. But the drugs approved to treat these disorders turned out to be as indiscriminate in their effects as Spitzer's colleagues were in their initial judgments.

By failing to distinguish clearly between shyness and social anxiety disorder, the task forces made every anxiety reaction fair game for medical attention. They lumped together routine traits that do not belong in a manual of mental disorders. And they quietly ignored the fact that shyness was once thought a positive characteristic, whereas anxiety can be a rational, even necessary, response to stress. Ironically, the drug the FDA licensed to treat social anxiety disorder, Paxil, is similarly all-inclusive, often blanketing the nervous system so completely it prevents the brain and nervous system from distinguishing between routine stress and chronic anxiety. The result is all manner of health risks that GlaxoSmithKline (GSK) now reluctantly acknowledges. Paxil's side effects also explain why a substantial number of patients (16.1 to 20 percent) discontinue treatment after several months and why, after doing so, they often feel worse than before.[1]

The hasty, overmedicated handling of anxiety is a direct result of *DSM-III* and the large number of new disorders it created. But an alarming medical problem now faces many patients taking Paxil, in particular. Doctors call it "rebound syndrome," because its symptoms—which stem from discontinuing drug treatment—can have a boomerang effect more intense

*"I think the dosage needs adjusting. I'm not nearly
as happy as the people in the ads."*

© *The New Yorker* Collection (August 6, 2001), Barbara Smaller, from cartoonbank
.com. All rights reserved.

and dangerous than the turmoil the patients first experienced. So many
Paxil users are in fact struggling with this syndrome that they have formed
support groups to share information, swap advice, and manage a health
crisis that GSK for many years tried to ignore.

Fueled by new research, health scares, and mounting skepticism about
GSK's promotional campaigns, public concern about rebound syndrome
has led many to ask whether drugs are the optimal or necessary way of
treating anxiety. This reevaluation is now sufficiently widespread and accepted among medical experts that the *Los Angeles Times* and *Newsweek*,
adjusting their earlier emphasis, ran parallel stories about it on the same
day in March 2006. "The nation's heady romance with antidepressant
medication appears to be over," the *Los Angeles Times* declared, while
Newsweek insisted, in a cover article, "Freud Is *Not* Dead. The Couch Is

Out, But the Culture of Therapy Is Everywhere—And Science Is Taking a New Look at His Theories."[2]

I do the same in this chapter, to provide a clear medical explanation for why some patients have an adverse reaction to drugs such as Paxil. Considering the many side effects of medications, I also assess different ways of viewing shyness and more effective ways of handling anxiety. Because therapists view anxiety less mechanistically than do neuropsychiatrists, they restore the phenomenon's complexity and reverse the impoverishment of human experience that dates to DSM-III. And though I focus partly on cognitive-behavioral theories, because they are considered a popular and efficient alternative to psychotherapy, like *Newsweek* I take a fresh look at Freud's theories of anxiety, because they point to more deep-seated conflicts that resist our culture's stress on quick fixes.

Kate is one of many patients who wishes a specialist had told her about potential withdrawal symptoms long before she began taking Paxil. "Ironically," she tells me, "I did ask for Paxil because I thought I had social anxiety disorder."[3] After enduring anxiety and bouts of menopausal depression, she responded well to the drug for three years, then carefully tapered her dose when she felt better. Hers would seem to be a simple success story. But as Kate stepped down her prescription, a new wave of problems hit her. "I immediately had a whopping reaction," she despaired. "Three months of quasimania, which made it seem as if I was very active and confident, followed by six months of anxiety, insomnia, periodic brain zaps, and total uninterest in sex."[4] Other drugs, such as trazodone, prescribed by "well-meaning psychiatrists," only worsened her anxiety, weepiness, and hopelessness. Coping with Paxil's aftereffects, she now feels worse than she did before starting treatment.

Kate does not represent every patient who has taken Paxil. She is, however, one of a disturbingly large number who are documenting their problems online because the drug companies, eager to promote remedies for the new anxiety disorders, are painfully slow in investigating the health-related side effects. The many expert pharmacologists I consulted when researching this chapter, who verified its medical claims and whose careers as researchers partly depend on the amount of external funding they can attract, are loath to bite the hand that feeds them by publishing findings at odds with the drug companies' largely upbeat reports. Consequently, it is extremely difficult to find articles about SSRI-related rebound syndrome in the nation's top peer-reviewed medical and psychiatric journals. For many years, moreover, doctors and psychiatrists would tell patients like Kate they were re-experiencing their original anxiety and should either raise their dose or change to another medication. Now they are more likely to recognize that she and many others are experiencing side effects stemming entirely from the drugs.

Of all the antidepressants and antianxiety remedies now available, Paxil has the worst track record for rebound syndrome, because it has additional side effects as an anticholinergic, a term I explain shortly. Indeed, the chorus of outrage, litigation, and bad press in 2005 became so deafening that GSK decided to revise the drug's "product monograph." It warned healthcare professionals about "adverse reactions" and "discontinuation symptoms" that include "agitation, anxiety, headache, tremor, confusion, diarrhea, nausea, vomiting and sweating."[5] These, the booklet stressed, supplement a litany of already well-known side effects: "dry mouth, constipation, decreased appetite, somnolence, tremor, decreased libido, yawn [*sic*], abnormal ejaculation, female genital disorders, and impotence."[6]

As GSK's altered rhetoric broke the dam, patients finally could account for the side effects deluging them. The company felt obliged to note "serious, sometimes fatal, reactions" to the drug, including "mental status changes that include extreme agitation progressing to delirium and coma." Other disturbing reports receiving brief, scattershot attention concerned newborns with serious birth defects, most of them heart related, when pregnant mothers continued taking Paxil into their third trimester. And GSK admitted that patients on Paxil had experienced seizures, kidney failure, and abnormal bleeding because of "impaired platelet aggregation."[7]

As if these revelations weren't shocking enough, the company stressed, in boldface type, that "recent analyses" of the drug's effect on patients under the age of 18 recognized "behavioral and emotional changes, including an increased risk of suicide ideation." GSK couldn't generalize about these "small denominators," it hastened to add. But since the list of "severe agitation-type adverse events" in children *and* adults included "self-harm or harm to others," as well as "disinhibition, emotional lability

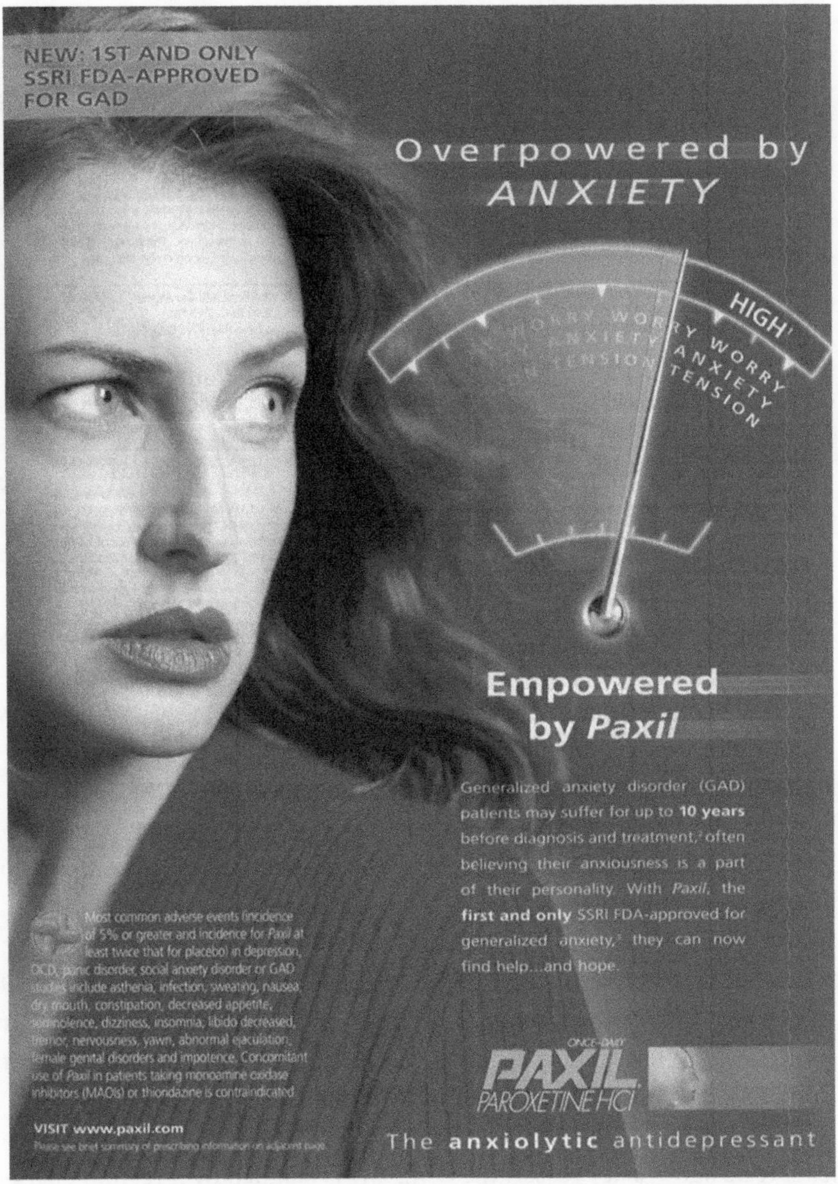

(Paxil, *American Journal of Psychiatry* 158, July 2001)

[unpredictable mood swings], hostility, aggression, depersonalization, [and] akathisia," a serious condition marked by extreme motor restlessness, apparently none of the several million people taking the drug could safely be said *not* to require "rigorous clinical monitoring for suicidal ideation"[8]— an almost unbelievable outcome, voiced by the drug manufacturer itself, for a company still encouraging the public to take Paxil for anxiety about going to parties and fear of being criticized.

If, according to our drug companies and psychiatrists, this list of side effects represents progress, then something is terribly wrong with their vision of mental health. The upshot of GSK's multimillion-dollar "awareness campaign"—certain to intensify the anxiety it was meant to quell—is mind-boggling, yet in the brochure, at least, the company scarcely breaks its stride. It continues to represent the drug as a key treatment "for the symptomatic relief of generalized social phobia (social anxiety disorder)," as well as depression, panic disorder, and premenstrual dysphoric disorder.[9]

It would have been better, of course, if the scale and gravity of Paxil's side effects had been broadcast long before millions of people began taking the drug. Even in 2002, the list of associated health problems GSK was required to mention was still relatively easy to downplay: "Paxil is generally well tolerated. As with many medications, there can be side effects. . . . Most people who experience [them] are not bothered enough to stop taking Paxil. . . . Talk to your doctor about non-habit-forming Paxil today. So you can see someone you haven't seen in a while . . . Yourself!"[10]

GSK's careful qualifiers ("generally well tolerated"; "most people"; "there can be side effects") give the company so much legal and clinical wiggle room that by the time one reaches its final, vacuous statement about seeing oneself, the copy might be advertising a window cleaner, not a powerful psychotropic with a laundry list of side effects.

The problem facing GSK today is that it knew about most of these problems years ago—a key reason the company is plagued by litigation charging gross negligence. It is well known among experts, as *USA Today*'s website still reports, that fully "20 percent of patients treated with Paxil in worldwide clinical trials in major depressive disorder and 16.1 percent of patients treated with Paxil in worldwide trials in social anxiety disorder . . . discontinued treatment due to an adverse event."[11] You will still hear

(Paxil, *American Journal of Psychiatry* 156, March 1999)

some psychiatrists, many of them paid consultants, question the significance of these figures while urging more people to seek treatment. Doing so must take real nerve: the fact that one in five patients has an adverse reaction to Paxil is, proportionally speaking, a staggering number. Even a small incidence of serious side effects would be cause for alarm, but the sheer scale of the problem facing the drug companies makes their unwillingness—and psychiatry's—to study it systematically a grave concern.

Fed up with GSK's half-truths, New York State Attorney General Eliot Spitzer decided to sue the company for fraud in June 2004, claiming it had concealed crucial information about the drug's track record.[12] The full extent of Paxil's side effects, Spitzer alleged, hadn't been disclosed to physicians—no real surprise when GSK advised its pharma reps not to discuss such matters with them.[13] The company said the charges were unfounded but decided to settle anyway, paying the State of New York $900,000 and promising to post on its website summaries of all its clinical trials since December 2000.[14]

In April 2006 the company also "agreed to pay U.S. states $14 million to resolve allegations it illegally blocked generic entry to the market of its antidepressant Paxil, which caused state healthcare plans to pay inflated prices for the drug." Indeed, GSK has "paid a total of *$165 million* under similar settlements stemming from class action lawsuits brought by pharmacies, consumers, and health insurers."[15]

Although the settlement with the attorney general's office paves the way for further industry reforms, $900,000 is but a fraction of GSK's revenue for the drug. And despite promises that it would disclose key information to the public and to researchers, GSK and other drug companies continue to withhold major documents and results.[16] Neither settlement nor promise is especially reassuring to Kate, whose full recovery from Paxil seemed so elusive fourteen months after ending treatment that she decided to learn more about the drug she had taken. What she read horrified her.[17]

Paxil, she discovered, is unusual among SSRIs in being a potent anticholinergic. That means, technically, that the drug tends to block receptors in our cholinergic system, an aspect of our central nervous system controlling many involuntary activities such as fight-or-flight reactions, the amount we sweat, and our ability to produce saliva and tears.[18] It is no surprise, then, that many taking the drug experience dry mouth and feel mildly sedated.

But Paxil doesn't just frequently jam the cholinergic system, to prevent it from going into overdrive. Because the drug is *not* sufficiently selective to distinguish between extreme and routine stress, it often blocks almost all signals from this system, including those that would alert us to undue stress and overexertion. Nor does the cholinergic system stand by and accept its altered condition. Sensing that something internally is wrong, it often tries to compensate for the false neuronal picture by sprouting new receptors, a process that in psychiatric jargon is called upregulating. The whole nervous system is thrown out of kilter, making it more difficult than ever for the body to distinguish between stress and anxiety.

Paxil's other deliberate and unintended effects can be equally erratic. Like all SSRIs (including Prozac, Zoloft, Effexor, and Lexapro), Paxil is meant to block the uptake of the serotonin that neurons normally discharge, thereby storing a greater amount of this messenger to activate neighboring neurons. Some neuropsychiatrists believe that over the long term a large amount of serotonin in the brain can stabilize extreme fluctuations in mood—a belief, we'll see shortly, that many of their colleagues have discredited.[19] Still, the serotonergic system doesn't ignore the artificially raised quantities of this messenger. It normally needs more 5-HT2 receptors to soak up the excess, a situation some researchers link to patients' widespread sexual dysfunction, because these receptors send saturation signals to the brain.[20] The system's excess serotonin has the opposite effect on our 5-HT1A receptors, however, which assume they're in less demand and downregulate accordingly. The combined effect of these alterations, as our body tries to adjust or compensate, is a key reason the drugs lose their kick (Lauren Slater calls this SSRI "poop-out") and patients are urged either to up their dose or to switch to another brand.[21]

Those trying to quit Paxil face an especially difficult dilemma, with few really equipped to guide them. For if they taper their dose when the drug stops working, they may experience an intense "cholinergic rebound."[22] Why?

There are three reasons. First, as the receptors in our cholinergic system try to outpace the drug, more of them will put the body in a state of permanent red alert, leaving patients at the mercy of hair-trigger symptoms such as intense anxiety, aggression, and insomnia. This is exactly what Kate endured. "I have never been prone to anxiety attacks," she reports, "but in April 2005, shortly after reducing my dose, I experienced an anxiety attack so severe I thought I would have a heart attack."

Second, although most people's nervous systems eventually adjust, the receptors in our serotonergic system—saturated artificially for several months—experience the drop to predrug levels as starvation. Kate puts it memorably, "Once well-fed, they're now like hungry baby birds, bitterly squawking for food."[23]

Third, our 5-HT1A receptors aren't as malleable as other kinds and take longer to sprout anew, delaying the return to neuronal health. Indeed, studies have found that in some patients these receptors fail to grow back at all, in effect leaving the patients worse off than before.[24]

Among medical experts, including the many I consulted, none of these statements is especially controversial. GSK's revised product manual even acknowledges the existence of rebound syndrome and other discontinuation symptoms. But it sugarcoats this process by saying "a gradual reduction in the dose rather than abrupt cessation" will minimize the problem.[25] That is misleading. Like many other patients, Kate was scrupulous in lowering her dose. She followed her doctor's recommendations to the letter. But that's when she experienced her worst difficulties.

When patients are at the mercy of such unpleasant mood swings, it's easy for harried doctors to misdiagnose the problem, insisting that the original anxiety has returned with a vengeance. For a long time, these assumptions masked rebound syndrome and put anxiety in a chronic light. Rather than tolerating such symptoms, perhaps for weeks or even months at a time, some patients understandably want to end them by switching to a new drug or taking an even higher dose of Paxil. Unfortunately, in most cases that simply prolongs the inevitable.

While for years the drug companies and their consultants blamed these problems on the disease, not the drug, the counterevidence pointing to SSRIs is now too massive—and widely accepted—to ignore.[26] Nevertheless, many experts still broadcast the discredited notion that our serotonin levels drop when we feel down, and underreport the neuronal crises besetting those who are trying to discontinue treatment.

Although the drug companies often suggest otherwise, there is no correlation between anxiety or depression and low levels of serotonin. Some people with symptoms of either have ordinary levels of serotonin, others high, and others low. Flooding the brain with this messenger therefore doesn't end, or even swiftly reduce, depression or anxiety. That interested clinicians and lobbyists for the pharmaceutical industry repeatedly claim otherwise is, as David McDowell of Columbia University says, "part of modern neuromythology."[27] Doubtless it is easier to accept that our suffering derives from faulty neurotransmitters than it is to concede that numerous factors—psychological, biological, social, and environmental—influence our states of mind.

If we are to understand why anxiety blights so many lives, we need a comprehensive picture of its causes and effects. Yet even after a century of wrangling, clinicians are no closer to agreeing about them.

Neuropsychiatrists favor drug treatments because they say anxiety stems largely, if not exclusively, from our nervous system's overreacting to situations that do not warrant extreme fight-or-flight responses. If a work-related presentation paralyzes us with dread, apparently it's because our nervous system has misread external cues as threatening or even dangerous. The office is suddenly a battleground; the meeting becomes a torture chamber, as GSK's year 2000 advertisement for Paxil tried to convey. The arguments—psychological, social, even ethical—for preventing these mistakes and the suffering they cause seem unambiguous, indeed commendable.

Yet this limited picture of our body's behavior tells us nothing about how the mind processes such information. After all, the office problem concerns *perception* as well as biology. The relationship between consciousness and our nervous system is far more open-ended and unpredictable than many neuropsychiatrists allow; it involves also family history, hereditary traits, our most vivid memories, and behavioral qualities we might loosely call temperament. Just as some people seem relatively untroubled by catastrophes while others find them traumatic, our perceptions are not limited to biological factors. Though our mental landscapes may be sufficiently resilient to influence us for years, our minds form new associations all the time, especially with the help of therapy—a point to which I'll return.

What it is.

What it feels like.

If this is how you feel, it could be social anxiety. Social anxiety disorder is an intense, persistent fear and avoidance of social situations. This extreme fear of being judged or embarrassed can put your life on hold. Those who suffer may blush, sweat, shake, or even experience a pounding heart around those they think may criticize them. To avoid this embarrassment, some drop out of school. Some refuse to date. Some turn down job promotions or choose unsatisfying jobs beneath their skill level.

Over 10 million people suffer from social anxiety, and a chemical imbalance could be to blame.

PAXIL – the only prescription medication proven effective for social anxiety disorder – works to correct this imbalance.

Talk to your doctor today. PAXIL is not for everyone. Lesser degrees of social anxiety usually do not require medication. Tell your doctor what medicines you're taking. People taking MAOIs should not take PAXIL. PAXIL is generally well-tolerated. As with many medications, there can be side effects. Side effects may include decreased appetite, dry mouth, sweating, nausea, constipation, sexual side effects in men and women, yawn, tremor or sleepiness. Most people who experience side effects are not bothered enough to stop taking PAXIL.

Call 1-800-454-6163 or visit paxil.com

Your life is waiting.

PAXIL
PAROXETINE HCl

PX5842 © SmithKline Beecham 2000

Please see the following page for important product information.

The office is a battleground, the meeting a torture chamber (Paxil, *New York Times Magazine,* October 29, 2000)

Even those insisting that biology is paramount must admit that the cholinergic and serotonergic systems vary greatly from person to person, with each of us responding differently over time to a range of conditions. One size (or dose) doesn't and couldn't fit all. And though drug companies and psychiatrists partly concede this by promoting a variety of "me-too" drugs with minor molecular differences and dosages, they don't broadcast that the millions of people taking these drugs will have enormously unpredictable responses to them over the short and longer terms.

Neuropsychiatrists often scoff when treatment and diagnosis issues even allude to consciousness. Science should focus only on what is known about our brains, they say, not dwell on the quirks and enigmas of our minds. Yet in the case of psychiatry, its practitioners seem largely to have forgotten, the quirky and enigmatic always assume a larger-than-usual significance. And what about the long-term effects of keeping our brains and nervous systems in such an artificial state? It's disturbing to underscore that neuropsychiatrists simply do not know. Doubtless fueled by excitement and good intentions, the mass consumption of these drugs is, at bottom, a colossal experiment. Whether some of us will respond well to them and others will suffer permanent brain or bodily damage remains a troubling—and, for many, unacceptable—gamble.

Consider the risks: We may be consigning those experiencing only mild shyness or anxiety to lifetime dependencies on SSRIs, and the young, in particular, to permanently producing less serotonin, dopamine, and norepinephrine. As the list of severe side effects for SSRIs lengthens, and associated health warnings sound increasingly shrill, a lifetime dependency on one or more of these drugs is not a treatment plan to undertake lightly.

Finally, as if these unknown factors weren't sufficiently troublesome, we must begin to assess collectively, across generations, what permanent neurochemical alterations of the brain could mean for the personalities, memories, passions, and even mental aptitude of millions of patients. Despite the growing urgency of these concerns, scientists simply cannot predict how or even whether we'll resolve them. Some researchers, however, are sufficiently concerned about long-term harm to ask if an entire generation will be too blunted emotionally to form lasting relationships, much less fall deeply in love.[28]

In short, the idea that neuropsychiatry holds all the explanatory cards

The "tender loving care" of an SSRI (Seroxat/Paxil, *British Journal of Psychiatry* 171,
October 1997)

must in good conscience be dispelled. With the long-term effects of SSRIs unknown, neuropsychiatrists are still working very much in the dark.

———————————

In a bracing, timely book, Elisabeth Roudinesco tackles some of these concerns. "Since neurobiology seems to affirm that all psychical disturbances are linked to an abnormality in the functioning of nervous cells," she remarks, "and since adequate medication exists, why should we worry?"[29]

The medical explanation I've given for why drug treatments often fail makes clear—as Roudinesco's book soon confirms—that the question is rhetorical and meant to shake us out of complacency. As Kate and many other patients have learned painfully, adequate medication for anxiety (meaning, medication without harmful side effects) does *not* exist. With their litany of associated symptoms and violent rebound syndromes, current treatments can leave patients feeling a great deal worse.

The meaning of *adequacy* in this context needs more thought and discussion, especially as patients routinely are "prescribed the same range of medications whatever their symptoms."[30] If a drug like Paxil can't reliably distinguish between acute anxiety and everyday stress, how could it parse the intricate differences among social phobia, major depression, premenstrual dysphoric disorder, generalized anxiety, and panic disorder—all illnesses the same pill is approved to treat?

Compounding this problem, many neuropsychiatrists suggest we really have no need to ask *why* people behave in certain ways. We need only find the quickest practical intervention: medication, perhaps with exposure and response prevention. With such mechanistic views of humanity, the cause of our distress translates neatly into behavioral effects, and our symptoms, unimpeded by consciousness, seem clear and uncomplicated.

The belief among many neuro- and cognitive scientists that "the machine person" simply replaces "the desiring person" stems, according to Roudinesco, from "a scientism elevated to the status of religion."[31] Our quasimystical faith in pharmacology is so unshakable, moreover, that it dictates treatment even when the effects are remote from our suffering, worsen our health, and are unable to gauge—much less cure—our underlying malaise.[32] Is it any wonder, she asks, that patients given almost identical treatments for varied, even unique predicaments will "seek another kind of outlet for their unhappiness"?[33]

Freud certainly thought these matters sufficiently urgent and misunderstood to issue, almost a century ago, a stern rebuke to detractors *and* supporters, urging them not to take anxiety at face value or to assume it would disappear after telling the patient what likely was wrong. Granted, today's treatment picture is more complex, but the underlying thinking—the literalism that Freud challenged—is in many respects the same. To proceed in that crude way, Freud declared, was grossly to underestimate the complexity of the mind, its emotional states, its capacity for distortion, and its defense mechanisms.

One of several examples Freud gave is of a "middle-aged lady . . . complaining of anxiety-states" who, around 1910, "had consulted a young physician" in her suburb. The doctor had promptly told her that "the cause of her anxiety was her lack of sexual satisfaction," owing to her divorce, and suggested she seek a fresh outlet by masturbating, starting an affair, or reuniting with her husband.[34]

When he learned of this case, because the woman went to see him more anxious than ever, Freud was both indignant and appalled by the physician's ignorance. As he put it: "The lady who consulted the young doctor complained chiefly of anxiety-states, and so he probably assumed that she was suffering from an anxiety neurosis, and felt justified in recommending a somatic therapy to her. Again a convenient misapprehension! A person suffering from anxiety is not for that reason necessarily suffering from anxiety neurosis; . . . one has to know what signs constitute an anxiety neurosis, and be able to distinguish it from other pathological states which are also manifested by anxiety."

The doctor did great damage, Freud claimed, by failing to heed the cause of her anxiety; by assuming that it constituted a neurosis; by presuming that sexual release would ease her mind; by telling her what to do; and by confusing a practical act with its psychological significance. Besides his questionable—even unethical—advice, the doctor broke a series of "*technical rules,*" due in part to his ignorance of "the *scientific theories* of psycho-analysis." The irony could not be plainer—not just because of the scorn heaped on Freud today, but also because he insisted that there are scientifically correct and incorrect ways of conducting analysis.

Freud's statement, "A person suffering from anxiety is not for that reason necessarily suffering from anxiety neurosis," is worth restating, given its relevance and magnitude. The young doctor's emphasis on finding a practical solution to the woman's anxiety completely overlooked the mental significance she had given her drives and the suffering that ensued from this internal judgment.

In the case of the middle-aged woman, Freud argued, her anxiety was so pervasive that treatment could proceed slowly—"through preparation"—only after she had "reached the neighbourhood of what [she'd] repressed." But that would never happen, he cautioned, unless she had enough time, and could develop enough trust, to form "a sufficient attachment (transference) to the physician for [her] emotional relationship to him to make a fresh flight impossible."

Why might the speed, not just the form, of treatment determine its chances of success? "Attempts to 'rush' [the patient] at first consultation," Freud warned, "by brusquely telling [her] the secrets which have been discovered by the physician, are technically objectionable." For they not only prevent the patient from making such links herself, which is paramount to lasting change, but also bolster the patient's resistance to such connections, making recovery all the more tenuous and difficult. They also "mostly bring their own punishment," he added, "by inspiring a hearty enmity towards the physician on the patient's part and cutting him off from having any further influence."

This example helps demonstrate what is lost, minimized, or ignored when psychiatry insists on quick fixes, whether through drugs or short-term therapies designed rapidly to alter our thinking. Put bluntly, if a patient is not ready to trust that there may be more to her behavior than meets the eye, why would she accept a hasty, consequential diagnosis based on a few minutes' consultation, or forthright, practical initiatives that may have no bearing on the internal significance of her distress?

If we are to assess these deeper conflicts properly, a literal approach to anxiety will not work and may, indeed, be part of the problem. We need different perspectives on shyness and more counterintuitive ways of thinking about anxiety. Adam Phillips usefully asserts of the latter, "What worries are used for—what kind of medium of exchange or currency they become in one's relationship with other people and oneself—may be as revealing as what prompts them." In practical terms, that is, "What are you

(Paxil, *American Journal of Psychiatry* 159, March 2002)

worried about?" may be a less useful guide to discovering what is wrong than asking, "Whom is this worry for?"

In asking this last question, Phillips doesn't mean that the worry is always meant for someone else. "We are," he says, "familiar with the notion of worrying away at a problem, like a dog gnawing a bone, but is it absurd to suggest that we are doing a kind of violence to ourselves when we worry?"[35] If we add such a question to Freud's later thoughts about anxiety and social phobia (outlined in Chapter 1), the notion that a "chemical imbalance" is the sole determinant of our emotions starts to crumble, leaving in stark relief the peculiar riddle of internalized hostility and its complex relation to social dynamics that may also be adverse.

Those experiencing social embarrassment and acute shyness often complain that they feel harassed by others' looks and perceived judgments. This sensation must be almost unbearable, blighting lives with fruitless torment. But while the effects of anxiety are doubtless palpable, the perceptions that give rise to them are not always so reliable. Granted there are exceptions, but the external judgment rarely matches the vehemence of the internal one.

Susie Scott captures this tension from a sociological perspective: "Shyness is motivated by great sociability (the wish to be with people and to belong to a group), but this is subsumed beneath anxieties about self-presentation. Shy [people] long to be recognized and included but doubt that they can make adequate, defensible contributions to the encounter."[36]

This passage well summarizes the conflict between yearning and hesitation, showing how anxiety often intercedes between the desire to participate and the fear of doing so unsuccessfully. Scott identifies most of the pressure to participate and conform in social dynamics, which, she argues, shyness challenges. It does so unintentionally by disrupting the conventions we affirm unthinkingly in meetings, over meals, on dates, and in routine exchanges.

If we view "every social encounter [as] a precarious balance of rules and assumptions," Scott urges, there's an expectation that everyone will "display a certain level of interactional competence." But "when a person appears shy, their 'moves' are unexpected and uncoordinated with those around them. It's as if the shy have conducted an unintentional breaching experiment" that often provokes indignation and hostility from others, whether in accusations that they're not "making an effort" and "pulling their weight," or that they're haughty, aloof, bored, and uninterested.[37]

The interviews Scott conducted with many shy people suggest they are usually not in the least aloof or disengaged. Most of the interviewees were deeply concerned about fitting in and more attentive to group dynamics than those around them. However, some tended to second-guess their contributions, to assume others were more adept than they themselves were, or to be so self-conscious that the moment to contribute passed and the conversation rolled on without them.

It is easy to see how such situations could spiral into frustration and even self-recrimination. Yet the specialists in emotion who are quick to call shyness "social anxiety" also compound the prejudices of a "culture obsessed with self-expression and communication," where everyone must be both individual and original.[38]

Nor is it wise to generalize about the shy, the introverted, or the avoidant. Not every shy person Scott interviewed berated himself or herself for not joining in. A few like being shy and view it a welcome idiosyncrasy; others see it as an unavoidable part of their personality, which they define as "quiet"; and still others happily invert the picture and stress "the perks of being a wallflower"—the unique perspective that comes from detaching oneself somewhat from group dynamics, the better to observe them more carefully, even guardedly.[39] From these perspectives, what passes for loquacious self-confidence could easily be seen as aggressive banter, even as vacuous blather. Both can be entertaining and occasionally quite useful, but why should they consistently trump introspection?

It is an important question to ask, not least because it calls attention to our shifting mores. Scott writes carefully about peer pressure, competitive group dynamics, and the growing need to be garrulous and assertive.[40] All the same, arguing that the shy and socially anxious have "internalized" these standards more stringently than others tells but one side of the story, largely pushing aside questions about the reason they have done so, including the *source* of anxiety, self-doubt, and even terror. To put this differently, the sociological perspective doesn't explain why some people view these standards as a forceful imperative and berate themselves for supposedly falling short, while others simply shrug, consider the standards impossible or inconsequential, and do the best they can. We've seen that bio-logical arguments are inadequate ways of determining human behavior. From the other side of the equation, though, sociologists face a problem explaining the asymmetry of anxiety relative to social pressure.

In the film *Dirty Filthy Love*, Adrian Shergold's 2004 romantic comedy about obsessive compulsive disorder, Charlotte (played by Shirley Henderson) makes this point unintentionally, in a scene otherwise devoted to neuropsychiatric and cognitive-behavioral explanations of the phenomenon. Charlotte leads a self-help group treating OCD, and after Mark's (Michael Sheen) first session with them they talk good-naturedly about his problems, which include obsessive ruminations on his failed marriage, endless rituals that eat up hours of his day, and compulsively blurting out obscenities, many of them hilarious, which prevent his keeping his job as a high-powered London architect.

While Charlotte carefully explains that Mark's problems are due to "faulty neurotransmitters" and that therapy—not drugs—will best help him, she adds that OCD sufferers can't "rationalize away unwanted thoughts." As if illustrating the point, her description of the illness quickly betrays how harshly she judges herself for falling prey to it: "It really is the most *ridiculous* illness . . . We're *completely* aware how *stupid* and *ridiculous* we're being, but we can't stop ourselves . . ."[41]

Although OCD isn't the same as social phobia, psychiatrists call them both anxiety disorders stemming from "chemical imbalances." The intelligence of *Dirty Filthy Love* lies in complicating this received wisdom by slyly disclosing the psychology that buttresses it. When Charlotte turns upon herself, we might say, she betrays less the success or failure of neurotransmission than how mercilessly she judges herself regarding a problem from which science apparently has exonerated her. Why, then, does her judgment persist, and with such vehemence?

To many neuropsychiatrists, any talk of self-directed hostility is too loose and abstract to be of lasting benefit. Charlotte is but a fictional character, moreover, and if she continues blaming herself long after science tells her she needn't, that's because the drugs haven't kicked in or because the disorder is so stigmatized that it is easier for her to internalize the taboo.

Further, people with social phobia know exactly what will trigger their anxiety: usually work-related speaking and other situations in which they are highly visible and prone to be assessed accordingly. They also can predict with awful certainty when blood will begin racing to their heads, their palms will become moist, and their voices are likely to quaver. There is no real mystery to these symptoms or their recurrence, experts opine; telling the socially anxious that they dread the unexpected, tend to swallow their anger, or may one day stop caring so much what others think of them does not really give them a handle on their difficulties.

That is true as far as it goes, and one should always balance short-term interventions with longer-term gain. Yet Adam Phillips calls worrying "often an *appropriate* response to ordinary demands that begin to feel excessive."[42] To grasp why we are right to chafe against such demands requires that we identify their source.

Roughly midway through his career, Freud struggled to account for the psychological causes of anxiety. He had begun to characterize physiological explanations as useful but insufficient, and could not yet determine what should replace them. "We know that the fear is of being overwhelmed or annihilated," he declared in *The Ego and the Id*, "but it cannot be grasped analytically."[43]

While Freud floundered over this problem, he began investigating why antagonism thrives so lopsidedly in our minds and culture. We may feel harried and miserable in times of peace, that is, but find that depression lifts in times of war or crisis. As he tried to explain why, Freud perceived "there must be some disturbing factor which we have not yet discovered." What baffled him especially was the "tormenting . . . anxiety" we experience if we are "prevented from carrying out certain actions." Not only is this unfair to those who forgo, but, more strangely, the anxiety persists whether we act on our desires or recognize merely a desire to do so.[44] A deity may spot this crucial distinction, Freud added wryly, but our baleful superego cannot. We are, as he put it memorably, "far more immoral than [we] believe . . . but also far more moral than [we] know."[45]

The superego, like the unconscious, has burrowed into the popular consciousness, but only, unfortunately, by sacrificing Freud's best point about it. Nowadays we commonly view it as equivalent to our "conscience"—a representative of social customs and laws that we internalize through fam-

ilies, schools, and environment. True enough, Freud spoke of the superego as "a continuation of the severity of the external authority."[46] But, he
added, the continuation is potentially limitless, installing an entity whose
stipulations may be as merciless as they are unfounded.

The punishment we receive as guilt, anxiety, and self-recrimination is often painfully unmerited. It also intensifies, Freud observed in several case
studies, the more we try to appease the persecutor. Finally, as if we had not
borne enough, this inner despot actually looks for ways to extort from us
greater suffering and anguish: "The superego torments" us, Freud wrote,
"with the same feeling of anxiety and is on the watch for opportunities of
getting [us] punished by the external world."[47]

In psychodynamic terms, we might say that the scrupulous care—indeed, vigilance—with which the socially anxious monitor their behavior
and speech, endlessly concerned with how they are coming across and
whether they are being judged, poignantly mirrors this scenario. The reason social phobes needlessly self-excoriate, turning mild assessments into
harsh judgments, is not brain chemistry, Freud and his supporters insist,
but rather a relentless internal force that is fueling their self-recrimination.
This is not to say our culture doesn't make fierce demands of its own or
frown on anything less than strident self-assertion. The enigma, rather, is
why some people compound these demands, adding an even stronger insistence that failing to comply with them is unacceptable. If falling ill
amounts to reprieve from such intolerable strictures, anxiety betrays the
effort to convey that all is well when falling ill is *not*, perhaps, an option.

To put the matter in this way may explain why anxiety is often so in-
tractable that trying to eliminate its worst symptoms through drugs is not
enough to allay our fundamental unease. We asked earlier whether anxiety
serves any purpose after the mind transforms its biological meanings (as,
say, a warning for survival), but the rejoinder is so poignant it is likely to
sadden or enrage us. The short answer is no. A tyrannical superego may induce us to work or love harder than we need to, but the misery that accrues
from such constant anxiety is more counterproductive than otherwise. We
would be better off taking a stand against this noxious neighbor, Freud implies, than trying pointlessly to appease the suffering or arguing, based on
faulty science, that our serotonin levels are to blame for its relentless cruelty.

Critics often say that psychoanalysis generalizes too much about people's problems, reducing them to simple formulas, but there is nothing trivial about self-recrimination or the unique and varied contortions it spawns. Based on what I have postulated and represented from case studies, I would upend the argument and ask why neuropsychiatrists so often turn this predicament into a medical condition requiring drug treatment. Why, moreover, do they think it is appropriate to prescribe one type of drug (an SSRI) for a complaint with so many mild-to-chronic psychological causes and repercussions?

I have discussed self-antagonism and hostility quite extensively in this chapter, arguing that drugs can neither fully address their causes nor alleviate their varied effects. Of the many articles published on how to treat social phobia, one of them makes quite similar observations without supporting psychoanalysis—a situation we have identified before, with anti-Freudians forced to reinvent the psychology they hastily eliminated. Among neuropsychiatrists and those practicing cognitive-behavioral therapy, the authors opine, it is notable that "anger" among social phobes "has received strikingly little attention."[48]

After conducting a clinical trial involving "234 persons with social anxiety disorder and 36 nonanxious controls," Brigitte Erwin and Richard Heimberg, principal authors of the paper, argue that the socially anxious show "a greater tendency to experience anger across a range of situations, an increased tendency to experience and express anger without provocation, and a greater propensity to express anger when criticized." Even so, after the individuals in their trial completed an "Inventory of Interpersonal Problems," their responses tended to fall broadly into two camps, with one set displaying "unassertiveness, exploitability, and overnurturance," and the other "problems with anger, hostility, and mistrustfulness."[49]

There are weighty matters of interpretation to assess here, including whether the type of anger expressed or swallowed is qualitatively the same; whether expressing anger lowers or heightens anxiety; and whether both groups are anxious because they fear incurring anger, or are anxious regardless and susceptible to other people's anger as a result. Erwin and Heimberg don't really commit to any of these key distinctions ("Anger may . . . elicit anxiety," they state rather vaguely, "and be suppressed in the service of anxiety reduction"). They do opt for saying the quick-tempered social phobe is liable to be judged negatively, thereby hinting that we should take the disorder more seriously than ever.

Scott reached a similar conclusion about negative assessments of the shy and withdrawn, without presenting such psychological effects as offshoots of medical disorders. Another reason for questioning Erwin and Heimberg's conclusion is their difficulty in distinguishing the quick-tempered who are "nonanxious" from those who are not, especially when everyone with a short fuse is likely to fall into yet another category: those with intermittent explosive disorder. How can we form meaningful psychiatric distinctions here? The simple answer is that we cannot. As the categories and subtypes proliferate, the psychiatrists' ability to parse, say, generalized anxiety disorder from avoidant personality disorder—or circumscribed social anxiety with intermittent explosive disorder from schizoid personality disorder with generalized social phobia—becomes illusory.[50]

The notion that expressing anger could diminish anxiety so effectively that the person would no longer have social anxiety disorder does not seem to be an option for Erwin and Heimberg. Even so, it seems necessary to ask whether other people are the sole cause of anger among social phobes or whether the type of self-recrimination just described contributes to their emotional instability.

Unfortunately, Erwin and Heimberg's article doesn't begin to assess such subtleties. Indeed, it is difficult to establish from it who, precisely, has the problem with these qualities: the person interviewed, the recipients of his or her changing emotions, or the interviewers adding their own judgments to the mix by deciding who belongs where and why. As Erwin and Heimberg are fond of the passive voice, they write ambiguously, "One [group] evidenced problems with unassertiveness," while "the other was characterized by problems with anger." Tantalizing insights are similarly unclear, as for instance, "Less belief in the trustworthiness and dependability of others has been associated with social anxiety."[51] Does that mean the socially anxious are less *trusting* or less *trustworthy* than their "nonanxious" counterparts?

One nugget does lie buried in the thicket of Erwin and Heimberg's prose: "Persons with social anxiety disorder may be more demanding and critical of others but hypersensitive to criticism themselves."[52] While this point is fairly close to some I've already raised, the authors fail to ask whether such demands are *extensions* of demands the anxious make on themselves.

The questions Erwin and Heimberg bring to their research preempt their answer. Who, after all, could gauge such complex matters by using a "12-item Brief Fear of Negative Evaluation Scale," which asks patients to rate (with one to five points) statements such as "When I am talking to someone, I worry about what they're thinking about me" and "Sometimes I think I'm too concerned with what others think of me."[53] These may now be tried and tested ways of gauging impairment by social anxiety disorder, but they don't reveal much about the relationship between anger and anxiety.

Another problem mars Erwin and Heimberg's work: the supposition that irate patients are displaying "maladaptive anger expression"—indeed, "maladaptive beliefs" and "maladaptive automatic thoughts." As the authors do not consider other causes of or explanations for the patients' anger, they see the aim of behavioral therapy, in groups or on a one-to-one basis, as being to "train [patients] in cognitive restructuring skills," so that they will learn to identify and "disput[e] cognitive errors in these automatic thoughts, and develop . . . rational responses" to them.[54]

Some of this makes sense. If patients consistently overreact to situations, based on recurring misperceptions, then encouraging them to reflect on their internal associations and imagine different outcomes could be enormously beneficial. But cognitive-behavioral therapy presupposes that the solution lies in "restructured" positive thoughts, an emphasis that minimizes not just the patients' resistance to change, but also their internal explanation for the anger and the sometimes unconscious reasons for its persistence. One wonders whether patients will have time to grasp such dynamics, for the small number of sessions set aside for their improvement is likely to leave them feeling so rushed and chivvied that the treatment will be proportionately shallow. If, moreover, the conclusions they draw must match their clinician's for treatment to be successful, the combined haste and need for consensus will merely result in the spoon-feeding of another's perspective, without the time or freedom necessary to establish their own.

Although these concerns make many chafe at the principles governing cognitive-behavioral therapy, the very phrase "maladaptive automatic thoughts" smacks of a *Brave New World* scenario. It implies that all our thoughts and beliefs must be "adaptive," regardless of their intention or effect. Erwin and Heimberg's emphasis recalls Freud's disquiet with the presumptuous doctor who believed that telling his patient why she was anxious and presenting her with (what were to him) rational ways of fixing it meant she would see the wisdom of changing and rapidly amend her behavior.

Recall Freud's indignation at such "attempts to 'rush'" the patient. The most relevant point here is that failing to give her time to generate a sufficient transference means the patient will not "reach . . . the neighbourhood of what [she's] repressed," meaning *the treatment will not have any lasting impact on her anxiety.* According to Freud, this approach actually worsens the patient's symptoms, because it increases resistance to change.[55]

If you don't believe patients have unconscious reasons for avoiding painful encounters, including the desire to banish inadmissible thoughts or fantasies, then treating them must seem entirely logical and straightforward. After all, while their anxiety is irrational, it is also quite obvious and, for cognitive-behavioral therapists, stems mostly from faulty reasoning. Moreover, if you can convince patients to change, even in the short term, why bother with deeper, enigmatic causes that may take months to fathom?

By way of an answer, I am reminded of Thomas Hardy's eloquent 1886 novel, *The Mayor of Casterbridge,* in which Elizabeth-Jane, the mayor's adopted daughter, voices a similar appeal to her painfully self-destructive father. When she grasps, however, that his obstinacy amounts to a perverse but not absurd wish to increase his suffering as self-punishment, she decides that Ovid has the best explanation: "*Video meliora proboque, deteriora sequor*" (I can see which is the better course to take, and I agree with it; but I follow the worse.)[56]

The statement, and various scenarios in the novel that give rise to it, are in several respects very moving. While Michael Henchard, the ousted mayor, flails for years in an alcoholic stupor, riven by jealousy and guilt, sadness and anxiety, he isn't blind to the consequences of his behavior. Like many of us, he simply does his best to avoid dwelling on them. Elizabeth-Jane quotes Ovid because she wants to dispel any lingering power of bad faith. "I follow the worse" ensues from a full recognition of—and even agreement with—"the better course to take." In other words, it's a judgment made in the best knowledge of likely causes and their consequences. Finally, as guilt exacerbates whatever social humiliation the community could devise for him (already heinous in Hardy's novel), Henchard's suffering propels him into decline just as others try to forgive and redeem him.

There is much more to say about the formidably complex, pre-Freudian psychology that Hardy outlines in the novel. I invoke it not to confuse fiction with treatise, or life with art; the point is rather that Hardy, Kraepelin's contemporary, sketches a form of austere anxiety that makes today's emphasis on "maladaptive anger expression" look, by comparison, painfully simplistic.[57]

What, then, of the long-term prospects of recovery by cognitive-behavioral therapy? Erwin and Heimberg admit, "Despite the demonstrated efficacy of CBGT [cognitive-behavioral group therapy] and other cognitive-behavioral techniques for social anxiety disorder, some patients do not achieve clinically significant improvement by the end of treatment." Rather than question the reason for this outcome and thus the validity of their approach, including its reliance on DSM categories, they insist, "There is a strong need to determine who will and will not complete or respond to cognitive-behavioral treatments for social anxiety disorder."[58]

Considering the differences we've unearthed among the neuropsychiatric, cognitive-behavioral, and psychodynamic approaches to social phobia, it may be surprising that Freud in his final years was willing to give biomedicine *more* credit than he had previously. "The future may teach us," he conceded, "to exercise a direct influence, by means of particular chemical substances, on the amounts of energy and their distribution in the mental apparatus."[59]

The statement helps to clarify that prioritizing the psychological elements that cause anxiety does not eclipse interest in its biological and even social underpinnings; it simply means that anxiety transposes them into a different key. The heart-pounding dread we may feel before giving a speech is not the same, psychologically, as the fight-or-flight response we might encounter in a state of nature, even if our adrenalin flows rapidly in both cases. The situations should not be confused, then, because to do so overdramatizes public speaking anxiety and ignores that anxiety can arise independently of external threats or danger. In psychoanalytic terms, one's perception of such threats (and, often, of their compounding internal cause) is both unexceptional and the true object of analysis.

We have also seen that medicating anxiety can have unforeseen psychological and physiological effects, and that SSRIs like Prozac and Paxil— with their many harmful side effects—are not the magic bullet Freud failed to predict. Despite mounting evidence of justifiable public concern about these drugs (including documentary investigations, troubling health reports, ever lengthier and more serious lists of side effects, and widespread litigation against their manufacturers), few neuropsychiatrists are willing to concede the true limitations of SSRIs. They may acknowledge, with regret, that the drugs cause many side effects, some of them very serious. They may also accept that patients who initially respond well to SSRIs (for a host of reasons, including the placebo effect) frequently revert to earlier behaviors and emotions the moment the treatment ends. For many prescribers, that simply means they await from the drug companies a more perfect remedy; meanwhile, their patients continue to take the existing drugs for months, if not years, even if they have to cycle through many different brands, each with sometimes wildly unpredictable effects, as well as symptoms ranging from sleeplessness and impotence to nausea, headaches, and periodic neurological shocks. It is less common to see neuropsychiatrists draw a very different conclusion: that the drugs are simply a stopgap that often fails to engage the underlying causes of anxiety, because the causes themselves are not always neurological or pharmacological.

We could put this differently. Even if Paxil and other SSRIs were entirely benign, with no side effects or emotional blunting, they could not address our existential malaise. Nor could they resolve the problems that neuropsychiatrists now represent as illnesses. If psychodynamic therapists are skeptical of treating minor ailments with serious drugs, it is less because they have overlooked the promise of neuroscience (how, in today's climate, could they?) and more that they consider mechanistic accounts of human behavior inadequate ways of addressing both ordinary and deep-seated fears and anxieties.

Especially given the sky-high relapse rates among those taking SSRIs for anxiety (one in five, according to SKB's own memo),[60] these candid assessments of our current malaise magnify the medical plight of the mildly anxious. Some pharmacologists now conduct drug treatments on shy six-year-olds in a fervent belief that they will nip the anxiety in the bud. Yet many doctors, wisely cautioning that some anxiety is useful and even necessary, are turning their patients to less drastic and more humane remedies, including what Freud euphemistically dubbed "the talking cure." What he meant by this is that the mind must first symbolize psychological anguish before any associated suffering can begin to dissipate. While cognitive-behavioral therapy works on a similar principle, I have argued that it underestimates the strength of a patient's resistance to recovery, including unconscious defenses that he or she must first relinquish before symptoms such as anxiety can diminish.

There are many other reasons for urging psychiatry to reconsider treatments it has spurned as protracted and unscientific. In general, psychodynamic therapists do not fix us in doubtful categories. Interested in engaging our unique histories, they are likely to equate shyness with introspection, not call it a medical disorder. Above all, since they tend to begin where drug treatments fail, psychodynamic therapists take social phobia in a direction quite different from that of neuropsychiatry. In the process, they overturn a host of fashionable assumptions, including that refusing to adapt to environment automatically means maladjustment and pathology. They help us see that "social phobia" and "avoidant personality disorder" can represent complex, sometimes appropriate, signs of noncompliance with social norms—meaning the problem extends from the individual to the wider community and culture.

6

A BACKLASH FORMS:
PROZAC NATION REBELS

It would be naive to think the wrangles we've observed in psychiatry had no effect on the wider culture. The conflicts troubling psychiatrists in the 1970s and 1980s have in fact saturated popular culture, especially in America, where writers, artists, and filmmakers have wrestled for years with the perils and opportunities of biotechnology. How, they wonder, should they convey inner turmoil in a climate that urges us to medicate it away? And can they portray character conventionally when drugs may have such transformative effects on our personalities that they can, for better or worse, render us quite different from ourselves?

"Psychotropic drugs and their supposedly problematic effects on human autonomy and identity," yawns David Gates in the *New York Times,* "is a topic as old as *Brave New World* and as new as Peter D. Kramer's *Listening to Prozac*—which is no longer all that new."[1] Although he is right about both books, one could easily best him by invoking Stevenson's *Strange Case of Dr. Jekyll and Mr. Hyde,* De Quincey's *Confessions of an English Opium Eater,* or even Plato's *Phaedrus,* in which the word *pharmakon* marks a disturbingly nebulous line between remedy and poison.[2] How one responds to Gates's statement depends on whether one can get past his laconic "supposedly." Some contemporary writers and filmmakers frankly disagree with him about the consequences of those effects and are sufficiently outraged to take action.

Can we afford to be blasé about psychotropic drugs, or is that response part of the problem? True, Aldous Huxley's novel about soma-popping citizens is now convenient shorthand whenever commentators want to invoke the risks of pharmacological dystopia. What is still striking about his novel, making it strangely bracing to teach, is how quickly its characters, given the chance to regulate their suffering, grow inured to even mild hints of distress. Even more presciently than brilliant counterparts like Orwell (in *1984*), Huxley understood that the ability to cauterize pain has surprisingly counterintuitive effects: what should be a net gain in humanitarian and technological terms turns out to be oddly enervating. The amount of ordinary suffering we should accept may be so difficult to gauge that it's easiest to block the matter completely, averting any incident that would give us even a foretaste of it.

"When the individual feels," one of Huxley's characters declares bitingly and aphoristically, "the community reels." So the totalitarian system Huxley satirized rejects feeling entirely, narcotizing its citizens into zombies and denouncing all who would live differently as "enem[ies] of Society."[3] By today's standards, the logic is rather crude; we tend to think of ideology as less brazenly manipulative and more consumer friendly. Perhaps we're merely grateful to be spared extreme suffering. But as Huxley later observed, a year before *DSM-I* appeared and pharmacologists announced that chlorpromazine has antidepressive effects, "The need for frequent chemical vacations from intolerable selfhood and repulsive surroundings will undoubtedly remain."[4]

Does that need remain today? Is it in fact stronger than ever? To think of Prozac and other SSRIs as "chemical vacations from intolerable selfhood" would appall those afflicted with chronic depression and anxiety, and rightly so. But as Kramer grasped in *Listening to Prozac*, the line between the sick and the well isn't always clear or easily drawn, and the drug companies—building on psychiatrists' already hazy distinctions—have done their best to muddy it further. They have also spent millions on advertising and giveaway samples, in a systematic bid to persuade us that even mild afflictions are dramatic problems in their own right.

As Kramer's book appeared amid a euphoric stampede for SSRIs, *Listening to Prozac*'s generally upbeat assessment spent more time documenting the antidepressant's apparently miraculous effects on patients than fretting whether such developments were entirely benign, mentally and physically. For good reason, Kramer was intrigued—even mesmerized—

by such changes, which struck him as faster than and qualitatively different from those brought about by the talking cure.[5] He couldn't know that support groups would soon spring up across the country to help many cope with the drugs' sometimes devastating side effects. Nor could he predict that even patients free of such effects would turn to these groups in an effort to integrate personality changes they first welcomed, then found bewildering and upsetting.

Kramer was more adept at asking related philosophical questions about these antidepressants, including whether his transformed patients became less or somehow more like themselves. Did Prozac and other SSRIs bring out aspects of their personality that depression once smothered, that is, or provoke a more ersatz transformation with little bearing on their past lives or the illness that blighted them? Who, indeed, could say either way—especially if the changes were irreversible and the patients' minds were altered beyond recognition?

These questions are not airy problems we can pose or solve in the abstract. They stem from not only our enthusiasm for medication, but also our unwillingness to face the consequences of a "neurochemical reshaping of personhood."[6] With the number of annual prescriptions for SSRIs in the United States alone racing toward two hundred million and the drug companies pushing the same drugs worldwide, the questions take on considerable urgency.[7] As it is well known that other drugs like lithium and Depakote have transformative effects on patients, often compelling them to form something resembling an emergency personality, distinguishing between medicated and unmedicated selfhood is paramount. How else could doctors know whether they are engaging, much less treating, real symptoms or abnormal states caused entirely by medication?[8]

Finally, Kramer wondered whether the drugs were having an unrealistic effect on Americans' expectations about happiness and well-being. That pharmaceutical companies came close to touting the drugs as miracle cures stoked, in Kramer's view, a demand that SSRIs do more than alleviate depression and anxiety; they must also somehow make people "better than well," a demand that soon amounted to mood brightening, personality sculpting, and "cosmetic psychopharmacology."[9] The orthodox role of psychiatrists changed accordingly; helping patients overcome the fundamental issues no longer seemed to either party a sufficient goal. Something else was wanted: a "designer" personality and pain-free living detectable amid the mantra of personal transformation and perfectibility that patients voiced with increasing stridency in the 1980s and 1990s.

Since the personality changes Kramer witnessed may be inseparable from permanent neurochemical changes to the brain, and since the effects of ssris may far exceed their intended goal, these questions are necessary to ask and still woefully difficult to answer conclusively. Pharmacologists, doctors, and psychiatrists ultimately must settle the medical side of this equation. Writers, filmmakers, and artists of all kinds are grappling with its social and cultural legacy.

To the stunned amazement of neuropsychiatrists and drug companies used to glowing cover stories in *Newsweek* and *Time,* a backlash against their work and products has begun viewing both with suspicion and scorn. Whether as a basis for blockbuster political thrillers (John Le Carré's *Constant Gardener*), less famous but still heartrending meditations on our unwillingness to face loss (Claudia Rankine's *Don't Let Me Be Lonely* and Charlie Kaufman and Michel Gondry's dazzling *Eternal Sunshine of the Spotless Mind*), or superb critiques of biochemical pollutants (Don DeLillo's *White Noise* and Todd Haynes's *Safe*), the backlash is helping to transform—even shatter—a host of neuropsychiatric assumptions about mental health and illness that prevailed almost unchallenged at the end of the twentieth century.

In Jonathan Franzen's poignantly hilarious novel *The Corrections,* to take a justly celebrated example, Enid Lambert is diagnosed in her late sixties as suffering from "subclinical dysthymia" (mild unhappiness) and given eight free "SampLpaks" of Aslan® Cruiser™ by a charming but distracted psychiatrist who can't remember her name.[10] Chirpy, manipulative, but also amazingly resilient for most of the novel, Enid hits a patch where her life starts to unravel, her husband beset by Parkinson's and her three grown-up children flailing about in confusion, much of it self created. As the full implications of these crises seem unbearable, she wants, understandably, for life to return to normal. She's used to thinking of her world as "like a lawn in which the bluegrass grew so thick that evil was simply choked out: a miracle of niceness" (117). But when she asks for an antidepressant while on a cruise ship, Dr. Hibbard quickly corrects her:

"Crude term. 'Personality optimizer' is the phrase I prefer."

"And 'Cruiser'?"

"Aslan optimizes in sixteen chemical directions," Hibbard said patiently. "But guess what? Optimal for a person enjoying a luxury cruise isn't optimal for a person functioning in the workplace. The chemical differences are pretty subtle, but if you're capable of fine control, why not offer it? Besides Aslan 'Basic,' Farmacopea sells eight custom blends. Aslan 'Ski,' Aslan 'Hacker,' Aslan 'Performance Ultra,' Aslan 'Teen,' Aslan 'Club Med,' Aslan 'Golden Years,' and I'm forgetting what? Aslan 'California.' Very popular in Europe. The plan is to bring the number of blends up to twenty within two years. Aslan 'Exam Buster,' Aslan 'Courtship,' Aslan 'White Nights,' Aslan 'Reader's Challenge,' Aslan 'Connoisseur Class,' yada, yada, yada. . . . If you're asking what's specific to 'Cruiser'? Mainly that it switches your anxiety to the Off position. Turns that little dial right down to zero." (318–19)

In such passages, Franzen clearly relishes chiding our quick-fix culture, with its credulous assumption that there's a pill for every ill, and the absurd hype of our pharmaceutical industry, which has done its best to magnify and confirm those beliefs. As his fictional psychiatrist declares, in a tautology reminiscent of the DSM-III task force, "A crippling fear of asking for Aslan is the condition for which Aslan is most commonly indicated" (315).

The satire may be welcome, but we might think it strains credulity. There could never, we insist, be so many "blends" of "personality optimizers" that our psychiatrists would rattle them off in a bored "yada yada yada." And surely we'd never reach the point where psychiatrists would be giving away pre–FDA-approved drugs to pensioners in international waters, because they couldn't do so legally elsewhere. Although literalism is of course beside the point here (and, by Franzen's reckoning, part of the problem),[11] let's see for a moment what happens if we push his analogy.

When Eli Lilly and Company was allowed in July 2000 to repackage Prozac as Sarafem, presenting the latter as a treatment for "Premenstrual Dysphoric Disorder," not depression, and turning the green-and-yellow pill into a "lavender-colored [one], . . . promoted with images of sunflowers and smart women,"[12] was its approach so different from that of Farmacopea? Post-1999 ads for Paxil are more sophisticated than Dr. Hibbard's pitch for Aslan, but even if we grant the immense complexity of neurotransmission, the main effect of the anticholinergic is principally to switch patients' anxiety "to the Off position." Else why would they take it?

"While he is eviscerating the Lamberts' pretensions—and by extension, the culture they represent," observes Michiko Kakutani, Franzen presents "a harrowing portrait of America in the late 1990s—an America deep in the grip of that decade's money madness and sick with envy, resentment, greed, acquisitiveness and self-delusion, an America committed to the quick-fix solution and determined to medicate its problems away."[13] Pharmacology in fact knits together the Lamberts' disparate traumas and stop-gap remedies, but Franzen doesn't lay all their problems at its door; he is keener to observe what fuels the Lamberts' demand for reprieve through its numbing effects.

The Corrections opens with an extended, and soon exhausted, metaphor about an "alarm bell of anxiety" that has been ringing unheeded in the Lamberts' household for years (3). Despite their best efforts at muffling this warning, Enid and Alfred are indeed "near to exploding with anxiety," the last word recurring several times in the opening chapter, to jarring effect, because the cause of their distress is not immediately obvious (4). The Lamberts want for nothing, are in decent health, and seem relatively happy.

But their otherwise perky household and pleasant community is suffused with unexamined disappointments, loneliness, paralysis, and boredom. A compulsive hoarder and spender, Enid is prone to saying things like, "And this is something else I'm very, very, very, very worried about" (71). When she's not sneaking quick gulps of wine, she's joining almost everyone else in the novel in taking an array of other mood stabilizers and drugs, prescription and otherwise, for a startlingly wide range of real and imaginary symptoms. The effect is so blunting that, for her and her family, "as in the country as a whole, life came to be lived underground" (10).

The Aslan helps to rout Enid's lingering depression and social phobia: "Your anxiety and oversensitivity will disappear," Dr. Hibbard assures her, "as will any morbid concern about the opinion of others. Anything you're ashamed of now—" (320).

Maybe such blithe unconcern is a mixed blessing. After all, her husband, immobilized by Parkinson's, has begun talking to his excrement; and Enid is soon reduced to asking puzzled neighbors to obtain illegal variants of the drug Aslan for her. The pill's "transformative blessings" are so promising that, after her first meeting with Dr. Hibbard, *she couldn't wait to take it*" (321). As Franzen is brilliantly—sometimes brutally—committed to making the scales fall from her eyes, however, he gradually forces Enid and her family to confront "gust after gust of disorder," a phrase that assumes increasing medical and psychiatric significance as the novel develops and the task evolves (3).

A prelude to this many-sided "disorder" is their youngest son, Chip, a professor of textual artifacts at D—— College. Everything is going splendidly with his career, despite (or perhaps because of) the fact that his scholarship is quite unreadable. But in a moment of delirious abandon, Chip confirms his ineligibility for tenure by starting a torrid affair with one of his students. This turn of events too may seem familiar, even predictable. But Melissa Paquette is savvy and wonderfully contemptuous in giving her hapless professor Mexican A, the black-market version of Aslan that his mother is soon reduced to taking, which on Chip has the combined effect of Prozac, Ecstasy, Xanax, and Viagra.[14] After a slight falling out with Chip, Melissa turns him in to his college administrators for helping her write a term paper.

Like Chip and, indeed, Peter Kramer, Franzen is not interested in merely the local, estranging effects of prescribed and illegal drugs. He wants to assess how profoundly they have infused our lives, transforming and sometimes overturning our notions of intimacy, purpose, and even responsibility. Ever mindful of the ironies that ensue, and ever willing to skewer his characters' pretensions, Franzen has Chip tell his sister: "The very definition of mental 'health' is the ability to participate in the consumer economy. . . . A lack of desire to spend money becomes a symptom of disease that requires expensive medication" (31). He speaks to his students along the same lines, though they turn a deaf ear and see nothing wrong with being medicated to the gills. Chip's critique of their "compensatory pleasures" doesn't long precede his own euphoric binge—and precipitous downfall—on Mexican A.

It would be easy to leave matters there, with Chip denuded as a Marxist hypocrite, stuck believing that "what made drugs perpetually so sexy was the opportunity to be other" (116). After all, the line between wanting to be someone else and resisting being oneself is tantalizingly elusive, its ambiguity gripping many other characters as well.[15] But Franzen is after deeper, more compromising dilemmas. As he put it in "Why Bother?" an eloquent essay first appearing in *Harper's:* "We live in a reductively binary culture: you're either healthy or you're sick, you either function or you don't. And if that flattening of the field of possibilities is precisely what's depressing you, you're inclined to resist participating in the flattening by calling yourself depressed. You decide that it's the world that's sick, and that the resistance of refusing to function in such a world is healthy."

In one respect, at least, such resistance *could* be healthy. Franzen isn't ruling conclusively either way. While he's fully prepared (as I am) to call depression a clinical condition and not reduce it to a cultural metaphor— adding that his own spirits lifted when he recognized his right to participate in the world as a "social isolate" committed to the imagination—he firmly maintains that his upturn lay in realizing "that my condition was not a disease but a nature." He is temperamentally suited to solitude and reflection, that is, and rightly says such perspectives should be cherished, not pathologized. The reason many of us still want serious, iconoclastic fiction, he adds, is because it's unpredictable, cogent, and records "the darkness of sorrows that have no easy cure."[16]

Franzen doesn't like laying down the law for novelists or artists—a stance that could seem hubristic, even messianic. Given the standoff between the word of art and that of commerce, however, he urges writers of realist fiction to engage "the degree to which a conversation about mental health and mental states has infiltrated all of our interior conversations, which are about how we understand ourselves, and exterior conversations, too. If you have a fight with your girlfriend, then you say 'You're the one who should be seeing a therapist, and not only that, but I have a diagnosis for you: I think you have mild OCD.' The way a medical understanding has displaced the old vocabularies of love and loss is interesting to me and I wouldn't want to tell a significant story of emotional pain without alluding to it."[17]

One consequence of this shift, which Franzen firmly rejects, is the notion that "you don't need to have a story anymore. Your story becomes: the chemicals in my brain were bad; I fixed those chemicals. From a humanitarian standpoint, that's great, but it makes for a less interesting world."[18] Franzen therefore writes about the consequences of medicated and nonmedicated responses to suffering, whether in a powerful essay on his father's death from Alzheimer's[19] (a disease Kraepelin first identified with his colleague Alois Alzheimer) or when he reveals that he once "made an appointment with a doctor who could prescribe antidepressants. In the end, unsure about how a substance like Prozac would affect a writer's brain, he decided not to go."[20]

Franzen's rejoinder to works like *Listening to Prozac* is most noticeable in *The Corrections* when he catches the zeal with which some of his characters press for a new identity. As Dr. Hibbard tells Enid, both confirming and undermining his point by mistakenly calling her Edie, Elinor, Eartha, Eden, Elaine, and Edwina, "We all have irrational attachments to the particular chemical coordinates of our character and temperament. It's a version of the fear of death, right? I don't know what it will be like not to be me anymore. But guess what. If 'I'm' not around to tell the difference, then what do 'I' really care?" (321).

One might feel a mix of shocked amazement and outrage that such a character is dispensing powerful, largely untested psychotropic drugs while treating his patients like guinea pigs. But Dr. Hibbard is by no means the only loose cannon in Franzen's arsenal; the statements he makes ricochet around the novel, striking almost everyone. When for instance Doug O'Brien, a mergers-and-acquisitions specialist, bumps into Chip at an upscale supermarket, he asks him straight out, "Do you have a second? Say somebody offered you a new personality: would you take it? Say somebody said to you, *I will permanently rewire your mental hardwire in whatever way you want.* Would you pay to have that done?" (96).

Doug's specialty is "trying [his] very hardest to persuade the average American to happily engineer his own financial ruin," but in Chip's case he's a fraction too late (96). Fired from his professorship, broke from a series of menial jobs, and trapped near the checkout with a fillet of stolen Norwegian salmon wedged down his trousers, Chip isn't sure how to respond so Doug helps him out:

> "The idea . . . is your basic gut cerebral rehab. Leave the shell and roof, replace the walls and plumbing. Design away that useless

> dining nook. Put a modern circuit breaker in. . . . You get to keep
> your handsome façade. . . . You still look serious and intellectual,
> a little Nordic, on the outside. Sober, bookish. But inside you're
> more livable. A big family room with an entertainment console. A
> kitchen that's roomier and handier. You've got your In-Sink-Era-
> tor, your convection oven. An ice-cube dispenser in the refrigera-
> tor door."
>
> "Do I still recognize myself?"
>
> "Do you want to? Everybody else still will—at least, the outside
> of you."
>
> [. . .]
>
> "My furnishings are my personality," Chip said.
>
> "Say it's a gradual rehab. Say the workmen are very tidy. The
> brain's cleared up every night when you get home from work,
> and nobody can bother you on the weekend, per local ordinance
> and the usual covenantal restrictions. The whole thing happens
> in stages—you grow into it. Or it grows into you, so to speak."
> (96–97)

Pitch perfect, the exchange epitomizes how in the 1990s home improvement and "do-it-yourself mental health care" came to mean virtually the
same thing.[21] But the extended metaphor takes us far beyond the excesses
of the housing market and the associated mantra of being what one owns.
If you can enjoy a "basic gut cerebral rehab" with no fuss and no muss,
Doug implies, then not only would you be foolish to delay, but hesitating
in fact confirms your need for the work: it showcases the low self-respect
that prevents you from wanting optimal brain performance.

––––––––––

Endlessly susceptible to such thinking, Franzen's characters monitor the
highs and lows of their emotions as obsessively as they watch the stock
market. Indeed, in a further sign that the two are intertwined (as Alan
Greenspan once hinted when coining the phrase "irrational exuberance"),
Franzen reveals how Gary Lambert, Chip's elder and increasingly alcoholic brother, perceives his inner world:

> Although in general Gary applauded the modern trend toward in-
> dividual self-management of retirement funds and long-distance

calling plans and private-schooling options, he was less than thrilled to be given responsibility for his own personal brain chemistry, especially when certain people in his life, notably his father [now seriously afflicted by Parkinson's], refused to take any such responsibility. But Gary was nothing if not conscientious. As he entered the darkroom, he estimated that his levels of Neurofactor 3 (i.e., serotonin: a very, very important factor) were posting seven-day or even thirty-day highs, that his Factor 2 and Factor 7 levels were likewise outperforming expectations, and that his Factor 1 had rebounded from an early-morning slump related to the glass of Armagnac he'd drunk at bedtime. (137)

"Posting highs," "outperforming expectations," "early-morning slump," and, before that, "leading indicators": one might be listening to a CNN report on the Dow-Jones average. A greater interest here, reversing Chip's meditation on drugs, is the extent to which Gary feels responsible for his brain chemistry, which he assumes is key to explaining his moods and malaise. Where did that assumption come from?

In Gary's warped version of 1990s business-speak, the rat race becomes "the race for mental health," for which elusive victory he stubbornly competes with his wife (157). So while her bedtime reading includes *Feeling GREAT!* (Ashley Tralpis, M.D., PhD.), he frets about anhedonia, a rather apt clinical term that Tralpis's amusingly titled book correctly calls an "inability to experience pleasure in normally pleasurable acts" (162). If his serotonin isn't "outperforming expectations," then something is terribly wrong and anhedonia may be looming, but brain chemistry apparently must be to blame. He or his marriage couldn't possibly be. Franzen's narrator completes the metaphor, capturing Gary's refusal to think about life with other metaphors: "His seasonally adjusted assessment of life's futility and brevity was consistent with the overall robustness of his mental economy. He was not the least bit clinically depressed" (138).

One of the few things that can lift Gary's Neurofactor 3, appropriately, is news about biotech stock for Axon Corporation. As this unscrupulous drug company holds most of the keys to the Lamberts' future, the family's dependency becomes a volatile brew of anxiety, panic, desperate hope, and frantic remorse—in short, collective addiction to another drug. As Alfred

Lambert has sold Axon his patent for "electrical anisotropy" for a song, Gary is determined to press the company for more money (189). In this way, he'll secure tangible and emotional dividends of his own. "He saw an opportunity here to make some money and avenge Axon's screwing of his father, and, more generally, be *bold* where Alfred had been *timid*" (187; emphasis in original).

The problem is not merely that the company has no intention of doing the right thing. Franzen raises the stakes by indicating, as in Plato's allegory, that the cure and the disease are quite inseparable. Axon's research in "neurochemotaxis," borrowing liberally from Alfred's patented work, shows great promise in treating Parkinson's, Alzheimer's, "and other degenerative neurological diseases," including depression (176, 187).

With enough foresight, then, the drug company could earn untold goodwill by helping to cure the disease of the man (Alfred) who made its research possible. Canny marketing could even sell this feel-good story to the public, branding the drug (or at least its manufacturer) as firmly altruistic, while hinting at the appropriateness of calling it "Corecktall."

But let's not be naive. Franzen is writing satire, in part, about the pharmaceutical industry. By blocking the Lamberts' hopes for a few thousand dollars more, Axon not only squanders goodwill but also punctures the illusion that its aims could be anything but mercenary. Perhaps appropriately, then, the drug's name turns out to be almost identical to that of a remedy for diarrhea.

We soon learn why (the reason isn't just because "Corecktall" sounds rather like "co-rectal"). At a key meeting for investors to pitch the first trials that Earl "Curly" Eberle has conducted at Johns Hopkins, the attorneys, deal brokers, and Axon CEO struggle to keep straight faces as they announce, "Folks, hello, we are dealing with clinical results that are *extremely interesting* but *extremely preliminary.* So caveat emptor. All righty? Wink wink wink. All righty?" (204). Given what happens in the novel, it's appropriate to ask: Are they smirking because of the massive profits they anticipate making, or the gross side effects they're struggling to conceal, or both?

When asked whether Corecktall isn't the name of a laxative, the CEO responds forthrightly: "Different spelling, but yes. Curly and I considered approximately ten thousand different names before we realized that branding isn't really an issue for the Alzheimer's patient, or the Parkinson's sufferer, or the massively depressed individual. We could call it Carcino-Asbesto, they'd still knock doors down to get it" (205). He adds that "reprogram[ming] the repeat offender to enjoy pushing a broom" (apparently a feasible outcome of the drug's revolutionary neurochemical potential) isn't just humane; it is also part of the company's "liberal *vision*: genuine, permanent, voluntary self-melioration" (206, 207).

The circle therefore closes on Doug O'Brien's earlier obsession with "your basic gut cerebral rehab" (96), the only distinction being that the drug promising this human reengineering has effects similar to those of Mexican A, itself an illegal variant of Aslan, the "personality optimizer" Dr. Hibbard gave Enid in international waters. The promised remedy for Alfred's Parkinson's disease, then, bears a likeness to the hallucinatory psychotropic that sped Chip to his euphoric downfall and later compelled Enid to score from her perplexed suburban neighbors.

With Plato one forerunner to Franzen's pharmaceutical satire, C. S. Lewis proves unexpectedly to be another. Strewing tantalizing hints of this connection throughout his novel, Franzen has Gary's young son Jonah read Lewis's *Chronicles of Narnia,* most famously *The Lion, the Witch, and the Wardrobe,* in which Aslan, the "Great Lion" and Narnian hero, is also, in Franzen's characterization, a "furry, four-pawed Christ figure" (139). Gary's wife, Caroline, predictably objects to Lewis's novel, calling him "a known Catholic propagandist" (139), which grossly overstates the aims and beliefs of the author of *Mere Christianity.*[22] Still, the furor in 2005 over Disney's dreadful film version made clear how difficult it is to advance secular and/or allegorical interpretations of Aslan as, say, king of a world of talking beasts, the principal figure of an adventure story, or simply a symbol of England—especially as it was under attack during World War II, when Lewis was writing.[23]

Our interest lies in *Franzen's* use of the analogy, because in connecting Corecktall and Mexican A to Aslan, he is close to saying that pharmacology, not myth or religion, is now America's cherished path to redemption, spiritual and otherwise. While Franzen isn't exactly alone in his belief, as Gates observed in the *New York Times,* his novel's intelligence lies not so much in unmasking our hopes for pharmacology as in gauging what, if anything, can or should replace them.

Although her quirks and foibles have contributed to her addiction to Aslan, for instance, Enid shows considerable courage and resilience toward the end by indicating that happiness is something for which she—not her husband, her family, or a "personality optimizer"—is responsible. Her visit to Dr. Hibbard delays that understanding, leading Franzen to hint that antidepressants may more often block than hasten self-knowledge.

A similar point recurs in Zach Braff's offbeat cinematic debut, *Garden State* (2004), in which the writer-director plays an overmedicated TV actor (Andrew Largeman) who floats through life in a chemical haze. When he's forced to return home to New Jersey for his mother's funeral, Largeman leaves his meds behind, perhaps hoping he won't need them, though he's still so numb that he can't shed a tear.

Despite his drug-induced stupor, Largeman is but an extreme case of the boredom and inertia afflicting almost every other character in the film. As one of his stoner friends from high school declares, "This town is so messed up. Everyone's got their drug of choice." Revealing his own drug-addled education, the friend adds: "It's like in *Brave New World*. Who wrote that? Um, Aldous . . . Aldous something. Anyway . . . there's like Alphas and Betas and Epsilons and all sorts of people. Huxtable. Aldous Huxtable." Amusingly, the stoner confuses Huxley's soma-dependent citizens with the Huxtables, the family depicted on *The Cosby Show*.

Despite its quirky humor, some reviewers dismissed *Garden State* as a standard Gen X lament against emotional blunting—a male version of, say, Elizabeth Wurtzel's one-dimensional *Prozac Nation*. Certainly, as the *Boston Globe* observed, "a prescription-drug fog hangs over" the film, making it feel "as if the entire picture were Paxilized."[24]

Perhaps it is striking that we now have a new adjective to describe the drug's effects. But to view *Garden State* only in this way lessens its best insights into the role pharmacology plays in our culture and its common effect on our relationships. Tackling these secondary effects means assessing what Largeman's stupor has cloaked and impeded.

Much of his plight, we learn, stems from his emotionally distant father, a psychiatrist who has prescribed Largeman a cocktail of SSRIs and lithium since the boy was ten. "All I ever wanted," his father protests when they finally confront each other, "was for everyone to be happy again." But as the film makes clear, there's a world of difference between trying to keep patients on an even emotional keel and hoping one's family will bear the brunt of one's disappointment and guilt. Dr. Largeman ultimately blames his son for a freak accident that paralyzed his wife, though her depression long preceded the accident, pointing to an unhappiness for which Andrew had no responsibility. Even so, coming into his own—partly by coming off meds—means not only that Andrew must stand up to his overbearing father, but also question the profession the father represents and the medical dogma he has espoused to his family.

Largeman junior, we soon learn, feels neither stressed nor anxious. He just wants to end the withdrawal symptoms he is now experiencing, including "really bad headaches" that feel like "little lightning storm[s] in my head." Assuming his son's numbness, guilt, and anger are brain-related imbalances that drugs can remedy, his father recommends a neurologist (played by Ron Liebman), which in itself conveys how poorly he understands such issues. Dr. Cohen is as quirky as most of the other characters. He pins a few of his copious certificates to the office ceiling, then rapidly undermines his credentials by explaining that an affair between his ex-wife and best friend meant he couldn't get an erection for a year and a half. This revelation is all in the service of explaining how anxiety can do strange things to our bodies, but it also confirms that Largeman is no more or less sane than anyone else.

The exchange continues thus:

> "How long have you been on the lithium?"
> "I've been on some form of it since I was ten or so."
> "And the Paxil, Zoloft, Celexa . . . Depakote . . . did they help you at all?"
> "No. [*Long pause.*] I mean, I don't know. . . . It's recently occurred to me I might not even have a problem. Only, I'd never know it because as far back as I can remember, I've been medicated."

Dr. Cohen can indeed find nothing physically wrong with Andrew. Instead, the neurologist, shifting gears, undermines his specialty by rebuking the notion that drugs are a long-term panacea: "Look, Andrew, first of all . . . I think you *do* need to find a psychiatrist that isn't your father.

That's something that should have been remedied years ago. He knows better. And secondly, I'm in no position to comment on whether you should stay on the meds or not because I don't know your story. But my *opinion*, since you're paying for it, is that, yeah, those drugs may help you as a means to an end. But sooner or later, if you're not in some sort of therapy, whatever's going on in your mind will find a way to peek its little head out of the water."

The point about the return of the repressed is well taken, even if a fictional character is stating it (the cases we invoked in the last chapter underscore this almost to the letter); and perhaps it is relevant to add that Braff's mother is a psychotherapist.[25] But Dr. Cohen's notion that SSRIs "may help . . . as a means to an end" ignores not only Andrew's almost zombie-like state and painful side effects, but also detailed research showing that such drugs are negligible improvements over placebos.[26]

The neurological zaps in Largeman's brain are both a medical problem and, for the film, a metaphor for his hard-fought autonomy. In this way, the film hitches its ambling progress to his quirky self-discovery. The lithium cloud soon vanishes, leaving him with a fuller, sometimes unsettling range of new emotions. By the end of the film, Largeman not only contradicts his father's diagnosis of his behavior, but also states he's willing to forgive *him* for prescribing a drug regimen that left him "numb to everything I have experienced in my life."

"At times *Garden State* feels like an homage," the *Austin Chronicle* observes, "as it rails against the current narcotized state of an overmedicated society that too often opts to throw a warm fuzzy Prozac blanket over the shivering shoulders of youthful angst."[27] The film does indeed have many debts, including to *Harold and Maude,* but its most obvious is to *The Graduate,* a now-iconic depiction of a quizzical, drifting returnee. In the case of Ben Braddock (the Graduate), the symbol of all that he rejects in the 1960s is plastics; for Largeman, it is pharmacology. And whereas Braddock was so anxious at the start of the film that he's "sort of disturbed about things in general," Largeman takes a while to get worked up about anything.

Nonetheless, both films are committed to viewing love as a redemptive force, an accent that caused many critics of *Garden State* to call its ending tacked on, sentimental, and oddly conventional. As Claudia Puig noted, "It is as if Andrew's epiphany, his thawing after so many years of numbness, dulls the film's cleverness."[28] *Garden State* may indeed be more adept at decrying the use of prescription drugs than at knowing how to reveal lives unfettered by them.

———————

Given Largeman's almost comatose state for much of the film, it is ironic to hear a psychiatrist tell Bill Chalmers, the distressed protagonist of Alan Lightman's third novel, *The Diagnosis,* "Let's start you on some medication to eliminate the numbness."[29] As in *Garden State* and *The Corrections,* the drugs compound his suffering, and the psychiatrists and doctors in the novel don't really have a clue what they're doing. Not surprisingly, just a few chapters later Bill is in worse shape than before: "'No, I'm not taking Prozac anymore,' [he] shouted into the phone" to his psychiatrist's receptionist. "'Dr. Petrov knows I'm not on Prozac. I'm on Paxil now.' . . . Was he in pain? 'I have no pain,' he screamed into the telephone. 'I can't feel anything. Can you hear that? I can't feel anything'" (264).

The Diagnosis, a finalist for the 2000 National Book Awards and Lightman's uneven successor to his acclaimed *Einstein's Dreams,* recounts the plight of Chalmers, a high-strung junior executive (rather like Gary Lambert in *The Corrections*) who processes information at a maniacal pace for no discernible reason. Out of the blue, he experiences chronic anxiety, then extreme amnesia on his way to work. Within hours, he is divested of everything that could identify him, including his briefcase, clothes, and, finally, all recollection of his name. The police find him naked on an empty subway train, talking to himself while clutching his cell phone—a haunting metaphor for "the discordance of our loud, congested, mechanized, toxic, and high-velocity world."[30]

Who experiencing for years the daily toll of intense corporate pressure could truly *escape* severe anxiety? Lightman's point, underscored in several interviews, is that the frantic pace of modern life ruptures any possible harmony with our surroundings, turning anxiety into a wearisome constant, and making illness a reprieve from alarming demands on our productivity, health, and availability for work. "We've lost our way," he says, "we have lost our centeredness. We don't have the time, literally, to think during the day. . . . We have become disembodied. By being always somewhere else we are nowhere."[31]

Lightman implies that one morning is all it takes to turn an ambitious corporate drone into a social leper caught up in the hell of a psychiatric hospital. Wandering from there into a church bingo game, however, gives Chalmers a chance encounter with someone who recognizes him, a meeting that helps him piece together enough of his life to return home. Miraculously—to a point straining credulity—he appears to recover enough to resume his former life.

Almost immediately a creeping numbness begins in his hands and spreads to the rest of his body. He is soon wheelchair-bound, susceptible to a profound malaise that a plethora of tests and drug trials can do nothing to remedy. "After a time," Lightman writes eloquently, "a great sadness would sweep over him, a sensation that he was the only human on earth watching these things, and he could not bear to look through the window any longer. Then he would close his eyes and let his head drop against his raised arms until the impotent legs finally crumpled beneath him" (276). The cause of the illness remains mysterious and, in the end, unfathomable. Doctor after doctor submits Chalmers to test after test. No one can determine whether his problem is physiological, psychological, or some combination of the two.

Lightman is best when satirizing doctors and psychiatrists who arrogantly portray themselves as omniscient, yet behave in ways both feckless and contemptuous of their patients. Some of Chalmers's physicians order expensive tests purely to explore the latest state-of-the-art technology; others barely look at their patient, much less give an answer to his frantic questions. One or two schedule multiple patients at the same time, prolonging the ordeal of the waiting room, while others try to assess Chalmers "using only test results and e-mail correspondence[;] and an addled psychiatrist . . . writes a paper about Chalmers for a journal on psychosomatic illnesses."[32]

Given the speed with which he degenerates physically, his wife's insistence that his illness is "all in his head" seems especially heartless. She screams in exasperation, "You just can't hack it, so you're self-destructing" (263). But she's having a cyberaffair with a professor she's never met, and rapidly becoming an alcoholic in the process, so the novel largely discredits her perspective.

Chalmers's psychiatrist is quite taken with her diagnosis, however, and puts him on 20 milligrams of Prozac per day, which, as we've seen, rapidly makes things worse: "Every few minutes [Chalmers] squeezed his hands to see if the numbness had lessened, but the only effect of the Prozac so far was to make him nauseous" (211). His mind soon starts racing, giving him uncharacteristic bouts of loquaciousness and insomnia, both adding turbulence to his already-rocky marriage: "That night, Prozac in his brain, Bill woke up a half-dozen times, with piercing dreams in between" (219). The sole response of his psychiatrist is to up the daily dose to 30 milligrams.

Eventually even Dr. Kripke concedes that Prozac is not helping his patient's nausea, insomnia, and paralysis. He switches Chalmers to Paxil, and the hapless protagonist promptly becomes more confrontational, yelling at his colleagues and wife until he's fired and his marriage turns to tatters. Glaxo's promotional campaign for Paxil, "Your Life is Waiting," seems especially ironic at such moments. As Claudia Rankine poignantly replies to this slogan in another work of fiction: "I think first, but then I wonder, for what, for what does it wait? For life I guess."[33]

While the same is doubtless true in *The Diagnosis*, the elusive cause of Chalmers's malaise underscores how difficult it is for his doctors and psychiatrists to determine what's wrong with him. Dr. Kripke eventually administers a Rorschach test, "having reluctantly agreed that the last month of Paxil was failing to produce any positive effects. 'There's plenty of anger here. . . . The anger is building,' said the psychiatrist. 'But it is too . . . unfocused and broad'" (280). What of the drug's negative effects on Chalmers, which seem glaringly obvious? The psychiatrist pays them no heed, leaving Chalmers and the reader unclear whether the Paxil has caused the patient's strong mood swings, exacerbated a minor trait to which he was prone, or helped him vent in ways he was too stressed to exploit before.

Given such open-endedness, we should doubtless read Lightman's title as ironic—the doctors in fact never *make* a diagnosis—and view their delay and imprecision as Lightman's frustrated diagnosis of our increasingly manic culture. But as he never gives a hint, and the novel ends with nothing resolved, several reviewers complained (quite reasonably) that he either has become as withholding as Chalmers's psychiatrists, or is unable to say conclusively what he imagines is wrong with his protagonist. As James Hynes put it aptly in the *Washington Post*, reading the novel is "a bracing but puzzling experience," leaving us "wondering just what exactly it [is] about. As a critique of money-grubbing and information overload, it peters out halfway through, and as an account of a man and his family's devastating illness, it is unrelievedly grim. . . . It becomes clear that the author is not planning on dispensing redemption of any kind."[34]

In this respect, of course, *The Diagnosis* differs somewhat from *Garden State* and *The Corrections,* only loosely suggesting Chalmers's spiritual uplift in the novel's final paragraphs. Yet it joins both works in voicing a powerful indictment of modern society, in which pharmacology and psychiatry are compounding symptoms of—rather than viable remedies for—ordinary suffering.

Like Franzen and Braff, Lightman also implies that while we need more imaginative and less commercial ways of thinking about redemption, our salvation will not come from medication. Pointing intelligently (as did the writings of Freud and others) to our broader malaise and discontents with civilization, their satires overturn the logic of maladaption. Laid at society's door, the problems they represent stem principally from cultures and communities that are insufficiently robust to absorb their citizens' diverse anxieties and eccentricities.

If anyone thought *The Diagnosis* a withering critique of psychiatry, it pales beside Will Self's darkly funny satire, *Dr. Mukti and Other Tales of Woe* (2004). Self is better known in Britain, his home, but on both sides of the Atlantic he has published four novels, several novellas, and three collections of journalism, many of them about mental health, a term he manages to twist into an amusingly misshapen euphemism.

Like his earlier irreverent works, *The Quantity Theory of Insanity* and *The Sweet Smell of Psychosis,* the novella *Dr. Mukti* deliberately frays the boundaries between sanity and schizophrenia. Its protagonist ostensibly treats patients suffering from the latter, but he resents every minute of his job, has contempt for his patients (indeed, for humanity at large), and gets snared in a bizarre, competitive vendetta with another psychiatrist that swiftly escalates into professional war and just as rapidly propels his breakdown into the very pathology he should be adept at treating.

Everything seems relatively calm when the novella begins. The opening sentences showcase Mukti's banter with a colleague, as well as Self's taut, crystalline prose, which manages to be brutally direct and slyly affectionate: "Dr. Shiva Mukti was a psychiatrist of modest achievements but vault-ing ambition. Not that he would've admitted it. Even if his oldest friend, David Elmley—a man of true mildness—had put it to him thus . . . , an absolute tirade of denials would've ensued. Whatdoyoumeanbythat? Mod-est by whose standards? By what measure? As for vaulting, why'dyousaythat? Because I dare to think that I should have a better job than this piss-poor consultancy at St. Mungo's? Is that a little too unEnglish for you? Not quite cricket, old boy?"[35]

Dr. Mukti is in one sense a highly appealing protagonist, not least be-cause his cynicism and general bolshiness don't "fit anyone's image of [a] submissive Hindu" (9). His ambition makes him susceptible to flattery and self-delusion, with at least one colleague sensing his fantasies of "padd[ing] through the mental miasma of Central London like a latter-day Sherlock Holmes" (120). The "downpour of self-justification" and "gale of resentment" that greet Elmley's observation nonetheless render Mukti appealingly human, and the chaos ensuing from his boredom and massively chipped shoulder is both horrifying and extremely entertaining (5).

Self, however, is more interested in satirizing the envy and hatred that swirl beneath Dr. Mukti's thin veneer of professionalism, where colleagues are only too willing to pathologize each other. They fabricate diagnoses in a desperate bid to get ahead, while offloading on each other their worst pa-tients in gestures of "titivating obsequiousness" (38).

The feud with Zack Busner starts as "a campaign of carpet bombing the culture with manufactured mental malaises," but it takes a sharp left turn when the suave Busner—imagining Mukti has snubbed him at a party—slyly retaliates by sending him a delirious patient (84). In one sense, Mukti's misanthropy and social awkwardness *could* be read as contemptu-ous indifference, but Busner is in no mood for forgiveness. He masks his fury in a short, chatty explanation:

> Dear Shiva—
> This is David Juniper, he's under the impression that he's a cre-osote man, both made out of creosote and with a mission to bring creosote ideas to the rest of mankind. He's undoubtedly schizoid, but he also has certain atypical symptoms consistent with hor-

monal imbalance. I happened to see your article in the *BJE* and thought you might be prepared to venture a second opinion in this case.

Thanks in anticipation,

Zack. (23)

Below this letter Self amusingly adds a faux footnote to the *British Journal of Ephemera,* issue 19, vol. 73, which ostensibly includes Dr. Mukti's treatise, "A Note on Endocrine Imbalance and Symptomatic Embellishment in Schizophreniform Disorders" (23, 24). The younger psychiatrist is flattered, outmaneuvered, and enraged at getting extra work under the pretext of generosity: "Unbelievable! The barefaced cheek of the man! The utter, self-serving, lazy, presumptuously familiar, self-regarding nerve" (23–24).

The incident leads to some wonderful comedy, including the line, "I hardly think his creosote delusion is to do with a creosote deficiency" (29), as well as revelations about Mukti's general philosophy of schizophrenia— "A third of them were untreatable, a third could be medicated into a shambling semblance of normality, and the final third would spontaneously recover" (18)—all of which render his profession valueless, dubious, or both.

The incident also prompts him to up the ante by sending Busner, as a professional courtesy, an even more volatile patient. He hopes that the patient (Rocky) "would, obligingly, transfer his fixation to Busner" and pester him instead: "This patient displays an uncannily consistent ametaphoric tendency. His total inability to enact analogous or comparative speech modes called forcibly to my mind your 1978 paper 'Intentionality Refracted: Schizophreniform Disorders and the Re-embodied Poetic.' I've no real belief that anything can be done for him, but thought that the intervention of a more experienced and perceptive therapist than myself might nevertheless throw up some interesting insights which might be applicable in other cases" (38). In such examples, Self displays an unnerving familiarity with psychiatric jargon and the way colleagues sometimes spar, in friendly and petty ways, over accurate diagnoses.

As in *The Diagnosis,* the serious question plaguing Dr. Mukti is whether these professional judgments have any real accuracy or whether the diagnoses simply "shoehorn" patients "into this or that dysfunctional slipper" out of medical expediency (99). It is a question recalling the debates we followed over *DSM-III*, *IIIR*, and *IV*, and Self ramps it up in two ways.

In sheer practical terms things with Rocky go horribly wrong. He attacks Busner and several colleagues, then dies when the drugs meant to restrain him lead to an overdose of chlorpromazine. Rather than taking his share of the blame, Busner ingeniously censures Mukti for pumping Rocky with too much of the drug, which he claims led to a heart attack.

Self also uses the incident (and the wider feud between Mukti and Busner) to view diagnostic inflections as professional fads that psychiatric interns and medical students start treating as gospel and simply disseminate by rote: "Early on in his career Shiva had kept up, wading his way through journals, papers and books, laboriously cross-referencing malaise with theory with treatment, until his head spun in a whirlpool of supposition. But now . . . well, what? Surely these academic theories were only hessian sacks stuffed full of dry-as-dust language then thrust in the path of the great inundations of despair which afflicted real patients?" (33).

The gap that Dr. Mukti encounters between diagnostic terms and his patients' delirium is both a pretext for Self's satire (the theory proves utterly inadequate to the practice) and an abyss into which Mukti imagines falling as his career flounders and his expertise fails even to keep up with his patients' burgeoning delusions, much less do anything to arrest them.

Before the feud with Busner gets out of control over Rocky, however, Mukti is revealed to be quite a dreamer himself. He imagines he's rather like Cortés, exploring virgin psychiatric territory before *DSM-III* tried to colonize every realm of the psyche. This path too is a pretext for satire: "How Shiva Mukti wished he had been practising in an earlier era, when the psychiatric field was yet to be enclosed. When across the open savannah of mental disorder ranged small bands of nomadic doctors, bagging whatever prey they could. Then no one had the temerity to stop any qualified man doing exactly as he pleased" (18).

"No one had the temerity," perhaps, because the psychiatrists were so adamant that they knew what they were doing: their diagnostic map was complete, their treatment methods watertight. The scenario is similar to that in Self's "Quantity Theory of Insanity," a deft story about psychiatric mentorship that goes painfully awry; it also includes an earlier incarnation of Busner as iconoclast. "We're really finding out," the youthful Busner declares, "the extent to which all these categories of psychopathology are just that: dry, empty categories, devoid of real content, representing only the taxonomic, psychic fascism of a gang of twisted old men."[36]

Betraying the signs of a zealot, Busner is all extremes and no gray areas, but it is also fair to say that neuropsychiatry bears most of the brunt of Self's lampooning: he views it as conceptually flawed, disdainful, and incompetent. As his narrator asks rhetorically, "How would Freud's own 'talking cure' have fared had it been introduced into the current age of anxiety, with its pill-pushing practitioners in vassalage to their pharmocorporate overlords? No doubt the Viennese would be tarred, feathered and run out of town on a couch-shaped rail" (18).

The question is certainly a necessary one to ask, even if the answer is painfully accurate. But Self doesn't balk at sending up psychodynamic treatments as well. He describes a secretary as "looking exactly like a receptionist at Kwikshrink plc" (93) and sums up psychodynamic methods in a bracing, memorable aphorism: "being in therapy meant paying for the slender reassurance of another's minor consideration" (92).

That would depend, of course, on whom one sees, but Mukti, in near-psychotic despair, eschews "the touchy-feeliness of interpersonality" and picks a man who takes a "mechanical approach to soul-doctoring." He brags: "If you went to [Gunnar] Grunbein you were paying to have your psyche stripped down to its core components then meticulously reassembled. Oily ego, beveled superego, vulcanised id, all were given a rub with the rag of his sensibility before being replaced in the engine compartment of identity" (90).

The fantasy here, as in neuropsychiatry, is so mechanistic that it aspires to an ideal balancing of our "bits and bytes of personality and emotion"[37] —a radical tune-up, perhaps, that transforms the jagged edges of our being into a well-oiled machine humming in every gear and giving the best possible mileage. In this respect Grunbein's approach, substituting Freudian terms for biochemical principles, simply mirrors the precepts of neuropsychiatry. It does not put an end to Mukti's one-upmanship and professional rivalry, as Self hints wittily when Mukti tries to outsmart his shrink with the same rampant egotism that first landed him in trouble: "Shiva decided to take a look in the *DSM-IV* when he reached home, although he was almost certain he knew already which personality disorder Gunnar Grunbein had" (93).

We don't learn much about Mukti's actual treatment with Dr. Grunbein, but it is worth noting, in closing, how Self depicts Shiva's social phobia. He starts out generalizing it so that it becomes a shared symptom among his protagonists. Then he subtracts its allegedly pathological standing so that it seems an unexceptional, even inevitable, reaction to the bizarre behavior that rivals and even professional groups sometimes act out.

True, Mukti's "social phobia" is almost indistinguishable from his aversion to everyone—he calls his patients "human rubbish" (16)—and his "social" anxiety is more often status anxiety than pathological embarrassment about how others judge him. Moreover, as Self's protagonists tend to be quite inept socially, quick to anger, and prone to exaggerate their standing among others, he doesn't lessen any of the comedy arising from their grandiose misperceptions.

However, if they are quite self-absorbed, as Dr. Mukti's serenely tolerant wife notes of her husband, the discrepancy between how they see the world and how others see them is an opportunity for farce, pathos, and, in the case of psychiatry, devastating critique. For Self, at least, it is never a reason to muzzle or medicate his characters' emotions.

7

FEAR OF OTHERS IN AN ANXIOUS AGE

Now that shyness has become a disease, which emotion will be next? The April 2005 issue of *NeuroPsychiatry Reviews* features two colleagues debating quite seriously whether the next edition of DSM should include criteria for a new psychiatric problem: *apathy*. According to James Duffy, a tenured professor at the University of Connecticut, apathy isn't just a state of mind; it's a "common" illness that "can occur alone and in conjunction with other disorders, [and] in percentages that translate into millions of people." The clincher for apathy's inclusion in the manual of mental disorders, he says (as if rehearsing a line from Self's *Dr. Mukti*), is that "psychotropics are a very potent cause of" it.[1] Instead of Duffy's questioning whether these drugs—with their terrible side effects—should be prescribed in such vast amounts, he argues that the medical problems they create should be pathologized.

Apathy is doubtless an extreme example of the "disorders" neuropsychiatrists have begun assessing for possible inclusion in DSM-V (slated to appear in 2011), but the logic behind its inclusion summarizes the bewildering confusion over cause and effect that we have witnessed repeatedly in this book. That sort of thinking has dominated American psychiatry since managed care began preferring drug treatments in the 1970s, even when drugs proved more expensive than therapy.[2] But as Robert Spitzer acknowledged, DSM approval for many disorders depended partly on whether researchers had a treatment for them—another case of putting the cart before the horse. To repeat his statement quoted in Chapter 3:

"If you have a treatment, you're more interested in getting the category in. If you have no treatment for it, there's not as much pressure to put the thing in."[3]

As neuropsychiatric, evolutionary biological, and even genetic explanations for a litany of modest ailments now reign supreme, it is time to gauge where they are likely to take us in the near future. For if anxiety is to be medicalized, why not an even greater range of human traits and emotions, such as envy, joy, or common unhappiness?

While psychiatrists are unlikely to scale back the seven anxiety disorders they created in 1980 (because doing so would look like an admission of weakness), several other conditions are almost certain to make the final cut for the fifth edition: compulsive buying disorder, Internet addiction, binge-eating disorder, compulsive sexual behavior disorder, and premenstrual dysphoric disorder (the last one only in the appendix to *DSM-IV*). Including the first of them would seem particularly ironic in light of Peter Kramer's concerns about "cosmetic psychopharmacology" and the widespread use of SSRIs to brighten our personalities. Even so, Susan McElroy and her colleagues tell us, "Compulsive buying is a probably common but little studied disorder" that "may co-occur with other psychiatric disorders; may be treatable; and, thus, should be further studied as a mental disorder in its own right."[4]

Another so-called illness, intermittent explosive disorder, dates to *DSM-III*, but the world press recently gave it a major boost after Ronald Kessler and his team at Harvard announced that up to 16 million Americans may be suffering from it. IED (not to be confused with ED, erectile dysfunction) is in large part a fancy euphemism for road rage, but 16 million potential patients is a figure to command attention. Funded by the National Institutes of Health, the researchers couldn't contact 16 million Americans, of course, much less form a reliable, long-term picture of their mental health. So they performed a now-standard procedure: Assess the fraying tempers of a fairly large sample; gauge the proportion of that sample relative to the population overall; then extrapolate the ratio and publish the upper range of Americans likely to be affected, as the largest number who "may" display the disorder.

Researchers know by now that the drug companies and the media are not interested in the lower likely figure (in this case, 11.5 million), much

"Drug signs" (Courtesy Ephemera Inc., Phoenix, Ore., 2001)

less how researchers came up with the figures in the first place. They want good copy, especially when it appears amid widespread concern over rising gas prices. Kessler's article in the *Archives of General Psychiatry* consequently received wide-eyed commentary around the world. Reports flowed off the newswires suggesting that the short-fused may be mentally ill.[5]

Perhaps most surprising of all, while the article said nothing about serotonin deficiency or preferred drug treatment, several journalists made the connection themselves. They explained that the cause was probably a chemical imbalance and urged treatment with all the usual pharmaceutical suspects: Prozac, Zoloft, and Effexor.[6] In this respect, the well-known caricature of our overmedicated culture shown above proves more relevant than ever.

The story follows a well-worn cycle that we have witnessed repeatedly in this book. Step One: Take the results of an ambiguous questionnaire to prove that the new disorder far exceeds psychiatrists' already ample expectations, leading them to suspect the presence of a widespread, underdiagnosed problem. Step Two: List the new disorder in the *DSM*, thereby inviting drug companies to treat it. Step Three: Shower doctors with free samples of newly minted pills, while bombarding television viewers with carefully crafted ads. Step Four: Castigate dissenters for failing to recognize the severity of the illness and for heartlessly prolonging patient suffering.

"Although the majority of people with IED (60.3%) obtained professional treatment for emotional or substance problems at some time in their life," Kessler and his colleagues stated, "only 28.8% ever received treatment for their anger."[7] While the first percentage may surprise us, especially for a disorder as loosely defined as IED, the second allows the team to focus on "unmet need," a phrase Kessler has used elsewhere to stress that "mild disorders should not be eliminated from the *DSM-V*."

This phrase is in fact the title of an article he and a slightly different group of colleagues published in 2003, four years before official discussions about *DSM-V* even get under way and eight years before the edition is due to appear—timing that suggests the high stakes for Kessler and likeminded neuropsychiatrists. The article indeed reads like a preemptive attack, designed to stop the DSM-V task force and its working groups from second-guessing earlier decisions. It even singles out Darrel Regier, a man "expected to play a prominent role in the development of *DSM-V*," and warns that he would be wrong to "support . . . similar restrictions" on the calculation of mild disorders.

But the article's main target was colleagues worried that diagnostic interviews in the National Comorbidity Survey "might be upwardly biased" and that "the *DSM* system itself is overly inclusive." Kessler had headed the survey, and his article states emphatically in response that bias was definitely not an issue.[8]

Perhaps Kessler doth protest too much, for he and his colleagues argue elsewhere, "About half of Americans will meet the criteria for a *DSM-IV* disorder sometime in their life."[9] Although that "about half" sounds rather casual, it has staggering implications for the country overall: if only half of us will avoid a *DSM* diagnosis, the rest will be saddled with them for most of their lives, and likely will be counted in the surveys even if they are asymptomatic. Consider the number of pills that would mean swallowing, the side effects they would cause, and the financial and logistical burden they would place on our already overstretched and massively expensive healthcare system.

But Kessler's colleagues aren't finished. "Interventions aimed at prevention or early treatment need to focus on youth," they say, to prevent nascent problems from developing into full-blown disorders.[10] If they can treat your shy child at age six, in other words, they will nip in the bud the "first onset" of social anxiety before it grows into full-blown public speaking anxiety. Kessler and his colleagues either haven't followed—or have chosen to ignore—the reason several drug companies were forced to add black-box warnings to antidepressants given to children: a number of them developed chronic side effects, including thoughts of suicide.[11]

Another strategy is switch and bait. David Healy explains:

> In the U.S., . . . they're even more enthusiastic about drug treatments than in the UK. But when they get negative results and side effects, they often say, "Well, we've been treating them for the wrong thing. The patients are actually, say, bipolar. So we need to treat them for bipolar disorder. We just didn't put them on the *right* pills. And the fact that we don't get great results when people are getting on in life, in their thirties and forties, just means we need to catch them when they're children. If we can treat this thing before it takes root, it won't be a problem later in life, so you get all these kids being put on really dangerous stuff. In some experiments the children's mean age is actually four, so there's two-year-olds being given these drugs.[12]

If we can stifle doubts that shy and anxious toddlers should be medicated at all—much less face the likelihood of permanently altered nervous systems and lifelong dependency on SSRIs[13]—there is simply no way of knowing whether a child displaying such behavior will continue to do so as an adult. Granted, some signs are noticeable by late childhood or adolescence, but these are traits, not full-blown disorders, and often characterize normal development. The catch-it-early approach stems from a grave fallacy that the first situation leads to the second. The net effect is to shower children indiscriminately with drugs, in a wild bid to stamp out anxiety— even when it can be useful and necessary for survival. What initially seems like a highly scientific approach therefore is anything but. The only certainty of the Kessler approach is that it will overmedicate a whole generation of children and adolescents, with untold health risks and staggering financial consequences.

Then too, in practical and statistical terms, treating incipient, mild, and chronic cases as equivalent grossly inflates the numbers and distorts the clinical picture. Additional arguments about "unmet need" become wholly unconvincing. The term applies, a skeptic would say, to those of us haplessly awaiting one of the many new disorders coming down the pike, such as apathy disorder, Internet addiction, or compulsive buying disorder. Yet as Healy points out, "Psychopharmacologists don't see any of this stuff as being constructed in any way. They see it as brute, material reality. . . . The idea that the disorders are partly a construction doesn't cross their radar."[14]

Anxiety disorders, combined, topped the list of symptoms in the National Comorbidity Survey, with almost a third of respondents saying they experienced some form of one.[15] While skeptics wonder why neuropsychiatrists are busy lowering the thresholds of the disorders to ratchet up the numbers, Kessler and his colleagues counter that it's unethical to ignore patients who haven't yet requested medication, because that would leave them to battle their problems unaided. The skeptics respond, in turn, that many of these problems don't warrant medication (people can resolve them in myriad other ways—including, when necessary, other forms of treatment); that the public could hardly be ignorant of these disorders when the drug companies have spent millions promoting them; that it's deeply unethical to blanket whole swaths of the population with powerful psychotropic drugs; and that Kessler's team is trivializing chronic illness by dissolving meaningful distinctions between severe and mild cases.

A 2006 essay on "Psychiatry by Prescription" quotes Arthur Kleinman, Harvard professor of psychiatry and medical anthropology, as saying, "By medicalizing ordinary unhappiness, we risk doing a disservice to those people who have severe mental illnesses." The article in *Harvard Magazine* amplifies his concerns:

> Kleinman fears that including mild forms of anxiety and depression under an ever-widening umbrella of mental disorders will di-

vert attention and resources from diseases like schizophrenia and major depression, which remain undertreated and stigmatized across much of the world. In his view, "We may turn off the public, who are a huge source of support for mental-health research, by telling them that half of them are mad."

Despite Kleinman's holding an endowed chair, Kessler dismissed his concerns as the "false enthusiasm of the noncombatant," by which he meant, according to the writer, "If you haven't worked directly with people who suffer from so-called mild disorders, it's easy to write them off as ordinary."[16] But Kleinman's hands-on experience includes developing mental-health policy and programs with the World Health Organization, as well as detailed clinical and cross-cultural knowledge of schizophrenia. His comments hardly convey "false enthusiasm"; they point to a deep-seated and justified concern that mental-health diagnoses, particularly in the United States, have gone haywire.

Part of this battleground is over ethics, in particular the ethics of diagnosis and treatment. Whereas skeptics fear that things have gotten out of hand, the subtext of "Mild Disorders Should Not Be Eliminated from the DSM-V" is that Kessler's team is facing these doubts from the other direction and clutching at every possible reason to keep psychiatric diagnoses as elastic as possible.

Why the urgency? A key concern running through their article is that many currently defined mental disorders, like social anxiety, "appear not to have meaningful thresholds." So if DSM-V were to raise the bar and set the threshold for inclusion higher, as critics have urged, "early interventions to prevent progression along a given severity continuum might reduce the prevalence of serious cases."[17]

Translation: Millions of patients would no longer be defined as ill. Whole segments of the population, here and abroad, currently buoying up the drug companies and their figures, would disappear at a stroke, to reemerge beyond their nets as something like the "worried well" or the "simply shy." Nor would Kessler's team be able to state, "About half of Americans will meet the criteria for a DSM-IV disorder sometime in their life."[18] If the criteria for every disorder were appropriately tightened, not relaxed, the upper range of each would plummet. The number of people seemingly afflicted by mental disorders would nosedive. It would be as if the DSM-V task force took a corrective pin to the manual's bloat and hype, leaving it suitably deflated to focus once more on those who are chronically ill.

It is useful here to recall Kutchins and Kirk's observation in *Making Us Crazy*: "By simply altering slightly the wording of a criterion, the duration for which a symptom must be experienced in order to satisfy a criterion, or the number of criteria used to establish a diagnosis, the prevalence rates in the United States will rise and fall as erratically as the stock market."[19] Because of this instability, Kessler and his colleagues want to keep the prevalence rates as high as possible, and the criteria defining them as expansive as the profession will allow—which is to say, as loose as the public will tolerate before we cry, "Enough is enough."

There are countless signs that this backlash is already under way. A bracing editorial in the *Washington Post* goes to work on the National Comorbidity Survey. According to Sally Satel and Christina Hoff Sommers (coauthors of *One Nation under Therapy*), the study indicated "a quarter of all adults in the United States—26 percent—qualified as having a mental illness within a given year," which already halves Kessler and his colleagues' emphasis on lifetime afflictions.

But Satel and Sommers are just getting going, and to the assertion about 26 percent of us they bluntly ask, "Can a rate so high be true? A closer look at the study," they insist, "reveals a less startling picture. . . . First, the survey used in the study was based on the standard psychiatric handbook—the *Diagnostic and Statistical Manual, 4th Edition* (*DSM-IV*)—which has a low threshold for calling a collection of symptoms a 'mental disorder.' For example, a balky, stubborn, aggressive child might well be diagnosed as having 'Oppositional Defiant Disorder' (ODD), according to the *DSM*, and sent to a therapist. Yet a layman might simply regard him as spoiled and in need of a strict British nanny."

Second, the survey included "moderate" and "mild" cases (each accounting for 10 percent, or 20 percent combined of the 26 percent cited), when mild cases either require no professional attention or "represent garden-variety anxieties and despair associated with problems in living—or moving. So, conservatively, 6 to 16 percent of us will suffer a mental condition this year, as defined by psychiatrists."[20]

We've gone from "about half of Americans" to as few as one sixteenth of them in just a few paragraphs. We've also seen in this book enough behind-the-scenes evidence sadly to view the phrase "as defined by psychiatrists" with profound skepticism. How, for instance, should one combine the *DSM-III* criteria for road rage with Roger MacKinnon's May 1978 observation that people with avoidant personality are so perverse they "frequently have not learned to drive a car" and "would suffer the inconvenience of public transportation in a situation where a private automobile is available"?[21] Or the *DSM-III* statement about schizoid personality disorder, "Individuals with this disorder are usually humorless or dull"?[22]

We need more professional skeptics like Satel and Sommers, and more attentive observers like Jonathan Franzen to correct the distorted picture *DSM* gives. While I certainly hope this book contributes to that goal, the chances of a full-scale revision to the manual are admittedly quite slim. One reason is the sheer amount of time, money, and effort devoted to creating—and, in *DSM-IIIR* and *DSM-IV,* to maintaining—the widespread category changes to *DSM-III.* To switch tracks at this point, one would first have to stop this speeding train, and the only entity capable of doing that, the American Psychiatric Association, is committed to its hurtling along even faster.

Another more general impediment to change is that psychiatry is caught in a Faustian pact with its pharmaceutical sponsors. It is almost impossible for experts to state even minor criticisms (or, more dangerously, negative trial results) without looking as if they are biting the hand that feeds. Colleagues I wanted to acknowledge for their invaluable advice actually told me, when I asked naively how to thank them, that the book could not name them anywhere; they needed to maintain an unblemished relationship with the drug companies, they admitted with a twinge of panic. That relationship is so fragile and so conditional that it relies on a high degree of unstated acquiescence. Meanwhile, those with detailed knowledge of the field not holding M.D.s are frequently attacked in print as straying beyond their expertise, as prolonging others' suffering, or both.

And it is not just psychiatrists who voice these attacks. One disturbing sign of the lengths to which the drug companies are willing to go became clear in the fall of 2005, when the *New York Daily News* and the *Los Ange-*

les Times reported "a tale worthy of a zany Washington satire—except for the lamentable fact that it's true."[23] "The rich and powerful pharmaceutical lobby," they revealed, had "secretly commissioned a thriller novel whose aim was to scare the living daylights out of folks who might want to buy cheap drugs from Canada."[24]

It turns out that the Pharmaceutical Research and Manufacturers of America, or PhRMA, which solicited the novel, has "vigorously fought all efforts to legalize the purchase of cheap drugs from Canada."[25] Indeed, the man recently appointed to head the agency, W. J. "Billy" Tauzin, was, just a few months earlier, "one of the principal authors of the Medicare prescription drug bill." That bill, according to the *Washington Post,* "included several provisions expected to vastly expand the market for prescription drugs among the elderly. In addition to adding hundreds of billions of dollars for drug benefits, the law bars the federal government from directly bargaining down the price of drugs, a provision PhRMA pressed for." Once one of the most powerful Republicans in the House, Tauzin decided abruptly to accept the presidency of PhRMA rather than seek reelection. Some of his colleagues voiced concern about the apparent conflict of interest, and Public Citizen, a public interest group, called for an ethics investigation.[26]

Sometime in 2003, however, PhRMA approached Michael Viner, publisher of Los Angeles–based Phoenix Books (a specialist in tabloid publishing and "tell-all books related to O. J. Simpson, Heidi Fleiss," and others), and offered "a six-figure sum for the marketing and production of a written-to-order fictional thriller." Tongue firmly in cheek, the *Los Angeles Times* explains that "the plotline was what Hollywood would term high-concept—a group of shadowy terrorists conspires to murder thousands of Americans by poisoning the medicine they're importing from Canada to beat U.S. drug prices. (Think *True Lies* meets the Physicians Desk Reference.)"[27]

"They said they wanted it somewhat dumbed down for women," explains Kenin Spivak, one of the authors, "with a lot more fluff in it, and more about the wife of the head Croatian terrorist, who is a former Miss Mexico." They also wanted "to change the motivating factor of the terrorists to greed, because they didn't want it to be politics," he adds. Finally, "lots of people [had] to die."[28]

When the deal came apart, because PhRMA allegedly didn't like the material, the group offered the authors $100,000 to sweep it all under the rug and "agree never to speak ill of PhRMA or the drug industry for the rest of their lives."[29] The writers refused, exposing the project and its amazingly ham-fisted plot. Confronted about the leaked story, Ken Johnson, executive vice president of PhRMA, backpedaled furiously: "The idea was brought to us by an outside consultant," he insisted. "We explored it, provided some background information, . . . but in the final analysis, decided it wasn't the right thing for us to do."[30]

The authors, however, say a PhRMA marketing executive "sedulously monitored the work by phone, e-mail and in person, often ordering changes in plot, characterization and tone."[31] And Johnson implicitly acknowledges it by calling the PhRMA executive a "renegade" who abused her "budgetary authority"—the authority, clearly, to make six-figure deals with tabloid publishers. Johnson also agrees with Tauzin that the organization needs "to turn [its] image around," presumably by not commissioning more thrillers about the dangers of Canadian prescription drugs.[32]

Clearly, we can't look to PhRMA to reform psychiatry. Who, then, will undertake this crucial task? While several brave colleagues with impeccable credentials have risked their careers in speaking out,[33] there is, I think, a significant chance that psychiatry will overreach itself so dramatically that it will shred its own credibility.

One might consider this the flip side of the gambit by Kessler, Duffy, and others in calling apathy, road rage, compulsive buying, and other run-of-the-mill traits illnesses that "can occur . . . in percentages that translate into millions of people."[34] For if these neuropsychiatrists continue pushing their claims so far that the illusion of scientific rigor bursts (and, relatedly, if half the country balks at being called crazy, as Kleinman warned), they will no longer be able to prescribe Paxil and other SSRIs so heavily for routine conditions like shyness and public speaking anxiety. Attuned to the hype and manipulation the drug marketers and PR companies have perpetrated so deftly, the public would differentiate more keenly, as *DSM* does not, between ordinary shyness and acute, paralyzing dread.

Kessler and his colleagues view that outcome as devastating for the public, but the mild cases they are intent on retaining as mental disorders could be addressed in far less dramatic and costly ways: by offering many more high school and college courses on public speaking, for instance, and by advocating low-cost, effective groups like Toastmasters. (Our culture might even ask whether gregarious and loquacious behavior is always more admirable than careful introspection, attentive listening, and scrupulous observation.) Above all, social anxiety disorder would shrink appropriately to the tiny number of chronically affected people who find social participation *terrifying*. Almost all the leading psychiatrists I interviewed affirmed they could distinguish within seconds between such acute dread and its more routine counterparts.[35]

Granted, one far-reaching consequence of this shift in perspective is that some patients would miss the comfort of being able to say their unease is due entirely to brain chemistry. As we quoted Donald Klein in Chapter 2, a "*biological dysfunction* . . . entitles the person to the exemptions inherent in the sick role."[36] Insisting that unease is not due to a "chemical imbalance" is neither callous nor judgmental; it is actually more respectful and scientifically accurate. Satel and Sommers add that it is also more compassionate and effective, because it restores a distinction between chronic and mild cases, treating the former with appropriate seriousness (and finite resources) while assuring the latter that their problems are both widespread and capable of being addressed in other ways. As they put it, in a phrase that is anathema to most of the psychiatric literature, "suffering is sometimes edifying."[37] I would add, with Freud, that such suffering and unease often result from complex adjustments to society, a point easily sidelined when even the mildest problem is couched as an individualized disorder. Inverting the psychiatric argument about "maladaptive beliefs . . . and thoughts," Freud's point is that this suffering is systemic, because it is an unavoidable consequence of our membership in communities.[38]

What about those "exemptions inherent in the sick role," as Klein put it? The reaction of many humanists, when they have heard me present parts of this book, is to express profound dismay over the growing number of students who press them each semester to be released from tests, exams, learning foreign languages, and even the reading of required texts on the grounds that they suffer from one or more disorders. Any teacher wondering why the student can't proceed—or, worse, doubting the severity of the disorder—will be challenging not only the student's integrity, but also the expertise of the doctor or psychiatrist making the diagnosis. Sadly, it is easier to say nothing, assign different work, and, if need be, create an entirely new exam for the student, even if one must do so year after year.

Those wondering whether the teachers' frustration is exaggerated may not have grasped the scale of this problem. A 2006 article in the *New York Times* on the sheer number of antidepressants and other medications handed out at summer camps was a wake-up call for many and hinted, for high school and university teachers, at worse problems to come.[39] The broader point is that viewing the students' or patients' problems in this way disempowers them. If a doctor or psychiatrist presumes that a person with public speaking anxiety or mild shyness needs a strong anticholinergic like Paxil, that caregiver is tacitly assuming the patient is too fragile or incompetent to resolve the problem in any other way.

––––––––––

Although it is relatively easy to state the challenges ahead, the possibilities for reform must for now remain conditional. All the evidence suggests that neuropsychiatrists have not only won the day, but also are busy trying to sew up the future of mental health. I documented earlier battles over brain and mind in order to reveal the controversial background to diagnoses that many now take for granted and ratify unthinkingly. Furthermore, despite the current illusion of consensus, the fundamental debate about mental health and illness will not go away, because it is far from resolved.

Despite the serene confidence of neuropsychiatrists wanting to reduce almost every emotion to brain chemistry, they simply don't know what they don't know. I mean this in two ways: First, the history of medicine and of psychiatry is full of cases (thalidomide and leukotomy, to name only two) where experts proceeded on well-meaning assumptions that hindsight and fuller research proved to be dreadfully misplaced. Second, because psychiatrists often downplay the role of consciousness in mental illness, they tend to reject it out of hand and, in so doing, fall back on facile explanations for cause and effect. These tell us nothing about the way the mind facilitates, blocks, or distorts social forces and biological stimuli. Psychiatry is greatly impoverished thereby, and broader philosophical arguments about the mind—developed and finessed across millennia—are shunted aside as inconsequential.

If this book has succeeded in revealing the poverty of these judgments and the troubling consequence of their effects, my hope is that it will spotlight social and psychological problems that psychiatry no longer can conceal: forms of disquiet that we trivialize by calling them "social phobia" or "avoidant personality disorder."

Are we really willing to attribute our complex moods and emotions to neurotransmitters and their alleged imbalance? And what, exactly, does our ferocious demand for "mood brighteners" and personality sculpting mask? These are questions we must try to answer together and alone. In part, they bring psychiatry into dialogue with philosophy (especially ethics); they also engage social policy in ways both surprising and alarming.

The Antisocial Behaviour Orders (ASBOs), which came into effect in Britain in 1999, reflect the kind of social policy to which the idea of a mechanistic brain lends support.[40] Indeed, neuropsychiatry has with a vengeance revived Karl Menninger's dictum about the individual's "adaptive failure" and turned it into a social problem requiring a large-scale intervention.[41] ASBOs have generated widespread debate in Britain, not least because they rely on implicit norms that are profoundly conservative and conformist. They also involve unstated but consequential decisions about what is and is not antisocial.[42] These issues, redolent of societal anxiety, quickly tilt toward shyness when one asks why our *cultures* are so troubled by not only antisocial behavior, but also traits that are in some respects its complete opposite: reticence, reclusion, and reserve.

In a piece in the London *Times* called "We're Sick of Being Shy," Roger Dobson suggests that the extent to which shyness preoccupies us tells us "more about society being uneasy with those who don't conform to the assertive, gregarious standards of the twenty-first century, than actually helping people."[43] He draws heavily on the work of Susie Scott, who argues, "Shyness has become an unhealthy state of mind for individuals living in contemporary Western societies." The fact that we are now medicating shyness implies that "bashful modesty and reserve are no longer so acceptable and that to succeed we must be vocal, assertive and capable of gregariously participating in social life."[44]

Why? Jonathan Rauch asks this key question in a delightful *Atlantic Monthly* piece called "Caring for Your Introvert." He observes: "Extroverts are energized by people, and wilt or fade when alone. They often seem bored by themselves, in both senses of the expression. Leave an extrovert alone for two minutes and he will reach for his cell phone. In contrast, after an hour or two of being socially 'on,' we introverts need to turn off and recharge. My own formula is roughly two hours alone for every hour of socializing. This isn't antisocial. It isn't a sign of depression. It does not call for medication. For introverts, to be alone with our thoughts is as restorative as sleeping, as nourishing as eating. Our motto: 'I'm okay, you're okay—in small doses.'"[45]

The problem is, many psychiatrists view those "doses" as pharmacological, and hope to increase them so that anything like an "avoidant personality" becomes a thing of the past.

I began this book noting that social phobia, the most enigmatic and poorly defined anxiety disorder, has rapidly become *the* psychosocial problem of our age, with many psychiatrists and doctors asserting that those who are not sufficiently outgoing may be mentally ill. Since 1980, when the DSM officially designated social phobia a psychiatric disorder, normal emotional states like shyness have been appropriated by the label and recast as a defect of brain chemistry.

The logical, perhaps inevitable, consequence of this biomedical turn in psychiatry is a growing consensus that traits once attributed to mavericks, skeptics, or mere introverts are psychiatric disorders that drugs should eliminate. With other contributing factors, this emphasis has transformed our expectations of the individual in society so dramatically that we now tend to believe that active membership in community activities, the cultivation of social skills (becoming a "people person"), and the development of group consciousness are natural, universal, and obligatory aims. We think the adjustment should be painless rather than a cause of unease and, sometimes, even of profound discontent. We tend, moreover, to attach such import to the attainment of these goals that psychiatrists are now licensed to regard as ill those manifesting even vaguely ungregarious behavior.

The meanings we attribute to apathy or shyness—for the meanings clearly change[46]—are less at issue here than the broader consequences of our intolerance for emotions we are encouraged to eliminate from ourselves and, indeed, to imagine eliminating from other people. Such concerns are not far-fetched. A 2003 government report, *Beyond Therapy,* asserts, in a statement so counterintuitive that it requires careful reading: "'Feeling good' may not always be good or good for us. . . . By seeking psychic detachment by means that pharmacologically insulate or remove us from the highs and lows of life, we may risk coming to love feebly or to care shallowly."[47]

Beyond Therapy questions the aspiration, voiced with increasing stridency in our culture, that we should polish our irregular edges and that society should function free of introverts, curmudgeons, misanthropes, pessimists, and the diffident or apathetic. One of several risks attached to medicating such people is that we'll accept as natural "a steady flow of re-socialised, conformist 'gingerbread men,'" a message telling everyone else they "have an obligation to change."[48]

This pressure is all the more ironic, in Susie Scott's eyes, as shyness "for a lot of people is actually not that debilitating."[49] Neuropsychiatry, seizing on the spurious logic of a "chemical imbalance" when no such ideal "balance" exists, implies that failing or refusing to strive for it means settling for less than optimal brain performance or unnecessary sadness.

We are understandably resistant to emotional pain, and SSRIs may help some with truly chronic depression and anxiety. Seeing limited value in these drugs does not override concern that quick-fix remedies for anxiety and ever-broader demands for cheerful social adaptation may in fact induce new and harsher varieties of suffering and anxiety, including, ironically, those from failing to adapt successfully and painlessly.[50] Eagerness for adaptation easily translates, moreover, into willingness to pathologize stoics—those who accept pain (and world-pain) as an unavoidable consequence of being human. Extroversion is becoming compulsory. As Margaret Talbot asks with appropriate humor and exasperation, "Is somebody out there inventing the drug to treat excessive perkiness?"[51]

The willingness to risk drug dependence and side effects in order to be "up" and "on" around the clock indicates a poor tolerance for the full range of human affect. As Andrew Hussey put it bluntly, "We're not allowed to be sad anymore."[52] Certainly we could, as a culture, contemn emotional intolerance rather than discourage introversion and brooding, but nonstop cheerfulness suggests productivity, malleability, and unreflec-

"Could we up the dosage? I still have feelings."

© *The New Yorker* Collection (January 22, 2007), Alex Gregory, from cartoonbank
.com. All rights reserved.

tive acquiescence in social norms. As Garret Keizer observes, in a statement extending beyond its immediate American context, "Our advertising and even our arts convey the idea that we as a society are brash, irreverent, and free of all constraint, when the best available evidence would
suggest that we are in fact tame, spayed, and easily brought to heel."[53]

The paradox here—and a surprising consequence for this book—is that
even the most mechanistic theory of subjectivity cannot mask the complexity of selfhood: the ambiguities of being human and the idiosyncrasies
they provoke. To some extent this complexity haunts, and may yet under-
mine, neuropsychiatry. As one clinician has observed perceptively, "one
could have," or believe oneself to have, "all the facts" about a patient "and
still not be in possession of the truth."[54]

Whether psychiatry ultimately accepts this predicament or continues
trying to medicate it away will be decisive for the profession. That there are
in all of us drives and fantasies that make us incapable of *complete* adaptation might indeed be the basis for an ethics that helps us live productively
and intelligently when we are "worried well," rather than wasting our energy aspiring to be "better than well," whatever that actually means.[55]

While neuropsychiatry offers us "chemical vacations from intolerable selfhood," then, we may become inured to routine fears and common un-happiness, and suffer more as a result.[56] As Hamm insists in Beckett's *Endgame*: "You're on earth, there's no cure for that!"[57] But neuropsychi-atrists and their corporate sponsors have spent countless hours and dollars trying to convince us otherwise.

NOTES

NOTE: The various editions of the *Diagnostic and Statistical Manual of Mental Disorders* will be referenced in the Notes as *DSM-I* and the like. The complete references appear below:

DSM-I   *Diagnostic and Statistical Manual of Mental Disorders, 1st Edition.* Washington, D.C.: American Psychiatric Association, 1952.

DSM-II   *Diagnostic and Statistical Manual of Mental Disorders, 2nd Edition.* Washington, D.C.: American Psychiatric Association, 1968.

DSM-III   *Diagnostic and Statistical Manual of Mental Disorders, 3rd Edition.* Washington, D.C.: American Psychiatric Association, 1980.

DSM-IIIR   *Diagnostic and Statistical Manual of Mental Disorders, 3rd Edition Revised.* Washington, D.C.: American Psychiatric Association, 1987.

DSM-IV   *Diagnostic and Statistical Manual of Mental Disorders, 4th Edition.* Washington, D.C.: American Psychiatric Association, 1994.

Introduction

1. Murray B. Stein, John R. Walker, and David R. Forde, "Setting Diagnostic Thresholds for Social Phobia: Considerations from a Community Survey of Social Anxiety," *American Journal of Psychiatry* 151.3 (1994), 408. Ronald C. Kessler and his colleagues put the combined percentage for any anxiety disorder at a staggering 28.8, but calculated that social phobia alone afflicts 12.1 percent of the population (roughly one person in eight). See their "Lifetime Prevalence and Age-of-Onset Distributions of *DSM-IV* Disorders in the National Comorbidity Survey Replication," *Archives of General Psychiatry* 62.6 (2005), 593.

2. John H. Greist, James W. Jefferson, and David J. Katzelnick, *Social Anxiety Dis-*

order: A Guide (Madison: Madison Institute of Medicine, 1997, rev. 2000), 2. The authors cite *The Book of Lists,* which claims that public speaking is the number one fear in the U.S. population, while fear of death is sixth.

3. Thomas Jefferson, letter to Martha Jefferson (March 28, 1787), *The Life and Selected Writings of Thomas Jefferson,* ed. Adrienne Koch and William Peden (New York: Random House, 1998), 387.

4. Stein, Walker, and Forde, "Setting Diagnostic Thresholds," 408. In their survey, the upper ceiling of those experiencing "social anxiety syndrome" is 18.7 percent.

5. "Social Phobia," *DSM-IIIR* (300.23), 241.

6. Robert L. Spitzer to the Advisory Committee on Personality Disorders, April 12, 1978. The psychiatrists apparently forgot that a major legal definition of privacy—first invoked in the 1890s, when their own field was undergoing a major shift—is the right "to be let alone." See Samuel Warren and Louis Brandeis, "The Right to Privacy," *Harvard Law Review* 4.5 (1890), 195.

7. Kessler et al., "Lifetime Prevalence and Age-of-Onset Distributions," 593: "About half of Americans will meet the criteria for a *DSM-IV* disorder sometime in their life."

8. Herb Kutchins and Stuart A. Kirk, *Making Us Crazy: DSM: The Psychiatric Bible and the Creation of Mental Disorders* (New York: Free Press, 1997), 22.

9. See Lynne Lamberg, "Social Phobia—Not Just Another Name for Shyness," *Journal of the American Medical Association* 280.8 (August 26, 1998), 685–86, and Claudia Kalb, "Challenging 'Extreme' Shyness," *Newsweek* (July 14, 2003), 47.

10. See Franklin R. Schneier et al., "The Social Anxiety Spectrum," *Psychiatric Clinics of North America* 25.4 (2002), 757–74.

11. Greist, Jefferson, and Katzelnick, *Social Anxiety Disorder,* 7. See also Samuel M. Turner, Deborah C. Beidel, and Ruth M. Townsley, "Social Phobia: Relationship to Shyness," *Behaviour Research and Therapy* 28.6 (1990), 497–505; and Joyce Libal, with Andrew Kleiman, *Antidepressants and Social Anxiety: A Pill for Shyness?* (Philadelphia: Mason Crest Publishers, 2007).

12. Colby Cosh, "You're Not Shy, You're Sick: Psychiatrists Discover a Crippling 'Social Anxiety Disorder' That Affects 13% of Us," *The Report* (June 19, 2000), 49–50.

13. Robert Langreth, "Drugs: Depression Pill May Help Treat the Acutely Shy," *Wall Street Journal* (May 3, 1999); and Elyse Tanouye, "Easing Stage Fright Could Be as Simple as Swallowing a Pill," *Wall Street Journal* (June 30, 1997; eastern ed.).

14. "Disorder of the Decade," *Psychology Today* 26.4 (July–August 1993), 22.

15. The 3.7 percentage is from the National Institute of Mental Health, *http://www. nimh.nih.gov/publicat/phobiafacts.cfm* (accessed June 8, 2006); the 18.7 is from Stein, Walker, and Forde, "Setting Diagnostic Thresholds," 408. The quotation is from David C. Rettew, "Avoidant Personality Disorder, Generalized Social Phobia, and Shyness: Putting the Personality Back into Personality Disorders," *Harvard Review of Psychiatry* 8.6 (2000), 285.

16. Lynne Henderson and Philip Zimbardo, *The Shyness Home Page* (Palto Alto, Calif., 2004): *www.shyness.com/encyclopedia.html* (accessed October 12, 2006).

17. Richard G. Heimberg et al., "The Issue of Subtypes in the Diagnosis of Social Phobia," *Journal of Anxiety Disorders* 7.3 (1993), 266.

18. Robert L. Spitzer and Janet B. W. Williams, "Proposed Revisions in the DSM-III Classification of Anxiety Disorders Based on Research and Clinical Experience," *Anxiety and the Anxiety Disorders,* ed. A. Hussain Tuma and Jack Maser (Hillsdale, N.J.: Lawrence Erlbaum, 1985), 769.

19. The Sunday magazine *Parade* plastered its March 7, 2002, cover with photos of celebrities such as Donny Osmond, Barbra Streisand, Donald Sutherland, Cher, and others apparently suffering from social phobia, then asked readers rather bluntly, "Do You Share Their Fear?"

20. *Oprah,* "People Who Are Afraid of People" (aired March 4, 2003): *http://tapes andtranscripts.oprah.com/product.aspx?ProductID=432848* (accessed October 12, 2006).

21. Barbara G. Markway et al., *Dying of Embarrassment: Help for Social Anxiety and Phobia* (Oakland, Calif.: New Harbinger, 1992); and Signe A. Dayhoff, *Diagonally-Parked in a Parallel Universe: Working through Social Anxiety* (Placitas, N.M.: Effectiveness-Plus, 2000). See also Barbara G. Markway and Gregory P. Markway, *Painfully Shy: How to Overcome Social Anxiety and Reclaim Your Life* (New York: Thomas Dunne, 2001); Bernardo J. Carducci with Lisa Kaiser, *The Shyness Breakthrough: A No-Stress Plan to Help Your Shy Child Warm Up, Open Up, and Join the Fun* (New York: Rodale, 2003); and Martin M. Antony and Richard P. Swinson, *The Shyness and Social Anxiety Workbook: Proven Techniques for Overcoming Your Fears* (Oakland, Calif.: New Harbinger, 2000). The now-classic study of shyness is Philip G. Zimbardo, *Shyness: What It Is, What to Do about It* (Reading, Mass.: Addison-Wesley, 1977).

22. Barry Wolfe, as quoted in "Disorder of the Decade," 22.

23. Isaac Marks, interview by author, November 1, 2005.

24. Michael R. Liebowitz et al., "Social Phobia: Review of a Neglected Anxiety Disorder," *Archives of General Psychiatry* 42.7 (1985), 729–36.

25. See IMS Health Data, *http://www.imshealth.com/ims/portal/front/articleC/0,2777,6599_18731_77056778,00.html* (accessed June 8, 2006).

26. The skit appears at *http://gorillamask.net/gaystrogen.shtml* (accessed August 25, 2006).

27. Emily Dickinson, "After great pain, a formal feeling comes," *The Complete Poems of Emily Dickinson,* ed. Thomas H. Johnson (Boston: Back Bay Books, 1976), 162.

28. Clark Davis, "Outside the Custom-House?: On the Philosophy of Shyness," *Common Knowledge* 12.3 (2006), 410–19.

29. Henry D. Thoreau, *Walden: A Fully Annotated Edition,* ed. Jeffrey S. Cramer (New Haven: Yale University Press, 2004), 88.

1. The Hundred Years' War over Anxiety

1. Jacques Lacan, *The Four Fundamental Concepts of Psycho-Analysis,* ed. Jacques-Alain Miller, trans. Alan Sheridan (1973; New York: Norton, 1981), 41.

2. Sir Thomas More, *A treatyse uppon these wordes of holye scripture* (1525), in *The*

vvorkes of Sir Thomas More Knyght, sometyme Lorde Chauncellour of England, wrytten by him in the Englysh tong (Printed at London: At the costes and charges of Iohn Cawod, Iohn VValy, and Richarde Tottell, 1557), 91.

3. Henry Power and Leonard W. Sedgwick, *The New Sydenham Society's Lexicon of Medicine and the Allied Sciences* (London: The Society, 1879–99), 5 vols., 1:n.pag. "Anxiety": s.v.

4. In addition to the OED, see Fay Bound, "*Anxiety*: Keywords in the History of Medicine," *The Lancet* 363 (April 24, 2004), 1407.

5. Hippocrates, described in Richard Burton, *The Anatomy of Melancholy: What It Is, with All the Kinds, Causes, Symptoms, Prognostics, and Several Cures of It* (1621; London: William Tegg, 1854), 253, also quoted in Isaac M. Marks, *Fears and Phobias* (New York: Academic Press, 1969), 152. Hippocrates's original account appears in *The History of Epidemics, in Seven Books*, trans. Samuel Farr (London: Printed for T. Cadell, 1780).

6. The Hippocrates quotation also appears in John H. Greist, James W. Jefferson, and David J. Katzelnick, *Social Anxiety Disorder: A Guide* (Madison: Madison Institute of Medicine, 1997, rev. 2000), 2–3.

7. Burton, *Anatomy of Melancholy*, 172.

8. Marks, *Fears and Phobias*, 152.

9. Isaac Marks, interview by author, November 1, 2005. Georges Canguilhem amplifies some of the broader consequences of this lost distinction in *The Normal and the Pathological*, trans. Carolyn R. Fawcett with Robert S. Cohen, introd. Michel Foucault (New York: Zone Books, 1991), esp. 275–87. See also Michel Foucault, *Psychiatric Power: Lectures at the Collège de France, 1973–1974*, ed. Jacques Lagrange, trans. Graham Burchell (2003; New York: Palgrave Macmillan, 2006), esp. 265–95.

10. David Healy, *Let Them Eat Prozac: The Unhealthy Relationship between the Pharmaceutical Industry and Depression* (New York: New York University Press, 2004), 264.

11. Charles Darwin, *The Expression of the Emotions in Man and Animals, 3rd Edition* (1872; New York: Oxford University Press, 1998), 329; second bracketed insertion mine.

12. Susan L. McElroy, "Recognition and Treatment of DSM-IV Intermittent Explosive Disorder," *Journal of Clinical Psychiatry* 60, suppl. 15 (1999), 12.

13. Helen Saul, *Phobias: Fighting the Fear* (New York: Arcade Publishing, 2001), 18.

14. Eric Lewin Altschuler et al., "Did Samson Have Antisocial Personality Disorder?," letters to the editor, *Archives of General Psychiatry* 58.2 (2001), 202–3.

15. Søren Kierkegaard, *The Concept of Anxiety: A Simple Psychologically Orienting Deliberation on the Dogmatic Issue of Hereditary Sin*, ed. Reidar Thomte (1844; Princeton: Princeton University Press, 1980).

16. Sharon Begley, "One Pill Makes You Larger, And One Pill Makes You Small," *Newsweek* (February 7, 1994), 1, 37–40; Richard Restak, as quoted on 37.

17. T. M. Luhrmann, *Of Two Minds: An Anthropologist Looks at American Psychiatry* (New York: Vintage, 2000), 286. Ronald W. Dworkin elaborates on this problem in

Artificial Happiness: The Dark Side of the New Happy Class (New York: Carroll and Graf, 2006).

18. Peter D. Kramer, *Listening to Prozac: The Landmark Book about Antidepressants and the Remaking of the Self,* rev. ed. (1993; New York: Penguin, 1997), xvi. See also Kramer, "The New You," *Psychiatric Times* (March 1990), 45–46.

19. Kutaiba Chaleby, "Social Phobia in Saudis," *Social Psychiatry* 22.3 (1987), 167–70; quotation on 169 (emphasis mine). See also Richard Morin, "Shy Nations," *Washington Post* (September 6, 1998). Those referencing Chaleby's essay include Leora R. Heckelman and Franklin R. Schneier, "Diagnostic Issues," *Social Phobia,* ed. Richard G. Heimberg et al. (New York: Guilford Press, 1995), 3–20.

20. Chaleby, "Social Phobia in Saudis," 169, 167.

21. Arthur Kleinman, "Do Psychiatric Disorders Differ in Different Cultures? The Findings," *Rethinking Psychiatry: From Cultural Category to Personal Experience* (New York: Free Press, 1988), 46. For further elaboration on taijin kyofusho, see Raymond Prince and Françoise Tcheng-Laroche, "Culture-Bound Syndromes and International Classification of Disease," *Culture, Medicine and Psychiatry* 11.1 (1987), 3–19; John E. Carr and Peter P. Vitaliano, "The Theoretical Implications of Converging Research on Depression and the Culture-Bound Syndrome," *Culture and Depression: Studies in the Anthropology and Cross-Cultural Psychiatry of Affect and Disorder,* ed. Arthur Kleinman and Byron Good (Berkeley: University of California Press, 1985), 244–66; Hisato Matsunaga et al., "Taijin Kyofusho: A Form of Social Anxiety Disorder That Responds to Serotonin Reuptake Inhibitors?" *International Journal of Neuropsychopharmacology* 4 (2001), 231–37; and Maggie Jones, "Shutting Themselves In," *New York Times Sunday Magazine* (January 15, 2006), 47.

22. Sigmund Freud, "Anxiety," Lecture 25 of the *Introductory Lectures on Psycho-Analysis* (1917), *Standard Edition of the Complete Psychological Works of Sigmund Freud,* ed. and trans. James Strachey (London: Hogarth, 1953–74), 24 vols., 16:393; Darwin, *Expression of the Emotions,* 340. See also Rollo May's classic study *The Meaning of Anxiety,* rev. ed. (1950; New York: Norton, 1977).

23. Greist, Jefferson, and Katzelnick, *Social Anxiety Disorder,* 11.

24. Elliot S. Valenstein, *Blaming the Brain: The Truth about Drugs and Mental Health* (New York: Free Press, 1988), 144, 126, 132, 134, 141.

25. Greist, Jefferson, and Katzelnick, *Social Anxiety Disorder,* 11, 15. See also Marianne Szegedy-Maszak, "Conquering Our Phobias: The Biological Underpinnings of Paralyzing Fears," *U.S. News and World Report* (December 6, 2004): *http://www.usnews.com/usnews/health/articles/041206/6fear.htm* (accessed October 12, 2006).

26. Wilhelm Griesinger, preface to *Archiv für Psychiatrie und Nervenkrankheiten* 1 (1868), iii–iv; idem, *Mental Pathology and Therapeutics, 2nd Edition,* trans. C. Lockhart Robertson and James Rutherford (London: New Sydenham Society, 1867), 1.

27. Emil Kraepelin, *Clinical Psychiatry: A Textbook for Students and Physicians,* rev. ed. abstracted by A. Ross Diefendorf (1902; London: Macmillan, 1921), 115.

28. Arnold I. Davidson, "Closing up the Corpses: Diseases of Sexuality and the

Emergence of the Psychiatric Style of Reasoning," *Homosexuality and Psychoanalysis,* ed. Tim Dean and Christopher Lane (Chicago: University of Chicago Press, 2001), 59–90.

29. Emil Kraepelin, "Lecture 1: Introduction: Melancholia," *Lectures on Clinical Psychiatry,* authorized translation from the second German edition, rev. and trans. Thomas Johnstone (1904; New York: William Wood, 1906), 1 (emphasis in original), xvii, 4, 5.

30. Kraepelin, *Clinical Psychiatry,* 348; idem, *Lectures,* 6.

31. Kraepelin, *Lectures,* 5; emphasis in original.

32. Ibid.; emphasis in original. Part (though by no means all) of what is surfacing here is a crucial distinction between "illness," which is the patient's experience and interpretation of his suffering, and "disease," which is how practitioners explain the symptoms relative to causality, pathology, and treatment. The distinction itself is in question here, not least because the practitioner (Kraepelin) offers a very simplistic explanation of the man's distress. For more on this distinction, see Arthur Kleinman, *The Illness Narratives: Suffering, Healing, and the Human Condition* (New York: Basic Books, 1988), ch. 1, 2.

33. See for instance Sigmund Freud, *Beyond the Pleasure Principle* (1920), *Standard Edition* 18:35–36.

34. Kraepelin, *Clinical Psychiatry,* 115, 116, 115; emphasis mine.

35. An unnamed psychoanalyst, as quoted in Luhrmann, *Of Two Minds,* 227.

36. David Healy, *The Antidepressant Era* (Cambridge, Mass.: Harvard University Press, 1997), 236.

37. Robert L. Spitzer, "A Manual for Diagnosis and Statistics," *The Psychopharmacologists III: Interviews with Dr David Healy* (London: Arnold, 2000), 421. The term *neo-Kraepelian* was Gerald Klerman's.

38. David H. Barlow and Michael R. Liebowitz, "Specific Phobia and Social Phobia," *Comprehensive Textbook of Psychiatry, 6th Edition,* ed. Harold I. Kaplan and Benjamin J. Sadock (Baltimore: Williams and Wilkins, 1995), 2 vols., 1:1213.

39. Hagop S. Akiskal and William T. McKinney, "Psychiatry and Pseudopsychiatry," *Archives of General Psychiatry* 28.3 (1973), 367.

40. Hagop S. Akiskal, "Mood Disorders," *Comprehensive Textbook of Psychiatry, 6th edition,* 1:1069. See also idem, "The Temperamental Foundations of Affective Disorders," *Interpersonal Factors in the Origin and Course of Affective Disorders,* ed. Christoph Mundt et al. (London: Gaskell, 1996), 3–30.

41. Barlow and Liebowitz, "Specific Phobia and Social Phobia," 1:1213.

42. Robert C. Carson, James N. Butcher, and Susan Mineka, eds., *Abnormal Psychology and Modern Life, 10th Edition, 1998 Update* (New York: Longman, 1998), 6–7. Although many books have been published on the problems of establishing and circumscribing cultural and psychological norms, including Michael Warner's *The Trouble with Normal: Sex, Politics, and the Ethics of Queer Life* (New York: Free Press, 1999), it is worth underscoring that William James and John Dewey argued for a broader, more pluralistic understanding of normality in America in the first half of the twentieth

century. See, for instance, James, "The Sick Soul" and "The Divided Self, and the Process of Its Unification," *The Varieties of Religious Experience: A Study in Human Nature* (1901–02; New York: Modern Library, 2002), 144–209; and Dewey, *Human Nature and Conduct: An Introduction* (1922; Kila, Mont.: Kessinger Publishing, 2005), esp. 65, 70.

43. Thomas Henry Burgess, *The Physiology or Mechanism of Blushing, Illustrative of the Influence of Mental Emotion on the Capillary Circulation, with a General View of the Sympathies* (London: John Churchill, 1839). See also Darwin, *Expression of the Emotions,* 335, where Burgess is quoted.

44. Darwin, *Expression of the Emotions,* 335.

45. Ibid.

46. Charles Bell and Alexander Shaw, *The Anatomy and Philosophy of Expression as Connected with the Fine Arts,* 3rd ed. (London: H. G. Bohn, 1844), as quoted in Darwin, *Expression of the Emotions,* 335. But Bell joined Burgess in thinking that our facial muscles are divinely created to convey feelings that separate us from other mammals. Although Darwin approved of Bell's point about surrogate expression, on the broader meaning of shyness they sharply disagreed.

47. Darwin, *Expression of the Emotions,* 324, 321. The scene is oddly reminiscent of the wincingly "wrong" after-dinner speech Mr. Dorrit gives in *Little Dorrit,* published two decades earlier. After lapsing into a trance, he stands to address Europe's elite at Mrs. Merdle's banquet, but welcomes them to the Marshalsea prison as if they were the debtors and criminals he'd earlier befriended. Charles Dickens, *Little Dorrit* (1857; Harmondsworth: Penguin, 1998), bk. 2, ch. 19, titled significantly "The Storming of the Castle in the Air."

48. Darwin, *Expression of the Emotions,* 340. For instance, he quotes Coleridge's comment on the blush: "account for that he who can." Samuel Taylor Coleridge, *Specimens of the Table Talk of the Late Samuel Taylor Coleridge* (London: John Murray, 1835), 2 vols., vol. 1, as quoted in Darwin, 325.

49. Carl Westphal, "Die Agoraphobie, eine neuropathische Erscheinung," *Archiv für Psychiatrie und Nervenkrankheiten* 3 (1871–72), 138–61; Pierre Janet, *Les Obsessions et la psychasthénie* (Paris: Félix Alcan, 1903), 2 vols., 1:205. For an excellent overview of this history, see R. P. Snaith, "A Clinical Investigation of Phobias," *British Journal of Psychiatry* 114 (1968), 673–97, and Edward Shorter, *A History of Psychiatry: From the Era of the Asylum to the Age of Prozac* (New York: John Wiley, 1997), esp. 81–87.

50. Janet, *Les Obsessions,* 1:210.

51. Paul Hartenberg, *Les Timides et la timidité* (Paris: Félix Alcan, 1901), 186, 188. The original reads "*La timidité pathologique réalise à la fois une maladie de l'émotivité et une maladie de la volonté*" (188).

52. The sole exception I could find is Nichole Fairbrother's essay "The Treatment of Social Phobia—100 Years Ago," *Behaviour Research and Therapy* 40.11 (2002), 1291–304, which argues (incorrectly, in my opinion) that Hartenberg's approach is similar to that of cognitive-behavioral therapy.

53. Hartenberg, *Les Timides*, 217, 158, 180.

54. Sigmund Freud, "The Justification for Detaching from Neurasthenia a Particular Syndrome: The Anxiety-Neurosis" (1894), *Freud: Early Psychoanalytic Writings*, ed. and introd. Philip Rieff, trans. John Rickman (New York: Collier, 1963), 112–13; emphasis in original. The essay also appears in *Standard Edition* 3:90–117, in a rather less elegant translation.

55. Adam Phillips, "Worrying and Its Discontents," *On Kissing, Tickling, and Being Bored: Psychoanalytic Essays on the Unexamined Life* (Cambridge, Mass.: Harvard University Press, 1993), 50.

56. Charles Shepherdson, foreword to Roberto Harari, *Lacan's Seminar on "Anxiety": An Introduction,* trans. Jane C. Lamb-Ruiz, rev. and ed. Rico Franses (New York: Other Press, 2001), xv. See also Jacques Lacan, *Le Séminaire, livre X: L'angoisse (1962–63),* texte établi par Jacques-Alain Miller (Paris: Seuil, 2004).

57. Freud, "Justification for Detaching," 93, 94.

58. Sigmund Freud, *Three Essays on the Theory of Sexuality* (1905, rev. 1920), *Standard Edition* 7:224n.

59. Freud, "Justification for Detaching," 95–96; emphasis mine.

60. Freud, "Anxiety," 16:393.

61. Shepherdson, foreword, xxx.

62. Sigmund Freud, *Civilization and Its Discontents* (1929, 1930), *Standard Edition* 21:135.

63. Sigmund Freud, *Inhibitions, Symptoms and Anxiety* (1926), *Standard Edition* 20:140.

64. Freud, *Civilization and Its Discontents,* 21:125.

65. Charles J. Rolo, "The Freudian Revolution," *Atlantic Monthly* 208.1, suppl.: "Psychiatry in American Life" (July 1961), 62. See also John R. Seeley, "The Americanization of the Unconscious," in the same issue, 68–72.

66. Norman E. Zinberg, "Psychiatry: A Professional Dilemma," *Daedalus* 92.4 (Fall 1963), 810.

67. Mitchell Wilson, "DSM-III and the Transformation of American Psychiatry: A History," *American Journal of Psychiatry* 150.3 (1993), 400.

68. Donald Klein, as quoted in Alix Spiegel, "The Dictionary of Disorder: How One Man Revolutionized Psychiatry," *New Yorker* (January 3, 2005), 58.

69. Dean and Lane, *Homosexuality and Psychoanalysis,* 12–13.

70. *Trends and Issues in Psychiatric Residency Programs: Report 31* (Topeka, Kans.: Group for the Advancement of Psychiatry, 1955), 1.

71. Healey, *Antidepressant Era,* 66.

72. Ibid., 46.

73. See Robert L. Spitzer and Paul T. Wilson, "A Guide to the American Psychiatric Association's New Diagnostic Nomenclature," *American Journal of Psychiatry* 124.12 (June 1968), 1620.

74. Robert L. Spitzer, interview by author, February 22, 2006.

2. The Diagnostic Battles

1. Alix Spiegel, "The Dictionary of Disorder: How One Man Revolutionized Psychiatry," *New Yorker* (January 3, 2005), 56.

2. Herb Kutchins and Stuart A. Kirk, *Making Us Crazy: DSM: The Psychiatric Bible and the Creation of Mental Disorders* (New York: Free Press, 1997), 40.

3. D. L. Rosenhan, "On Being Sane in Insane Places," *Science* 179 (n.s.; January 19, 1973), 251, 252.

4. T. M. Luhrmann, *Of Two Minds: An Anthropologist Looks at American Psychiatry* (New York: Vintage, 2000), 224.

5. For a significant account of this problem, see Joel Paris, *The Fall of an Icon: Psychoanalysis and Academic Psychiatry* (Toronto: University of Toronto Press, 2005). Blue Cross in fact reduced its psychiatric coverage in the mid-1970s to 20 outpatient visits and 45 inpatient hospital days per year on grounds that clearly favored neuropsychiatry over psychoanalysis. As its vice president explained, "Compared to other types of [mental health] services [the psychotherapeutic model offers] less clarity and uniformity of terminology concerning mental diagnosis, treatment modalities, and types of facilities providing care. . . . One dimension of this problem . . . arises from the latent or private nature of many services; only the patient and the therapist have direct knowledge of what services were provided, and why." "Blue Cross VP [Robert J. Laur] Says MH Prospects Cloudy," *Psychiatric News* (August 6, 1975), 1, 6, 7.

6. Melvin Sabshin, as quoted in Leslie Knowlton, "Melvin Sabshin: A Profile," *Psychiatric Times* 15.5 (May 1998). The point here is not that psychoanalytic practice had no interest in description, simply that neuropsychiatrists and managed-care companies viewed it as operating according to loose empirical guidelines. For elaboration on matters of psychiatric description and diagnosis, see Karl Jaspers, *General Psychopathology*, trans. J. Hoenig and Marian W. Hamilton (1948; Chicago: University of Chicago Press, 1963).

7. *ICD-9* was published in May 1978, two years before *DSM-III*.

8. Although the phrase mirrors Sabshin's approach, it is actually that of Robert L. Spitzer and his coauthors in Spitzer, Michael Sheehy, and Jean Endicott, "*DSM-III:* Guiding Principles," *Psychiatric Diagnosis*, ed. Vivian M. Rakoff, Harvey C. Stancer, and Henry B. Kedward (New York: Brunner/Mazel, 1977), 1. See also Allen Frances and Arnold M. Cooper, "Descriptive and Dynamic Psychiatry: A Perspective on *DSM-III*," *American Journal of Psychiatry* 138.9 (1981), 1198–202.

9. Robert L. Spitzer, interview by author, February 22, 2006.

10. Spiegel, "Dictionary of Disorder."

11. Spitzer, interview; and Wilhelm Reich, *Character Analysis*, 3rd ed., trans. Theodore P. Wolfe (1933; New York: Orgone Institute, 1949), 165.

12. Spitzer, interview. He adds, with regret, that he didn't keep the letter.

13. Ibid.

14. Many psychiatrists (including Spitzer) had sided with gay rights groups in argu-

ing that homosexuality should no longer be considered a mental illness. Disagreeing vehemently, other psychiatrists resisted this move. As neither side would back down, the wrangle dragged on for several years, spilling into *DSM-III* discussions. Although the conservative psychiatrists ended up losing that battle, Spitzer came up with a compromise term ("Sexual Orientation Disturbance"); although imperfect to both sides, it nonetheless paved the way for a more constructive dialogue. Indeed, by 1977 the discussion had shifted to ego-dystonic homosexuality, the term finally appearing in *DSM-III*. Even so, a large number of psychiatrists petitioned for its removal, on the grounds that it appeared to pathologize "homosexual arousal." See "Ego-dystonic Homosexuality," *DSM-III* (302.00), 281; and Ronald Bayer, *Homosexuality and American Psychiatry: The Politics of Diagnosis* (New York: Basic Books, 1981).

15. Allen Frances, as quoted in Spiegel, "Dictionary of Disorder," 60.

16. Donald F. Klein, as quoted in ibid., 58.

17. All but two of the task force were male, though Jean Endicott and Rachel Gittelman joined a group of four outside consultants. The principal members ultimately were Robert L. Spitzer (chair), Nancy Andreasen, Robert L. Arnstein, Dennis Cantwell, Paula J. Clayton, William A. Frosch, Donald W. Goodwin, Donald F. Klein, Z. J. Lipowski, Michael L. Mavroidis, Henry Pinsker, George Saslow, Michael Sheehy, Robert Woodruff, and Lyman C. Wynne. Consultants in addition to Endicott and Gittelman were Morton Kramer and Theodore Millon. Woodruff died before *DSM-III* appeared.

18. David Healy, *The Antidepressant Era* (Cambridge, Mass.: Harvard University Press, 1997), 237.

19. David Healy, *Let Them Eat Prozac: The Unhealthy Relationship between the Pharmaceutical Industry and Depression* (New York: New York University Press, 2004), 2; emphasis in original.

20. Spitzer, undated interview by Ray Moynihan, quoted in Moynihan and Alan Cassels, *Selling Sickness: How the World's Biggest Pharmaceutical Companies Are Turning Us All into Patients* (New York: Nation Books, 2005), 108.

21. Peele to Spitzer, June 4, 1979. From the highly condensed and rather self-flattering version of events that Spitzer coauthored with Ronald Bayer, "Neurosis, Psychodynamics, and *DSM-III*: A History of the Controversy," *Archives of General Psychiatry* 42.2 (1985), 187–96, one would know only a fraction of the arguments documented by the unpublished correspondence.

22. Theodore Millon, as quoted in Spiegel, "Dictionary of Disorder," 59.

23. David Shaffer, as quoted in ibid.

24. An unidentified participant, as quoted in ibid.

25. Klein to Spitzer, March 29, 1978, entitled "Emotionally Unstable Character Disorder."

26. Spitzer to Klein, April 5, 1978. The letter is entitled "Emotionally Unstable Character Disorder—Revisited Once Again."

27. Spitzer to Klein, February 27, 1978.

28. Jean Endicott, as quoted in Spiegel, "Dictionary of Disorder," 60.

29. Renee Garfinkel, as quoted in Jamie Talan, "Diagnosis by the Book: Controversy over Revisions of the Manual Psychiatrists Use," *Newsday* (March 11, 1986).

30. Leonore Walker, as quoted in ibid.

31. Irwin H. Marill et al. to Peele, June 6, 1977.

32. Waugh to Spitzer, July 11, 1975.

33. N. S. Lehrman, "'Borderline Personality Disorders' Should Be Discarded (The Emperor's New Jockstrap)," unpublished, 9, 10.

34. Spitzer, interview by author.

35. Fink to Grinspoon, May 15, 1978.

36. Spitzer, interview by author.

37. Ibid.

38. L. J. Davis, "The Encyclopedia of Insanity: A Psychiatric Handbook Lists a Madness for Everyone," *Harper's Magazine* (February 1997), 61–66; and Peter T. Janulis, "Tribute to a Word: Neurosis," *Archives of General Psychiatry* 39.5 (1982), 623. See also David Gelman, "Beyond Neurosis," *Newsweek* (January 8, 1979), 68.

39. Editorial, "Goodbye Neurosis?" *The Lancet* 2.8288 (July 3, 1982), 29.

40. Robert L. Spitzer, Andrew E. Skodol, and Miriam Gibbon, "Reply," *Archives of General Psychiatry* 39.5 (1982), 623–24.

41. Healy, *Antidepressant Era*, 233.

42. William A. Frosch, telephone interview, August 18, 1989, as quoted in Mitchell Wilson, "DSM-III and the Transformation of American Psychiatry: A History," *American Journal of Psychiatry* 150.3 (March 1993), 407.

43. Otto Kernberg, as quoted in Healy, *Antidepressant Era*, 234.

44. Spitzer, interview by author.

45. Richard G. Heimberg et al., "The Issue of Subtypes in the Diagnosis of Social Phobia," *Journal of Anxiety Disorders* 7.3 (1993), 263, 265.

46. Ronald C. Kessler et al., "Mild Disorders Should Not Be Eliminated from the *DSM-V*," *Archives of General Psychiatry* 60.11 (2003), 1118.

47. Spitzer, interview by author.

48. Ibid.

49. Spitzer to Sachar and Klein, July 12, 1977. The one-sentence letter, prefacing Spitzer's July 8 "invitation" to Thomas Lynch, president of the Baltimore–District of Columbia Society of Psychoanalysis, for "input into the further development of DSM-III," reads simply: "You may enjoy the enclosed as an example of my strategy of entrapment."

50. Spiegel, "Dictionary of Disorder," 59–60.

51. Shaffer, as quoted in ibid., 59.

52. Fink to Grinspoon, May 15, 1978.

53. Robert L. Spitzer, "A Manual for Diagnosis and Statistics," *Psychopharmacologists III:* Interviews with Dr David Healy (London: Arnold, 2000), 418; Spitzer, interview by Mitchell Wilson, September 17, 1989, as quoted in Wilson, "DSM-III and the Transformation," 404; and Bayer and Spitzer, "Neurosis, Psychodynamics, and *DSM-III*," 188.

54. Spitzer, "Manual for Diagnosis and Statistics," 424.

55. Klein, as quoted in Spiegel, "Dictionary of Disorder," 61.

56. Spitzer, interview by author.

57. See his reply to Leo Madow, January 30, 1978, which unfortunately is much too long to reproduce, but which outlines a number of responses to Rockland's work and its implications for the task force.

58. See Benedict Carey, "For Therapy, A New Guide With a Touch of Personality," *New York Times* (January 24, 2006), on the Alliance of Psychoanalytic Organizations' recently published *Psychodynamic Diagnostic Manual* (Silver Spring, Md.: Psychodynamic Diagnostic Manual, 2006).

59. Lawrence Rockland, "Some Thoughts on the Subject: Should Psychodynamics Be Included in the DSM III?" (unpublished and undated, c. January 1978).

60. Madow to Spitzer, January 4, 1978.

61. Spitzer, interview by author.

62. Hector Jaso and Howard E. Berk, Memo to the Task Force, June 11, 1976.

63. Spitzer, "Manual for Diagnosis and Statistics," 424.

64. Ibid., 427.

65. See for instance the memo from Millon to Spitzer, "On Neuroses," September 18, 1974. Also Millais Culpin, "The Conception of Nervous Disorder," *British Journal of Medical Psychology* 35 (1962), 73–80.

66. Minutes of the September 4, 1974, meeting of the Task Force on Nomenclature and Statistics, as quoted in Wilson, "DSM-III and the Transformation," 405.

67. Wilson, "DSM-III and the Transformation," 406. See also Stuart A. Kirk and Herb Kutchins, *The Selling of DSM: The Rhetoric of Science in Psychiatry* (New York: de Gruyter, 1992), 103–5.

68. Spitzer, "Manual for Diagnosis and Statistics," 424–25.

69. Spitzer, as quoted in Spiegel, "Dictionary of Disorder," 59.

70. Spitzer, Memo to Task Force Members, April 2, 1979, entitled "The Beginning of the End, Neurotic Disorders and My Neurotic Behavior"; Spitzer, Memo to Task Force Members, April 25, 1979, entitled "Our Travails Never Seem to End"; and Spitzer, Memo to the Assembly Liaison, Joint American Psychoanalytic Association, and American Academy of Psychoanalysis Committees, March 27, 1979, entitled "April 7th Meeting and Possible Neurotic Peace Treaty."

71. Spitzer to Task Force Members, April 25, 1979; Masserman to H. Keith Brodie, April 24, 1979.

72. Spitzer, "Manual for Diagnosis and Statistics," 424.

73. Alvan R. Feinstein, "A Critical Overview of Diagnosis in Psychiatry," paper presented at the Fourth C. M. Hincks Memorial Lectures, Toronto, November 19, 1976.

74. Spitzer to Quen, February 19, 1976.

75. Robert L. Spitzer and Paul T. Wilson, "Classification and Nosology in Psychiatry and the Diagnostic and Statistical Manual of the American Psychiatric Association," unpublished (courtesy of Spitzer). The intriguing epigraph was deleted in the published version, "Nosology and the Official Psychiatric Nomenclature," *Comprehensive*

Textbook of Psychiatry, 2nd Edition, ed. Alfred M. Freedman, Harold I. Kaplan, and Benjamin J. Sadock (Baltimore: Williams and Wilkins, 1975), 1:826–45.

76. Jules H. Masserman, "On Indefinite Definitions," *The Proposed DSM-III: Critiques by Participants of the Conference on "Improvements in Psychiatric Classification and Terminology: A Working Conference to Critically Examine DSM-III in Midstream"* (St. Louis, June 1976), 7d; and Lehrman, "'Borderline Personality Disorders,'" 9–10, 4–5.

77. John Frosch to Spitzer, December 4, 1978.

78. Bayer and Spitzer, "Neurosis, Psychodynamics, and *DSM-III*," 190.

79. Ibid. The authors' own footnotes here refer to two unpublished interviews with the Frosches in May and June 1982.

80. John Frosch to Spitzer, December 4, 1978.

81. Spitzer, interview by author.

82. Pardes to Grinspoon, May 19, 1978.

83. Spitzer, "Manual for Diagnosis and Statistics," 419.

84. Ibid., 421.

85. See for instance David Dorosin to Spitzer, May 17, 1976.

86. Wilson, "DSM-III and the Transformation," 404.

87. John P. Feighner et al., "Diagnostic Criteria for Use in Psychiatric Research," *Archives of General Psychiatry* 26.1 (1972), 59. Robert A. Woodruff, one of the authors, later served on the DSM-III task force.

88. Ibid., 57.

89. Bayer and Spitzer, "Neurosis, Psychodynamics, and *DSM-III*," 188.

90. Gerald L. Klerman, "The Advantages of *DSM-III*," in "A Debate on *DSM-III*" with George E. Vaillant, Robert L. Spitzer, and Robert Michels, *American Journal of Psychiatry* 141.4 (1984), 541.

91. Spitzer, interview by author.

92. Spitzer to Professor Sir Martin Roth, June 3, 1976.

93. Donald F. Klein, "Definition of Disorder," *The Proposed DSM-III: Critiques,* 1d.

94. Jaso and Berk, Memo to the Task Force, June 11, 1976.

95. Chodoff to Spitzer, June 16, 1976.

96. Richard A. Schwartz, "Personality Disorders," *The Proposed DSM-III: Critiques,* 8d.

97. Pinsker to Members of the Task Force on Nomenclature and Statistics, June 4, 1975.

98. Madow to Grinspoon, September 14, 1978. Stanford's David Dorosin also concluded to Spitzer, "In our search for a 'truth and reliability in diagnosis' nosology, I'm still not convinced that we have to go back as far as Kraepelin to maintain the integrity of a profession with our range and depth of responsibilities in contemporary society" (Dorosin to Spitzer, May 17, 1976).

99. Spitzer to Offenkrantz and Jaso, March 19, 1979.

100. Spitzer to Task Force Members, April 2, 1979.

101. Jaso and Berk, Memo to the Task Force, June 11, 1976.

102. See, in particular, Robert L. Spitzer and Jerome C. Wakefield, "DSM-IV Diagnostic Criterion for Clinical Significance: Does It Help Solve the False Positives Problem?" *American Journal of Psychiatry* 156.12 (1999), 1856–64.

103. George E. Vaillant, "The Disadvantages of *DSM-III* Outweigh Its Advantages," *American Journal of Psychiatry* 141.4 (1984), 545.

104. Marill et al. to Peele, June 6, 1977; emphasis in original.

105. Klein, "Definition of Disorder," id.

106. Marill et al. to Peele, June 6, 1977.

107. Spitzer, interview by author.

108. Concerning the term *labile personality,* Arthur Rifkin wrote to Spitzer, June 30, 1978: "You ask if this should be considered for personality disorder or affective illness. My honest answer is to send it to both groups. Maybe one will buy it." For discussion of the proposed term "malingering," see Steven E. Hyler to Spitzer, May 17, 1978.

109. Steven E. Hyler, "Chronic Undifferentiated Unhappiness" (CUU) and "Chronic Complaint Disorder" (CCD), which Spitzer forwarded to the task force for consideration on May 10, 1977. His cover letter reads, doubtless with some irony, "Enclosed are draft versions of two new disorders for possible inclusion in DSM-III . . . It is gratifying to see that the methodology that we have so painstakingly developed for the 'traditional' disorders, applies equally well to disorders yet awaiting discovery."

110. "Academic Problem," "Marital Problem," and "Other Interpersonal Problem," *DSM-III* (V62.30, V61.10, V62.81), respectively 332, 333, and 334.

111. Jules H. Masserman, "A Critique of the Current Version of DSM-III," unpublished paper appended to his April 11, 1979, letter to Boyd L. Burris.

112. Healy, *Antidepressant Era,* 175.

113. Luhrmann, *Of Two Minds,* 54.

114. Ibid., 229. See also Kirk and Kutchins, *Selling of DSM,* esp. 56–63.

115. Kutchins and Kirk, *Making Us Crazy,* 244.

116. Spitzer, interview by author.

117. Barlow to Spitzer, July 26, 1985.

118. Healy, *Antidepressant Era,* 175.

119. David Faust and Richard A. Miner, "The Empiricist and His New Clothes: *DSM-III* in Perspective," *American Journal of Psychiatry* 143.8 (1986): 962–67.

120. Marill et al. to Peele, June 6, 1977.

3. A Decisive Victory

1. David Healy, *The Antidepressant Era* (Cambridge, Mass.: Harvard University Press, 1997), 188.

2. Pierre Janet, *Les Obsessions et la psychasthénie* (Paris: Félix Alcan, 1903), 2 vols., 1:210; I. M. Marks and M. G. Gelder, "Different Ages of Onset in Varieties of Phobia," *American Journal of Psychiatry* 123.2 (August 1966), 218.

3. Marks and Gelder, "Different Ages of Onset," 218.

4. Ibid., 220. Based on the different ages of onset for such phobias and their lim-

ited symptoms, however, they did suggest that "there is heuristic value in classifying phobias of animate objects separate from the other varieties of phobia." It was a recommendation that might have led to a specific subtype of "anxiety neurosis" in the *DSM*.

5. See for instance Kutaiba Chaleby, "Social Phobia in Saudis," *Social Psychiatry* 22.3 (1987), 167.

6. I. M. Marks, "The Classification of Phobic Disorders," *British Journal of Psychiatry* 116.533 (April 1970), 386, 383.

7. Chaleby, "Social Phobia in Saudis," 167.

8. Eliot Slater and Martin Roth, *Clinical Psychiatry, 3rd Edition* (Baltimore: Williams and Wilkins, 1969), 95–96; and R. P. Snaith, "A Clinical Investigation of Phobias," *British Journal of Psychiatry* 114 (June 1968), 673–97, esp. 693. See also F. Kräupl Taylor, *Psychopathology: Its Causes and Symptoms, Revised Edition* (1966; Baltimore: Johns Hopkins University Press, 1979), 160.

9. I. M. Marks, *Fears and Phobias* (New York: Academic Press, 1969), 152; and Marks, interview by author, November 1, 2005.

10. Healy, *Antidepressant Era,* 188.

11. Colby Cosh, "You're Not Shy, You're Sick: Psychiatrists Discover a Crippling 'Social Anxiety Disorder' That Affects 13% of Us," *The Report* (June 19, 2000), 49–50; Michael R. Liebowitz et al., "Social Phobia: Review of a Neglected Disorder," *Archives of General Psychiatry* 42 (July 1985), 729–36; and "Disorder of the Decade," *Psychology Today* 26.4 (July/August 1993), 22.

12. Healy, *Antidepressant Era,* 188.

13. "Social Phobia," *DSM-III* (300.23), 228: "Prevalence: The disorder is apparently relatively rare."

14. Healy, *Antidepressant Era,* 188. See also Liebowitz et al., "Social Phobia."

15. Robert L. Spitzer, "A Manual for Diagnosis and Statistics," *The Psychopharmacologists III: Interviews with Dr David Healy* (London: Arnold, 2000), 424–25.

16. Spitzer to William Offenkrantz and Hector Jaso, March 19, 1979.

17. N. S. Lehrman, "'Borderline Personality Disorders' Should Be Discarded (The Emperor's New Jockstrap)," unpublished, 7.

18. Spitzer to Klein, February 27, 1978.

19. Marks, interview.

20. Marks to Spitzer, March 25, 1986.

21. Marks, interview.

22. All of the remarks quoted above are from Spitzer, interview by author, February 22, 2006.

23. Spitzer, "Manual for Diagnosis and Statistics," 419.

24. Healy, *Antidepressant Era,* 193.

25. Spitzer, interview.

26. I elaborate on this point in my previous book, *Hatred and Civility: The Antisocial Life in Victorian England* (New York: Columbia University Press, 2004 and 2006), esp. xiii–xxviii, 1–33.

27. Spitzer, interview.

28. Klein, telephone interview August 18, 1989, as quoted in Mitchell Wilson, "DSM-III and the Transformation of American Psychiatry: A History," *American Journal of Psychiatry* 150.3 (1993), 407. He had earlier told Spitzer (in a March 7, 1978, memo entitled "DSM-III Classification"): "I'm not happy to find that category IV is more or less analogous to traditional neuroses. In fact, it seems to me that's leading with your chin."

29. Klein to Spitzer, July 17, 1985, entitled "A Criteria [*sic*] for Panic Disorder."

30. Peter D. Kramer, *Listening to Prozac: The Landmark Book about Antidepressants and the Remaking of the Self*, rev. ed. (1993; New York: Penguin, 1997), 15.

31. Quenk to Spitzer, March 5, 1978. Another critic was Robert J. McCarthy, writing to Spitzer on March 3, 1978.

32. Will to Spitzer, March 15, 1978; Crowley to Spitzer, February 16, 1978.

33. Klein to Spitzer, March 7 and April 4, 1978.

34. See for instance Spitzer's reply to Klein, quoted at note 18, where the "intensive case study" forming the basis of a field trial concerned just one patient he had monitored intensively.

35. "Schizoid Personality," *DSM-I* (000-x42), 35.

36. "Schizoid Personality," *DSM-II* (301.2), 42.

37. Spitzer to unnamed colleagues, March 19, 1985.

38. Spitzer to Mary H. McCaulley, April 6, 1978; emphasis mine.

39. Ibid.

40. Kirsch to Spitzer, March 3, 1978.

41. Ray Moynihan and Alan Cassels give a compelling history of the term's partial inclusion in the *DSM* in *Selling Sickness: How the World's Biggest Pharmaceutical Companies Are Turning Us All into Patients* (New York: Nation Books, 2005), 107–18. See also Joan C. Chrisler and Paula Caplan, "The Strange Case of Dr. Jekyll and Ms. Hyde: How PMS Became a Cultural Phenomenon and a Psychiatric Disorder," *American Review of Sex Research* 13 (2002), 274–306. The article first outlining the new category is Robert L. Spitzer et al., "Late Luteal Phase Dysphoric Disorder and *DSM-III-R*," *American Journal of Psychiatry* 146.7 (1989), 892–97.

42. Spitzer to McCaulley.

43. McCaulley to Spitzer, March 21, 1978.

44. Ibid.

45. Will to Spitzer, March 15, 1978.

46. Spitzer to Will, March 29, 1978.

47. Spitzer to the Advisory Committee on Personality Disorders, Drs. Rachel Gittelman and Richard Jenkins, April 12, 1978. The subject header is "Introverted Personality Disorder, Introverted Disorder of Children, and Jungian Psychology."

48. Chappell to Spitzer, April 13, 1978; second emphasis mine.

49. In 1781, for instance, the poet William Cowper glossed the effects of "self-searching with an introverted eye," an idea William Hazlitt echoed in 1822; eight years later, Henry Coleridge was writing that "the mind of the old poets"—unlike those of his

contemporaries—"was rarely introverted on itself." See William Cowper, *Conversation* (1781; London: Wright and Albright, 1840), 35; William Hazlitt, "On the Pleasure of Painting," *Table Talk: Opinions on Books, Men, and Things* (New York: Wiley and Putnam, 1845), 2 vols., 1:6; and Henry N. Coleridge, *Introductions to the Study of the Greek Classic Poets* (1830; London: John Murray, 1846), 3rd ed., 22.

50. Lion to Spitzer, April 14, 1978.

51. Klein to Spitzer, April 21, 1978.

52. Spitzer, "TO ALL THOSE WHO HAVE EXPRESSED THEIR CONCERN ABOUT THE INCLUSION OF INTROVERTED PERSONALITY DISORDERS," April 20, 1978.

53. Frances to Spitzer, April 17, 1978.

54. Klein to Spitzer, May 8, 1978.

55. Klein to Spitzer, August 4, 1978.

56. Klein to Spitzer, May 8, 1978.

57. Madow to Spitzer, January 4, 1978.

58. James A. Hall, president of the Inter-Regional Society of Jungian Analysts, to Spitzer, May 2, 1978.

59. Millon to the Advisory Committee on Personality Disorders, June 28, 1978.

60. MacKinnon to the Advisory Committee on Personality Disorders, May 22, 1978.

61. See "Schizoid Personality Disorder," *DSM-III* (301.20), 310.

62. Hyler to Spitzer, May 3, 1978.

63. Arnstein to the Advisory Committee on Personality Disorders, June 15, 1978.

64. Finney to Spitzer, July 31, 1978.

65. Elder to Spitzer, July 11, 1978; and Santiago to Spitzer, c. June 1978.

66. Spitzer to Elder, July 20, 1978.

67. Forman to Hall, December 8, 1978.

68. Spitzer to the Advisory Committee on Personality Disorders, Drs. Gittelman and Jenkins, April 12, 1978; emphasis mine.

69. "Schizoid Personality Disorder," *DSM-III* (301.20), 311.

70. "Schizoid Personality Disorder," *DSM-IIIR* (301.20), 340.

71. "Schizoid Personality Disorder," *DSM-III* (301.20), 310.

72. The same incremental logic would rapidly infiltrate the U.S. Food and Drug Administration. Once a drug had been approved to treat, say, panic disorder, it was much easier (and far less costly and time-consuming) to license it for additional disorders such as social phobia and depression, than to review a brand-new drug. As the FDA tends to evaluate drugs on the basis of comparative efficacy with existing treatments, arguably it was already predisposed to the "new psychiatry." Certainly the drug companies, which many critics complain have a cozy relationship with this agency, were quick to seize on the economic benefits of proceeding in this way. They found it far more lucrative to nudge through "me-too" drugs with minor molecular variants than to start each review from scratch and put a new drug through a host of clinical trials and comparative studies, some of which might yield results so unfavorable that the drug would have to go back into development.

73. Lion to Spitzer, April 14, 1978.

74. Klein to Spitzer, May 8, 1978.

75. Anonymous vote on "Introverted Personality Disorder," April 12, 1978.

76. See for instance Richard G. Heimberg et al., "The Issue of Subtypes in the Diagnosis of Social Phobia," *Journal of Anxiety Disorders* 7.3 (1993), 249–69.

77. Betty Friedan, *The Feminine Mystique* (1963; New York: Norton, 2001), 15.

78. Ibid.

79. Michael R. Liebowitz, interview by author, May 7, 2005.

80. David Healy, interview by author, October 9, 2005.

81. Spitzer to the Advisory Committee on Personality Disorders, Drs. Gittelman and Jenkins, April 12, 1978.

82. Millon to the Advisory Committee on Personality Disorders, June 28, 1978.

83. Klein, "Definition of Disorder," *The Proposed DSM-III: Critiques by Participants of the Conference on "Improvements in Psychiatric Classification and Terminology: A Working Conference to Critically Examine DSM-III in Midstream"* (St. Louis: June 1976), 1d.

84. MacKinnon to the Advisory Committee on Personality Disorders, May 17, 1978.

85. Klein to Spitzer, February 23, 1978.

86. Klein to the Advisory Committee on Personality Disorders, April 5, 1978.

87. Millon to Spitzer, March 21, 1978. Spitzer heeded Millon's first recommendation but quietly ignored the second (*DSM-III* acknowledges Millon's role elsewhere, but not on that committee).

88. Frances to the Advisory Committee on Personality Disorders, c. May 1978 (curiously, the document is undated).

89. Klein to Spitzer, May 17, 1978.

90. Lion to the Advisory Committee on Personality Disorders, May 1, 1978. See also Roy Jenkins to Spitzer, May 16, 1978: "I feel that avoidant personality should be grouped together with introverted and schizotypal personality for easier comparison of diagnostic criteria, since all three are similar."

91. Klein to Spitzer, May 17 and August 4, 1978.

92. "Avoidant Personality Disorder," *DSM-III* (301.82), 323.

93. Ibid.

94. Spitzer, interview.

95. Minutes of the DSM-IIIR Anxiety Disorders meeting October 4–5, 1984.

96. Liebowitz, interview.

97. "Avoidant Personality Disorder," *DSM-IV* (301.82), 664.

98. Michael R. Liebowitz et al., "Social Phobia or Social Anxiety Disorder: What's in a Name?" letter, *Archives of General Psychiatry* 57.2 (2000), 191–92.

99. "Patient Testimonials Reintroduce an Old Drug in a New Market," *PR News* 56.20 (May 15, 2000), 1.

100. Liebowitz et al., "Social Phobia or Social Anxiety Disorder," 192.

101. "Social Phobia," *DSM-III* (300.23), 228.

102. Liebowitz to Spitzer, March 31, 1986.

103. "Social Phobia," *DSM-IIIR* (300.23), 242; emphasis mine.

104. Ibid.; Liebowitz et al., "Social Phobia or Social Anxiety Disorder," 192.

105. "Social Phobia," *DSM-IIIR* (300.23), 242.

106. "Social Phobia," *DSM-III* (300.23), 227.

107. "Social Phobia," *DSM-IIIR* (300.23), 241; emphasis mine.

108. David C. Rettew, "Avoidant Personality Disorder, Generalized Social Phobia, and Shyness: Putting the Personality Back into Personality Disorders," *Harvard Review of Psychiatry* 8.6 (December 2000), 285.

109. Liebowitz, interview.

110. Murray B. Stein, quoted in Shankar Vedantam, "Drug Ads Hyping Anxiety Make Some Uneasy," *Washington Post* (July 16, 2001).

111. Ibid.

112. Healy, interview.

113. Murray B. Stein, "How Shy Is Too Shy?" *The Lancet* 347.9009 (April 27, 1996), 1131.

114. Murray B. Stein, John R. Walker, and David R. Forde, "Setting Diagnostic Thresholds for Social Phobia: Considerations from a Community Survey of Social Anxiety," *American Journal of Psychiatry* 151.3 (1994), 408.

115. Ibid.

116. Michael R. Liebowitz, "Pharmacotherapy of Social Phobia," *Journal of Clinical Psychiatry* 54.12 (suppl.; December 1993), 32.

117. The first percentage is from the National Institute of Mental Health, *http://www.nimh.nih.gov/publicat/phobiafacts.cfm* (accessed June 22, 2006); the second is from Stein, Walker, and Forde, "Setting Diagnostic Thresholds," 408.

118. Stein, Walker, and Forde, "Setting Diagnostic Thresholds," 412.

4. Direct to Consumer

1. "Social Phobia," *DSM-IIIR* (300.23), 241.

2. Although this rejection intensified in the 1990s, it began much earlier, with psychiatrists such as Martin Fleischman lamenting his own profession's "quasi-religious revulsion against the pill" (by which he meant all pharmacology), and Gerald Klerman two years later decrying what he called "Pharmacological Calvinism" (by which he meant "if a drug makes you feel good it must be bad"). See Martin Fleishman, "Will the Real Third Revolution Please Stand Up?" *American Journal of Psychiatry* 124.9 (1968), 1262; and Gerald L. Klerman, "Drugs and Social Values," *International Journal of the Addictions* 5.2 (1970), 316.

3. Murray B. Stein, John R. Walker, and David R. Forde, "Setting Diagnostic Thresholds for Social Phobia: Considerations from a Community Survey of Social Anxiety," *American Journal of Psychiatry* 151.3 (1994), 408.

4. "Patient Testimonials Reintroduce an Old Drug in a New Market," *PR News* 56.20 (May 15, 2000), 1.

5. SmithKline Beecham press release, "First Medication for the Treatment of So-

cial Anxiety Disorder Approved by the FDA: SmithKline Beecham's Paxil® to Treat Highly Debilitating Condition" (May 11, 1999), 1. Obtained from Cohn and Wolfe, SKB's public relations company.

6. SmithKline Beecham PLC, "Seroxat/Paxil Fact File" (Abingdon, Oxfordshire: The Medicine Group [Education], 1998), sec. 1: "Towards the Second Billion," 2. Obtained from David Healy.

7. Ibid., and sec. 3: "Issues Management," n.pag. See also Shankar Vedantam, "Drug Ads Hyping Anxiety Make Some Uneasy," *Washington Post* (July 16, 2001).

8. Isaac Marks, interview by author, November 1, 2005.

9. David Healy, interview by author, October 9, 2005.

10. Barry Brand, as quoted in Vedantam, "Drug Ads Hyping Anxiety."

11. Brendan I. Koerner, "Disorders Made to Order," *Mother Jones* 27.4 (July/August 2002), 60. As Seroxat, the drug had entered the British market two years earlier, in 1991.

12. Beth Hawkins, "Paxil Is Forever: Doctor Please, Some More of These," *City Pages* 23.1141 (October 16, 2002): *http://citypages.com/databank/23/1141/article 10788.asp* (accessed April 30, 2006).

13. Ray Moynihan and Alan Cassels, *Selling Sickness: How the World's Biggest Pharmaceutical Companies Are Turning Us All into Patients* (New York: Nation Books, 2005), 120; Hawkins, "Paxil Is Forever."

14. Peter Landers, "Waiting for Prozac: Drug Companies Push Japan to Change View of Depression," *Wall Street Journal* (October 9, 2002).

15. Ray Moynihan, "Celebrity Selling—Part 2," *British Medical Journal* 325.7358 (August 3, 2002), 286.

16. David Healy, *The Antidepressant Era* (Cambridge, Mass.: Harvard University Press, 1997), 76.

17. Mickey C. Smith, *A Social History of the Minor Tranquilizers: The Quest for Small Comfort in the Age of Anxiety* (1985; Binghamton, N.Y.: Pharmaceutical Products Press, 1991), 67.

18. Anne E. Caldwell, "History of Psychopharmacology," *Principles of Psychopharmacology, 2nd Edition*, ed. William G. Clark and Joseph del Guidice (New York: Academic Press, 1978), 35; emphasis in original.

19. Morton Mintz, "Drug Success = News; Drug Failure = Non-News," *The Therapeutic Nightmare: A Report on the Roles of the United States Food and Drug Administration, the American Medical Association, Pharmaceutical Manufacturers, and Others in Connection with the Irrational and Massive Use of Prescription Drugs That May Be Worthless, Injurious, or Even Lethal* (Boston: Houghton Mifflin, 1965), 53–70, summarized in Smith, *A Social History,* 65.

20. Subcommittee on Intergovernmental Relations to Study the Safety and Effectiveness of New Drugs, as quoted in Smith, *A Social History,* 183.

21. Hawkins, "Paxil Is Forever."

22. Moynihan and Cassels, *Selling Sickness,* 23, 101.

23. David Healy, *Let Them Eat Prozac: The Unhealthy Relationship between the Phar-

maceutical Industry and Depression (New York: New York University Press, 2004), 272; emphasis in original.

24. Shankar Vedantam, "Experts Defining Mental Disorders Are Linked to Drug Firms," *Washington Post* (April 20, 2006). See also Benedict Carey, "Study Cites Links to Firms by Psychiatrists," *New York Times* (April 20, 2006).

25. See for instance Shankar Vedantam, "FDA Told U.S. Drug System Is Broken: Expert Panel Calls for Major Changes," *Washington Post* (September 23, 2006).

26. See Healy, *Antidepressant Era,* 61. Monoamine oxidase inhibitors (MAOIs) were so named because they increased monoamine levels in the brain, an outcome said to have antidepressive effects. SSRIs—particularly Prozac—soon eclipsed pharmacological interest in MAOIs, however, because they are comparatively safer and generate fewer side effects. Regarding chronic cases of depression, there are still claims that MAOIs are the more effective treatment.

27. Consequently, my perspective differs substantially from that of antipsychiatry gurus such as Thomas Szasz, who has insisted in a litany of popular books that mental illness is a "myth" designed to categorize and control us. As Peter Kramer and others have pointed out in brilliant rejoinders to Szasz, the net effect of his thinking about mental *illness* (rather than its sometimes questionable *treatment*) is to romanticize depression and schizophrenia by turning them into badges of political honor, symptoms of existential depth, or signs of tortured genius. Missing from Szasz's writing, in particular, is any sense of the acute, involuntary misery that depression, schizophrenia, and other illnesses cause, as well as the way they tug on hidden psychological and biological sources. See Thomas S. Szasz, *The Myth of Mental Illness: Foundations of a Theory of Personal Conduct* (New York: Harper and Row, 1961); and Peter D. Kramer, *Against Depression* (New York: Viking, 2005), esp. 63–84.

28. Susie Scott, interview by author, July 13, 2006.

29. Because the company's name changed shortly after it received FDA approval to treat social phobia, and because my text moves back and forth across several years, to avoid additional complexity I refer throughout this chapter to "SmithKline," even after the company technically had become GlaxoSmithKline, or GSK.

30. Cohn and Wolfe, Partners in Wellness, "Launching Paxil for the Treatment of Social Anxiety Disorder," *http://members.fortunecity.com/partnersinwellness/id23. htm* (accessed May 1, 2005).

31. Healy, *Antidepressant Era,* 168, and *Let Them Eat Prozac,* 270 and 337–38 n42, which refers to Healy's unpublished 2003 essay, "SSRIs and Withdrawal/Dependence." Among a long list of sources documenting these problems are the Committee on Safety of Medicine and the Medicines Control Agency, "Dystonia and Withdrawal Symptoms with Paroxetine (Seroxat), *Current Problems in Pharmacovigilance* 19.1 (February 1993), 1; Linda C. Barr, Wayne K. Goodman, and Lawrence H. Price, "Physical Symptoms Associated with Paroxetine Discontinuation" (letter), *American Journal of Psychiatry* 151.2 (February 1994), 289; Charles Debattista and Alan F. Schatzberg, "Physical Symptoms Associated with Paroxetine Withdrawal" (letter), *American Journal of Psychiatry* 152.8 (August 1995), 1235–36; Fiona J. Mackay et al., "A Com-

parison of Fluvoxamine, Fluoxetine, Sertraline and Paroxetine Examined by Observational Cohort Studies," *Pharmacoepidemiology and Drug Safety* 6.4 (1997), 235–46.

32. Healy, *Let Them Eat Prozac,* 27. See also David Healy and B. E. Leonard, "Monoamine Transport in Depression: Kinetics and Dynamics," *Journal of Affective Disorders* 12.2 (1987), 91–105; and Danish University Antidepressant Group, "Paroxetine: A Selective Serotonin Reuptake Inhibitor Showing Better Tolerance, but Weaker Antidepressant Effect than Clomipramine in a Controlled Multicenter Study," *Journal of Affective Disorders* 18.4 (1990), 289–99.

33. Healy, *Let Them Eat Prozac,* 27.

34. Irving Kirsch and Thomas J. Moore, with Alan Scoboria and Sarah S. Nicholls, "The Emperor's New Drugs: An Analysis of Antidepressant Medication Data Submitted to the U.S. Food and Drug Administration," *Prevention and Treatment* 5, Article 23 (July 2002): *http://content.apa.org/journals/pre/5/1/23* (accessed August 14, 2006). See also Irving Kirsch and Guy Sapirstein, "Listening to Prozac but Hearing Placebo: A Meta Analysis of Antidepressant Medication," *Prevention and Treatment* 1, Article 0002a (1998): *http://www.journals.apa.org/prevention/volume1/pre0010002a. html* (accessed August 24, 2006). The articles, which share the same principal author, did not appear in a peer-reviewed psychiatric journal.

35. See for instance R. C. Casper et al., "Somatic Symptoms in Primary Affective Disorder: Presence and Relationship to the Classification of Depression," *Archives of General Psychiatry* 42 (1985), 1098–104; J. Bobes et al., "Evaluating Changes in Sexual Functioning in Depressed Patients: Sensitivity to Change of the CSFQ [Changes in Sexual Functioning Questionnaire]," *Journal of Sex and Marital Therapy* 28 (2002), 93–103; and, most recently, Anita Clayton, Adrienne Keller, and Elizabeth L. McGarvey, "Burden of Phase-Specific Sexual Dysfunction with SSRIs," *Journal of Affective Disorders* 91 (2006), 27–32.

36. GlaxoSmithKline Inc., *Paxil CR™: Paroxetine Hydrochloride Controlled Release Tablets* (Mississauga, Ontario: Health Canada), rev. November 1, 2005, 7–10. I discuss these issues more extensively in the next chapter.

37. *Panorama,* "The Secrets of Seroxat" (BBC One, October 13, 2002). The transcript is available at *http://news.bbc.co.uk/2/hi/programmes/panorama/2310197.stm;* see also Healy, *Let Them Eat Prozac,* 283–84.

38. Healy, *Let Them Eat Prozac,* 284.

39. Craig J. Whittington et al., "Selective Serotonin Reuptake Inhibitors in Childhood Depression: Systematic Review of Published versus Unpublished Data," *The Lancet* 363 (April 24, 2004), 1341–45.

40. Gardiner Harris, "Spitzer Sues a Drug Maker, Saying It Hid Negative Data," *New York Times* (June 3, 2004); Barry Meier, "Two Studies, Two Results, and a Debate over a Drug," *New York Times* (June 3, 2004); Gardiner Harris, "FDA Toughens Warning on Antidepressant Drugs," *New York Times* (October 16, 2004).

41. Ed Silverman, "Sales Reps Told Not to Divulge Paxil Data: Drug Maker Memo Cited Risks to Youth," New Jersey *Star-Ledger* (September 29, 2004), citing an inter-

nal GSK memo that read: "This letter is for your informational purposes only. Although you should read the letter carefully, please do not discuss the contents with your customers." GSK's explanation was that only Prozac had received FDA approval to treat depression in children and adolescents, so its own material was "off-label" information. But medical ethics experts argue that the company had a "moral duty" to distribute the results of negative trials, and that GSK's explanation was suspicious.

42. Healy, *Let Them Eat Prozac,* 270, 337–38 n42.

43. SmithKline Beecham press release, "First Medication," 2; emphasis mine.

44. Healy, *Let Them Eat Prozac,* 270, 337–38 n42.

45. Moynihan and Cassels, *Selling Sickness,* 134.

46. Healy, *Let Them Eat Prozac,* 248, 213.

47. SmithKline Beecham PLC, "Seroxat/Paxil Fact File," sec. 3: "Issues Management: Managing the Discontinuation Issue," 3.

48. Ibid., sec. 1: Foreword, 3.

49. Ibid., sec. 3: "Issues Management: SB's Discontinuation Strategy," 6.

50. Ibid., "Issues Management: Background to Discontinuation," 5.

51. Ibid., "Issues Management: Rebutting the Lilly Myths," 19, 20.

52. Ibid., "Issues Management: Key Messages," 4, no. 6; Introduction, 3.

53. Ibid., "Issues Management: Discontinuation," 21.

54. Ibid., sec. 1: "Towards the Second Billion," 2.

55. Healy, *Let Them Eat Prozac,* 27, 296 n96.

56. See the articles cited in notes 31, 32, and 34.

57. *http://www.cohnwolfe.com* (accessed October 5, 2005). The company has since revised this claim, though it has been reproduced several times elsewhere.

58. *http://www.cohnwolfe.com/Content.aspx?NodeID=12* (accessed April 21, 2006).

59. "Patient Testimonials," 1.

60. SmithKline Beecham PLC, "Seroxat/Paxil Fact File," sec. 2, "The Burden of Social Anxiety Disorder/Social Phobia," 6.

61. Colby Cosh, "You're Not Shy, You're Sick: Psychiatrists Discover a Crippling 'Social Anxiety Disorder' That Affects 13% of Us," *The Report* (June 19, 2000), 49–50.

62. Ibid.

63. A direct-to-consumer (DTC) advertisement appearing in *Reader's Digest* (November–December 2001).

64. Moynihan and Cassels, *Selling Sickness,* 48.

65. Koerner, "Disorders Made to Order," 61.

66. Cohn and Wolfe, as quoted in Hawkins, "Paxil Is Forever," n.pag.

67. Koerner, "Disorders Made to Order," 62.

68. Cohn and Wolfe, "Launching Paxil": *http://members.fortunecity.com/partners inwellness/id23.htm* (accessed May 1, 2005).

69. Ibid.

70. "Can You Imagine Being Allergic to People?" *Spotlight on Health,* North American Précis Syndicate, *www.napsnet.com/pdf_archive/53/49514.pdf* (accessed April 30, 2006).

71. "It's Not Your Fault," part of the National Mental Health Awareness Campaign,

cosponsored with MTV in 2001: *www.nostigma.org/PDF/nostigma.pdf* (accessed April 30, 2006).

72. Osnat Benshoshan, "Celebrity Public Relations: An Alternative to DTC," *DTC Perspectives* 2 (2003): *http://www.dtcperspectives.com/content.asp?id=149* (accessed May 22, 2006).

73. Barry Brand, as quoted in Vedantam, "Drug Ads Hyping Anxiety."

74. Moynihan and Cassels, *Selling Sickness,* 131.

75. Vince Parry, "The Art of Branding a Condition," *MM and M: Medical Marketing and Media* (May 2003), 46.

76. Ibid., 44.

77. For elaboration see Moynihan and Cassels, *Selling Sickness,* and Ray Moynihan and David Henry, "The Fight against Disease Mongering: Generating Knowledge for Action," *PloS Medicine* 3.4 (April 2006), 0425–28: *www.plosmedicine.org* (accessed August 3, 2006), as well as essays in the same special edition by David Healy, Steven Woloshin plus Lisa M. Schwartz, and Christine B. Phillips on the selling of, respectively, bipolar disorder, restless legs syndrome, and attention deficit hyperactivity disorder.

78. "Social Phobia Inventory": *http://www.paxilcr.com/Social_Anxiety_Disorder_Test.jsp* (accessed April 30, 2006).

79. John R. Marshall, with the assistance of Suzanne Lipsett, *Social Phobia: From Shyness to Stage Fright* (New York: Basic Books, 1994), 171–73.

80. Michelle Cottle, "Selling Shyness: How Doctors and Drug Companies Created the 'Social Phobia' Epidemic," *New Republic* (August 2, 1999), 27, 28.

81. Lynne Henderson and Philip Zimbardo, *The Shyness Home Page* (Palto Alto, Calif.): *http://www.shyness.com/shyness-institute.html* (accessed October 12, 2006).

82. Marcia Vickers, "Help for the Chutzpah-Challenged: Shy New Yorkers Turn to Support Groups, If They Get the Courage to Show Up," *New York Times* (April 11, 1999).

83. Ibid.

84. Harriet Goodheart, "Heimberg Ahead of the Curve in Targeting Social Anxiety Disorder," *Temple Times* (April 21, 2005): *http://www.temple.edu/temple_times/4-21-05/heimberg.html* (accessed October 12, 2006).

85. Moynihan and Cassels, *Selling Sickness,* 10, citing "Health Campaigners, Fundraising, and the Growth of Industry Involvement," *Health and Social Campaigner's News* 6 (April 2004), *http://www.patient-view.com/news.htm* (accessed October 10, 2006); emphasis mine.

86. SmithKline Beecham PLC, "Seroxat/Paxil Fact File," sec. 2, "The Burden of Social Anxiety Disorder/Social Phobia," 6.

5. Rebound Syndrome

1. "Paxil: Adverse Reactions," *USA Today: http://www.healthscout.com/rxdetail/68/13/2/main.html* (accessed October 12, 2006).

2. Marianne Szegedy-Maszak, " . . . but still sad: Antidepressants Aren't the Magic That Millions Hoped. For the First Time, Prescriptions Fall," *Los Angeles Times* (March 27, 2006); Jerry Adler, "Freud in Our Midst," *Newsweek* (March 27, 2006), 43–49.

3. Kate, a member of the Paxil Databases Support Group, in personal correspondence with me, January 22, 2006. I have respected her desire for anonymity by not supplying her last name.

4. Kate first sent these particular words to the Paxil Databases Support Group on December 9, 2005, then relayed them to me, in slightly altered form, during follow-up email exchanges.

5. GlaxoSmithKline Inc., *Paxil CR™ Paroxetine Hydrochloride Controlled Release Tablets* (Mississauga, Ontario: Health Canada), rev. November 1, 2005, 7.

6. SmithKline Beecham press release, "First Medication for the Treatment of Social Anxiety Disorder Approved by the FDA," 2.

7. GlaxoSmithKline, *Paxil Tablets,* 5, 7, 8.

8. Ibid., 6.

9. Ibid., 4.

10. Advertisement for Paxil, *People Magazine* (2002).

11. "Paxil: Adverse Reactions."

12. Gardiner Harris, "Spitzer Sues a Drug Maker, Saying It Hid Negative Data," *New York Times* (June 3, 2004); see also Barry Meier, "Two Studies, Two Results, and a Debate over a Drug," *New York Times* (June 3, 2004).

13. Ed Silverman, "Sales Reps Told Not to Divulge Paxil Data: Drug Maker Memo Cited Risks to Youth," New Jersey *Star-Ledger* (September 29, 2004).

14. Harris, "Spitzer Sues a Drug Maker."

15. "GSK Agrees to Pay $14 Million to Settle Multistate Paxil Lawsuits," *Washington Drug Letter* 38.14 (April 3, 2006); emphasis mine. See also Dan Robrish, "GlaxoSmithKline, Attorneys General Settle Paxil Dispute," *Business News* (March 28, 2006).

16. Alex Berenson, "Despite Vow, Drug Makers Still Withhold Data," *New York Times* (May 31, 2005). See also Berenson, "Big Drug Makers See Sales Erode with Their Image," *New York Times* (November 14, 2005).

17. The following section owes much to Kate's initial description of her problems.

18. David S. Janowsky and David H. Overstreet, "The Role of Acetylcholine Mechanisms in Affective Disorders," *Neuropsychopharmacology: The Fifth Generation of Progress* (2000), *http://www.acnp.org/g4/GN401000095/CH.html* (accessed October 12, 2006); M. Bourin, P. Chue, Y. Guillon, "Paroxetine: A Review," *CNS Drug Review* 7.1 (Spring 2001), 25–47, *http://www.biopsychiatry.com/paroxetine.html* (accessed October 12, 2006).

19. David Healy, *Let Them Eat Prozac: The Unhealthy Relationship between the Pharmaceutical Industry and Depression* (New York: New York University Press, 2004), 11, 263–64.

20. See Robert Taylor Segraves, "Antidepressant-Induced Sexual Dysfunction," *Journal of Clinical Psychiatry* 59 (suppl. 4; 1998), 48–54; Sidney H. Kennedy et al.,

"Antidepressant-Induced Sexual Dysfunction during Treatment with Moclobemide, Paroxetine, Sertraline, and Venlafaxine," *Journal of Clinical Psychiatry* 61.4 (2000), 276–81; and Anthony J. Rothschild, "Sexual Side Effects of Antidepressants," *Journal of Clinical Psychiatry* 61 (suppl. 11; 2000), 28–36.

21. Lauren Slater, *Prozac Diary* (1998; Harmondsworth: Penguin, 1999), 118.

22. Richard C. Shelton, "Steps Following Attainment of Remission: Discontinuation of Antidepressant Therapy," *Primary Care Companion to the Journal of Clinical Psychiatry* 3.4 (2001), 168–74; R. Judge et al., "Discontinuation Symptoms: Comparison of Brief Interruption in Fluoxetine and Paroxetine Treatment," *International Clinical Psychopharmacology* 17.5 (2002), 224; Jun Fujishiro et al., "Comparison of the Anticholinergic Effects of the Serotonergic Antidepressants, Paroxetine, Fluvoxamine and Clomipramine," *European Journal of Pharmacology* 454 (2002), 183–88; David Healy, "SSRIs and Withdrawal/Dependence," a briefing paper (June 20, 2003): *www.socialaudit.org.uk/58092-DH.htm* (accessed August 14, 2006); and David S. Baldwin et al., "Discontinuation Symptoms in Depression and Anxiety Disorders," *International Journal of Neuropsychopharmacology* 19 (2005), 1–12.

23. Kate, Paxil Databases Support Group, December 9, 2005.

24. See for instance "Dissociation of the Plasticity of 5-HT1A Sites and 5-HT Transporter Sites," *Paxil Research Studies* 19.3 (1994), 311–15: *http://www.anti-depression.net/article/nlm-8177370/Paxil.html* (accessed August 24, 2006).

25. GlaxoSmithKline, *Paxil Tablets*, 7.

26. In addition to the articles listed above in notes 18 and 20, see Healy, *Let Them Eat Prozac*, 270.

27. David McDowell, as quoted in Andrew Solomon, *The Noonday Demon: An Atlas of Depression* (New York: Scribner, 2001), 22.

28. One of many possible citations on this topic is Adam Opbroek et al., "Emotional Blunting Associated with SSRI-induced Sexual Dysfunction. Do SSRIs Inhibit Emotional Responses?" *International Journal of Neuropsychopharmacology* 5.2 (2002), 147–51. This group found that of those in its sample, "80% of patients with SSRI-induced sexual dysfunction also describe clinically significant blunting of several emotions" (147). Ronald W. Dworkin assesses the broader philosophical implications of such findings in *Artificial Happiness: The Dark Side of the New Happy Class* (New York: Carroll and Graf, 2006).

29. Elisabeth Roudinesco, *Why Psychoanalysis?* trans. Rachel Bowlby (1999; New York: Columbia University Press, 2001), 6.

30. Ibid., 4.

31. Ibid, 4. See also Adam Phillips, "A Mind Is a Terrible Thing to Measure," *New York Times* (February 26, 2006).

32. I do not mean to rule out gratitude for other kinds of medical technology, on which our livelihoods sometimes depend.

33. Roudinesco, *Why Psychoanalysis?* 4.

34. Sigmund Freud, "'Wild' Psycho-Analysis" (1910), *Standard Edition of the Complete Psychological Works of Sigmund Freud*, ed. and trans. James Strachey (London:

Hogarth, 1953–74), 24 vols., 11:221. The next section of the text derives from 11:224, 222, and 226.

35. Adam Phillips, "Worrying and Its Discontents," *On Kissing, Tickling, and Being Bored: Psychoanalytic Essays on the Unexamined Life* (Cambridge, Mass.: Harvard University Press, 1993), 49, 54.

36. Susie Scott, "The Red, Shaking Fool: Dramaturgical Dilemmas in Shyness," *Symbolic Interaction* 28.1 (2005), 97. See also Jonathan M. Cheek and Arnold H. Buss, "Shyness and Sociability," *Journal of Personality and Social Psychology* 41.2 (1981), 330–39.

37. Susie Scott, "The Shell, the Stranger and the Competent Other: Towards a Sociology of Shyness," *Sociology* 38.1 (2004), 128. Scott here draws partially on the work of Harold Garkinkel, especially his *Studies in Ethnomethodology* (Englewood Cliffs, N.J.: Prentice-Hall, 1967).

38. Susie Scott, "The Medicalisation of Shyness: From Social Misfits to Social Fitness," *Sociology of Health and Illness* 28.2 (2006), 139.

39. Stephen Chbosky, *The Perks of Being a Wallflower* (New York: Pocket Books, 1999).

40. Scott, "The Red, Shaking Fool," 107. See also Scott, "The Shell, the Stranger and the Competent Other," 121–37.

41. *Dirty Filthy Love*, dir. Adrian Shergold (Manchester: Granada Television, 2004).

42. Phillips, "Worrying and Its Discontents," 58; emphasis mine.

43. Sigmund Freud, *The Ego and the Id* (1923), *Standard Edition* 19:57.

44. Sigmund Freud, *Civilization and Its Discontents* (1929, 1930), *Standard Edition* 21:109, 135, 124, 137.

45. Freud, *The Ego and the Id*, 19:52.

46. Freud, *Civilization and Its Discontents*, 21:127.

47. Ibid., 125.

48. Brigette A. Erwin et al., "Anger Experience and Expression in Social Anxiety Disorder: Pretreatment Profile and Predictors of Attrition and Response to Cognitive-Behavioral Treatment," *Behavior Therapy* 34.3 (2003), 333.

49. Ibid., 331, 332. The authors reference Leonard M. Horowitz et al., "Inventory of Interpersonal Problems: Psychometric Properties and Clinical Applications," *Journal of Consulting and Clinical Psychology* 56.6 (1988), 885–92.

50. See Richard G. Heimberg et al., "The Issue of Subtypes in the Diagnosis of Social Phobia," *Journal of Anxiety Disorders* 7.3 (1993), esp. 259.

51. Erwin et al., "Anger Experience and Expression," 332.

52. Ibid., 345.

53. See Mark R. Leary, "A Brief Version of the Fear of Negative Evaluation Scale," *Personality and Social Psychology Bulletin* 9.3 (1983), 371–75.

54. Erwin et al., "Anger Experience and Expression," 346, 338.

55. Freud, "'Wild' Psycho-Analysis," 11:226.

56. Thomas Hardy, *The Mayor of Casterbridge* (1886; Harmondsworth: Penguin, 1985), 288.

57. Erwin et al., "Anger Experience and Expression," 345.

58. Ibid., 333.

59. Sigmund Freud, *An Outline of Psycho-Analysis* (1940), *Standard Edition* 23:182.

60. "Duration of Treatment and Depression Relapse and Recurrence Rates," a confidential February 2001 memo prepared for GlaxoSmithKline by CMAT-Neurosciences, page 2. Obtained from David Healy.

6. A Backlash Forms

1. David Gates, "American Gothic," *New York Times* (September 9, 2001).

2. For an elaborate reading of this metaphor in Plato's *Dialogues,* see Jacques Derrida's long essay, "Plato's Pharmacy," *Dissemination,* trans. Barbara Johnson (1972; Chicago: University of Chicago Press, 1981), esp. 117–34.

3. Aldous Huxley, *Brave New World* (1932; New York: HarperPerennial, 1998), 94, 149.

4. Aldous Huxley, "The Doors of Perception," *The Doors of Perception and Heaven and Hell* (1954; New York: HarperPerennial, 1990), 64.

5. Peter D. Kramer, *Listening to Prozac: The Landmark Book about Antidepressants and the Remaking of the Self,* rev. ed. (1993; New York: Penguin, 1997), esp. xiv–xv.

6. Nikolas Rose, "Becoming Neurochemical Selves," *Biotechnology: Between Commerce and Civil Society,* ed. Nico Stehr (New Brunswick, N.J.: Transaction Publishers, 2004), 122.

7. See IMS Health Data, *http://www.imshealth.com/ims/portal/front/articleC/ 0,2777,6599_18731_77056778,00.html* (accessed August 14, 2006); also, as one of many related news items, Peter Landers, "Waiting for Prozac: Drug Companies Push Japan to Change View of Depression," *Wall Street Journal* (October 9, 2002).

8. David Healy outlines the case of one man who, in the course of just two years, received flupenthixol, Parstelin, alprazolam, thioridazine, viloxazine, and maprotiline, along with Valium, dothiepin, amoxapine, various tranquilizers, trazodone, and then Prozac. Two weeks after beginning the Prozac he experienced repeated suicidal thoughts, went on erratic, unplanned trips he couldn't account for, then walked into the sea fully clothed. See Healy, *Let Them Eat Prozac: The Unhealthy Relationship between the Pharmaceutical Industry and Depression* (New York: New York University Press, 2004), 46. See also Gogo Lidz, "My Adventures in Psychopharmacology," *New York Magazine* (January 8, 2007), 24–29.

9. Kramer, *Listening to Prozac,* xvi. See also Peter D. Kramer, "The New You," *Psychiatric Times* (March 1990), 45–46.

10. Jonathan Franzen, *The Corrections: A Novel* (2001; New York: Picador, 2002), 316. Subsequent references give page numbers in the main text.

11. Jonathan Franzen, "Why Bother?" *How to Be Alone: Essays* (New York: Farrar, Straus and Giroux, 2002), esp 66. "We live in a tyranny of the literal."

12. Vince Parry, "The Art of Branding a Condition," *MM and M: Medical Marketing and Media* (May 2003), 49.

13. Michiko Kakutani, "Books of the Times; a Family Portrait as Metaphor for the 90's," *New York Times* (September 4, 2001).

14. Theo Tait, "Lifestyle Flavours," *Times Literary Supplement* (December 21, 2001), 19.

15. We later learn, for instance, that as a young man Alfred Lambert daydreams "of radical transformation: of one day waking up and finding himself a wholly different (more confident, more serene) kind of person, of escaping that prison of the given, of feeling divinely capable" (270). And the narrator ably vocalizes the thinking that spurs Enid to take Aslan Cruiser: "How universal the craving to escape the givens of the self" (321).

16. Franzen, "Why Bother?" 72, 94, 79.

17. Laura Miller, "Only Correct," interviewing Jonathan Franzen, *Salon.com* (September 7, 2001), *http://archive.salon.com/books/int/2001/09/07/franzen/index.html* (accessed August 14, 2006).

18. Emily Eakin, "Jonathan Franzen's Big Book," *New York Times* (September 2, 2001).

19. Jonathan Franzen, "My Father's Brain," *How to Be Alone*, 7–38.

20. Eakin, "Jonathan Franzen's Big Book."

21. Jacket blurb on the Picador edition of *The Corrections*.

22. C. S. Lewis, *Mere Christianity: A Revised and Enlarged Edition, with a New Introduction of the Three Books, The Case for Christianity, Christian Behaviour, and Beyond Personality* (New York: Macmillan, 1952).

23. Among other symbols (including the Saint George's Cross), England is represented by lions, as in the Three Lions Crest.

24. Wesley Morris, "Over-tended 'Garden' Fails to Fully Bloom," *Boston Globe* (August 6, 2004).

25. Joel Stein, "Zach Braff Has a Big Laugh," *Time* 164.4 (July 26, 2004), 68–69.

26. Irving Kirsch and Thomas J. Moore, with Alan Scoboria and Sarah S. Nicholls, "The Emperor's New Drugs: An Analysis of Antidepressant Medication Data Submitted to the U.S. Food and Drug Administration," *Prevention and Treatment* 5, Article 23 (July 2002): *http://content.apa.org/journals/pre/5/1/23* (accessed August 14, 2006). See also Irving Kirsch and Guy Sapirstein, "Listening to Prozac but Hearing Placebo: A Meta Analysis of Antidepressant Medication," *Prevention and Treatment* 1, Article 0002a (1998): *http://www.journals.apa.org/prevention/volume1/pre0010002a. html* (accessed August 24, 2006).

27. Marc Savlov, "Garden State," *Austin Chronicle* (August 20, 2004): *www. austinchronicle.com/gyrobase/Calendar/Film?Film=oid%3A224510* (accessed July 18, 2006).

28. Claudia Puig, "'Garden State' Graduates with Honors," *USA Today* (July 28, 2004).

29. Alan Lightman, *The Diagnosis: A Novel* (New York: Pantheon, 2000), 203. Subsequent references give page numbers in the main text.

30. Donna Seaman, "Net Escape: Alan Lightman's Provocative Vision of Our Spiritually Debilitating Technocracy," *Chicago Tribune* (September 24, 2000).

31. Alan Lightman, interviewed by Robert Birnbaum, *identitytheory.com* (August 2000): *http://www.identitytheory.com/people/birnbaums.html* (accessed August 14, 2006).

32. Floyd Skloot, "Technology Drone Disconnects from the Human World," *San Francisco Chronicle Book Review* (September 17–23, 2000), 5.

33. Claudia Rankine, *Don't Let Me Be Lonely: An American Lyric* (Saint Paul, Minn.: Graywolf Press, 2004), 29.

34. James Hynes, "Out of Touch," *Washington Post Book World* (November 26, 2000), 7. See also Megan Milks, "Lightman's 'Diagnosis' Stretches Itself Too Thin," *The Cavalier Daily* (November 18, 2000): *http://www.cavalierdaily.com/CVArticle. asp?ID=6637&pid=656* (accessed October 12, 2006); and Bikram Chatterji, "The Illness of Modern Life: A New Novel about a Man Who Forgets His Culture," *Yale Review of Books* 4.2 (2001), 3.

35. Will Self, *Dr. Mukti and Other Tales of Woe* (New York: Penguin, 2004), 5. Subsequent references give page numbers in the main text.

36. Will Self, "The Quantity Theory of Insanity," in *The Quantity Theory of Insanity: Together with Five Supporting Propositions* (1991; New York: Vintage, 1996), 119.

37. Andrew O'Hehir, review of *The Corrections* at *Salon.com* (September 7, 2001): *http://archive.salon.com/books/review/2001/09/07/franzen/index.html* (accessed October 12, 2006).

7. Fear of Others in an Anxious Age

1. Michelle Stephenson, "Should Apathy Be Included in the DSM-V?" *NeuroPsychiatry Reviews* 6.3 (April 2005): *http://www.neuropsychiatryreviews.com/apros/apathy. html* (accessed August 14, 2006). James D. Duffy quoted there.

2. T. M. Luhrmann, *Of Two Minds: An Anthropologist Looks at American Psychiatry* (New York: Vintage, 2000), 210; and Joan Acocella, "The Empty Couch: What Is Lost When Psychiatry Turns to Drugs?" *New Yorker* (May 8, 2000), 115.

3. Robert Spitzer, interview by author, February 22, 2006.

4. Susan L. McElroy et al., "Compulsive Buying: A Report of 20 Cases," *Journal of Clinical Psychiatry* 55.6 (1994), 242.

5. Ronald C. Kessler et al., "The Prevalence and Correlates of DSM-IV Intermittent Explosive Disorder in the National Comorbidity Survey Replication," *Archives of General Psychiatry* 63 (June 2006), 669–78.

6. See for instance Jim Ritter, "Reason for the Rage? 'Explosive Disorder' More Common Than Thought: Researchers," *Chicago Sun-Times* (June 6, 2006); and "Road Rage? It May Be a Clinical Disorder," *ABC News* (June 3, 2006): *http://www. abcnews.go.com/GMA/Health/story?id=2035780* (accessed October 12, 2006).

7. Kessler et al., "Prevalence and Correlates," 669.

8. Ronald C. Kessler et al., "Mild Disorders Should Not Be Eliminated from the DSM-V," *Archives of General Psychiatry* 60.11 (2003), 1117–22. See also T. S. Brugha, P. E. Bebbington, and R. Jenkins, "A Difference That Matters: Comparisons of Struc-

tured and Semi-Structured Psychiatric Diagnostic Interviews in the General Population," *Psychological Medicine* 29.5 (1999), 1013–20; H.-U. Wittchen, T. B. Üstün, and R. C. Kessler, "Diagnosing Mental Disorders in the Community: A Difference That Matters?" *Psychological Medicine* 29.5 (1999), 1021–27; Darrel A. Regier et al., "Limitations of Diagnostic Criteria and Assessment Instruments for Mental Disorders: Implications for Research and Policy," *Archives of General Psychiatry* 55.2 (1998), 109–15; T. Bedirhan Üstün, Somnath Chatterji, and Juergen Rehm, "Limitations of Diagnostic Paradigm: It Doesn't Explain 'Need,'" *Archives of General Psychiatry* 55.12 (1998), 1145–46; and Harold Alan Pincus, Deborah A. Zarin, and Michael First, "'Clinical Significance' and *DSM-IV*," *Archives of General Psychiatry* 55.12 (1998), 1145.

9. Ronald C. Kessler et al., "Lifetime Prevalence and Age-of-Onset Distributions of *DSM-IV* Disorders in the National Comorbidity Survey Replication," *Archives of General Psychiatry* 62.6 (2005), 593.

10. Ibid.

11. See Erica Goode, "British Warning on Antidepressant Use for Youth," *New York Times* (December 11, 2003); Shankar Vedantam, "Child Antidepressant Warning Is Urged; Panel's Recommendation to FDA Comes as Use of Medications Has Soared," *Washington Post* (September 15, 2004); Jonathan Mahler, "The Antidepressant Dilemma," *New York Times Sunday Magazine* (November 21, 2004), 59–65, 100, 118–19.

12. David Healy, interview by author, October 9, 2005.

13. For corroboration see Glen R. Elliott, *Medicating Young Minds: How to Know if Psychiatric Drugs Will Help or Hurt Your Child* (New York: Stewart, Tabori, and Chang, 2006); Benedict Carey, "What's Wrong with a Child? Psychiatrists Often Disagree," *New York Times* (November 11, 2006); and Gardiner Harris, "Proof Is Scant on Psychiatric Drug Mix for Young," *New York Times* (November 23, 2006).

14. Healy, interview. See for instance M. S. Marcin and C. B. Nemeroff, "The Neurobiology of Social Anxiety Disorder: The Relevance of Fear and Anxiety," *Acta Psychiatrica Scandinavica* 108 (suppl. 417; 2003), 51–64; and Jonathan R. T. Davidson, "Pharmacotherapy of Social Anxiety Disorder," *Journal of Clinical Psychiatry* 59 (suppl. 17; 1998), 47–51.

15. Kessler et al., "Lifetime Prevalence," 595. As noted in my Introduction, the exact percentage reported was 28.8.

16. Ashley Pettus, "Psychiatry by Prescription: Do Psychotropic Drugs Blur the Boundaries between Illness and Health?" *Harvard Magazine* (July–August 2006), 38–40.

17. Kessler et al., "Mild Disorders," 1118.

18. Kessler et al., "Lifetime Prevalence," 593.

19. Herb Kutchins and Stuart A. Kirk, *Making Us Crazy: DSM: The Psychiatric Bible and the Creation of Mental Disorders* (New York: Free Press, 1997), 244.

20. Sally Satel and Christina Hoff Sommers, "Defining Down Mental Illness (editorial)," *Washington Post* (August 14, 2005).

21. Roger A. MacKinnon to members of the Personality Disorders Advisory Committee, May 17, 1978.

22. "Schizoid Personality Disorder," *DSM-III* (301.20), 310.

23. Lloyd Grove, with Hudson Morgan, "Drug Business Prescribes a Novel Cure for Its Ills," *New York Daily News* (October 17, 2005). See also Michael Hiltzik, "Fiction Genre Fits Big Pharma," *Los Angeles Times* (October 27, 2005).

24. Grove, "Drug Business."

25. Ibid.

26. Frank Ahrens, "Tauzin Quits Chairmanship, Will Retire From House," *Washington Post* (February 4, 2004). See also Robert Pear, "Drug Industry Is on Defensive as Power Shifts," *New York Times* (November 24, 2006).

27. Hiltzik, "Fiction Genre Fits Big Pharma."

28. Grove, "Drug Business."

29. Hiltzik, "Fiction Genre Fits Big Pharma."

30. Grove, "Drug Business."

31. Hiltzik, "Fiction Genre Fits Big Pharma."

32. The novel appeared in 2005 via Phoenix Books as *The Karasik Conspiracy*, complete with a foreword explaining its unusual gestation. Its published incarnation is a somewhat recast version of the earlier proposal, with Bosnian terrorist Ken Karasik seeking revenge against Serbian ethnic cleansing and the killing of his own family by unleashing tainted drugs on them. "The irony," as the novel's jacket description puts it, is that "pharmaceutical giant PharmCorp has the same plan; with loyalty to no one, its goal is to protect billions of profit."

33. For instance, Kutchins and Kirk, *Making Us Crazy*; Joseph Glenmullen, *Prozac Backlash: Overcoming the Dangers of Prozac, Zoloft, Paxil, and Other Antidepressants with Safe, Effective Alternatives* (2000; New York: Touchstone Books, 2001); David Healy, *Let Them Eat Prozac: The Unhealthy Relationship between the Pharmaceutical Industry and Depression* (New York: New York University Press, 2004); Marcia Angell, *The Truth about the Drug Companies: How They Deceive Us and What to Do about It* (New York: Random House, 2004); Ray Moynihan and Alan Cassels, *Selling Sickness: How the World's Biggest Pharmaceutical Companies Are Turning Us All into Patients* (New York: Nation Books, 2005); and, most recently, Greg Critser, *Generation Rx: How Prescription Drugs Are Altering American Lives, Minds, and Bodies* (Boston: Houghton Mifflin, 2005).

34. Duffy, as quoted in Stephenson, "Should Apathy Be Included?"

35. Healy (interview), for instance, says that of the twenty-five thousand people who live in the area for which he has clinical responsibility, he "would see every two years one person who is *classically* socially phobic. They walk in through the door and you don't even have to ask them any questions" to know how they view social interactions. One person every two years is "pretty rare," he underscores.

36. Donald F. Klein, "Definition of Disorder," *The Proposed DSM-III: Critiques by Participants of the Conference on "Improvements in Psychiatric Classification and Ter-*

minology: A Working Conference to Critically Examine DSM-III in Midstream" (St. Louis, June 1976), 1d; emphasis mine.

37. Sally Satel and Christina Hoff Sommers, "Therapy Nation: Really, We're OK," *Orlando Sentinel* (June 19, 2005). See also Ian Craib, *The Importance of Disappointment* (New York: Routledge, 1994), esp. 1–11. Satel and Sommers would, however, recast my statement about psychological conflicts, since they believe the result is "therapism," a doctrine that "extols openness, emotional self-absorption, and the sharing of feelings."

38. Brigette A. Erwin et al., "Anger Experience and Expression in Social Anxiety Disorder: Pretreatment Profile and Predictors of Attrition and Response to Cognitive-Behavioral Treatment," *Behavior Therapy* 34.3 (2003), 345, 338. See, by contrast, Sigmund Freud, *Civilization and Its Discontents, Standard Edition of the Complete Psychological Works of Sigmund Freud,* ed. and trans. James Strachey (London: Hogarth, 1953–74), 24 vols., 21:108–16; and Georges Canguilhem, *The Normal and the Pathological,* trans. Carolyn R. Fawcett, with Robert S. Cohen (New York: Zone Books, 1991), esp. 275–87.

39. Jane Gross, "Checklist for Camp: Bug Spray. Sunscreen. Pills," *New York Times* (July 16, 2006).

40. ASBOs came into effect on April 1, 1999, as a key element of Britain's Crime and Disorder Act (1998). Ranging from a minimum of two years to no upper ceiling, the orders are civil not criminal sanctions, though they can result in prison sentences. According to *www.crimereduction.gov.uk,* the total number of ASBOs reported to the Home Office by the end of March 2004 was 2,455 (accessed October 12, 2006). One of many recent articles voicing concern about the misuse of ASBOs is Sarah Lyall, "Britain Cracks Down on Nasties Like the 'Neighbor from Hell,'" *New York Times* (April 2, 2004). See also Michael White, "Blair Admits ASBOs Have Yet to Beat the Louts: Prime Minister Says Crackdown on Hooligans Has Still to Reach 'Critical Mass,'" *The Guardian* (September 1, 2004); and Martin Bright, "Residents Delight as Anti-Social Teenagers Are Named and Shamed," *The Observer* (October 12, 2003).

41. Mitchell Wilson, "*DSM-III* and the Transformation of American Psychiatry: A History," *American Journal of Psychiatry* 150.3 (1993), 400, summarizing the neo-Kraepelinian study of Karl Menninger, with Martin Mayman and Paul Pruyser, *The Vital Balance: The Life Process in Mental Health and Illness* (New York: Viking, 1963), esp. 77–80. For a contrasting perspective, see Philippe van Haute, *Against Adaptation: Lacan's "Subversion" of the Subject: A Close Reading,* trans. Paul Crowe and Miranda Vankerk (New York: Other Press, 2002).

42. See for instance Dolan Cummings, "Don't Conform, Break the Rules: Observations on Antisocial Behaviour," *New Statesman* (September 27, 2004), 16–18, which concludes: "The problem . . . is not so much rampant individualism as shrinking-violetism. New laws, rules, and regulations simply reinforce the public's passivity. The [Blair] government's fondness for 'contracts' to promote neighbourliness on estates and good behaviour in schools reflects a desire to harness conformism in the service of

public spirit, but the result is a distinctly spiritless public." See also Craig O'Malley and Stuart Waiton, *Who's Antisocial? New Labour and the Politics of Antisocial Behaviour,* introd. Dolan Cummings (London: Academy of Ideas, 2005), and its counterpoint, Frank Field, *Neighbours from Hell: The Politics of Behaviour* (London: Politico's, 2003).

43. Roger Dobson, "We're Sick of Being Shy: Is Bashfulness a Personality Disorder? Or Are We in Danger of Medicalising a Harmless Trait?" *The Times* (London; April 8, 2006).

44. Susie Scott, as quoted in ibid. See also her essay "The Medicalisation of Shyness: From Social Misfits to Social Fitness," *Sociology of Health and Illness* 28.2 (2006), 133–53, and her forthcoming book, *Shyness and Society: The Illusion of Competence* (London: Palgrave, 2007).

45. Jonathan Rauch, "Caring for Your Introvert: The Habits and Needs of a Little-Understood Group," *Atlantic Monthly* (March 2003), 133.

46. See for instance Patricia A. McDaniel, *Shrinking Violets and Caspar Milquetoasts: Shyness, Power, and Intimacy in the United States, 1950–1995* (New York: New York University Press, 2003), esp. 2–20; and Joanna Bourke, *Fear: A Cultural History* (Emeryville, Calif.: Shoemaker and Hoard, 2006).

47. Leon R. Kass et al., *Beyond Therapy: Biotechnology and the Pursuit of Happiness: A Report of the President's Council on Bioethics,* introd. William Safire (Washington, D.C.: Dana Press, 2003), 291. See also Jim Holt, "Against Happiness," *New York Times* (June 20, 2004); and Darrin M. McMahon, "From the Happiness of Virtue to the Virtue of Happiness: 400 B. C.–A. D. 1780," *Daedalus* 133.2 (2004), 5–19.

48. Scott, as quoted in Dobson, "We're Sick of Being Shy," 4.

49. Susie Scott, interview by author, July 13, 2006.

50. See for instance Carl Elliott, "Pursued by Happiness and Beaten Senseless: Prozac and the American Dream," *Prozac as a Way of Life,* ed. Carl Elliott and Tod Chambers (Chapel Hill: University of North Carolina Press, 2004), 127–40; and Carl Elliott, "Medicate Your Dissent," *Speakeasy Magazine* (May/June 2003), reprinted at *http://www.tc.umn.edu/~elli0023/medicate.htm* (accessed August 14, 2006).

51. Margaret Talbot, "The Shyness Syndrome: Bashfulness Is the Latest Trait to Become a Pathology," *New York Times Sunday Magazine* (June 24, 2001), 12. See also Michelle Cottle, "Selling Shyness: How Doctors and Drug Companies Created the 'Social Phobia' Epidemic," *New Republic* (August 2, 1999), 24–29.

52. Andrew Hussey on "Start the Week," Britain's BBC Radio 4 (July 17, 2006): *http://www.bbc.co.uk/radio4/factual/starttheweek_20060717.shtml* (accessed August 14, 2006). See also H. Gilbert Welch, Lisa Schwartz, and Steven Woloshin, "What's Making Us Sick Is an Epidemic of Diagnoses," *New York Times* (January 2, 2007).

53. Garret Keizer, *The Enigma of Anger: Essays on a Sometimes Deadly Sin* (San Francisco: Jossey-Bass, 2002), 10.

54. As quoted, anonymously, in Luhrmann, *Of Two Minds,* 253.

55. I am slightly rephrasing Leo Bersani's point about the need to "adapt to that which makes us incapable of adaptation," in his introduction to Sigmund Freud, *Civilization and Its Discontents,* trans. David McLintock (London: Penguin, 2002), xxii.

See also Carl Elliott, *Better Than Well: American Medicine Meets the American Dream* (New York: Norton, 2003), xix–xx, 10; Adam Phillips, *Going Sane* (London: Hamish Hamilton, 2005); and Arthur Kleinman, *What Really Matters: Living a Moral Life Amidst Uncertainty and Danger* (New York: Oxford University Press, 2006).

56. Aldous Huxley, "The Doors of Perception," *The Doors of Perception and Heaven and Hell* (1954; New York: HarperPerennial, 1990), 64.

57. Samuel Beckett, *Endgame,* trans. Samuel Beckett (1957; New York: Grove, 1970), 68.

ACKNOWLEDGMENTS

It's a pleasure to thank the many people who have helped me complete this book. At an early stage in the writing, Mitchell Wilson in Berkeley and Cristina Hanganu-Bresch at the University of Minnesota were kind enough to share their stashes, respectively, of unpublished *DSM-III* correspondence and pharmaceutical ads. Their personal archives spurred me to undertake a great deal more intensive research, including at the American Psychiatric Association library; they also sharpened my project and saved me countless hours. I'm extremely grateful for their generous support and advice.

A further guide to research, someone whom it's difficult to acknowledge properly, is "Kate." Her thoughtful, anonymous posts to a web-based support group prompted me to investigate Paxil's "rebound syndrome" more thoroughly. Her follow-up recommendations were similarly helpful, and my chapter on the topic owes a great deal to her.

I cannot fail to thank the many psychiatrists and clinicians I interviewed, in both the United States and Britain. They gave up hours of their time, shared their doubts, insights, and victories, sent me unpublished work, cheerfully answered follow-up questions, and guided me to new sources and experts. I am enormously grateful to David M. Clark, Richard Heimberg, Michael Liebowitz, Isaac Marks, Robert Spitzer, and especially David Healy. Although my thinking and conclusions sometimes differ considerably from theirs, I found them fascinating, thoughtful interlocutors. Many thanks, as well, to Susie Scott, who helpfully answered questions about her work and shared a number of valuable sources.

Beth Hawkins at the *City Paper*, Brendan Koerner at *Mother Jones*, Trish Kane at IMS Health, and Martin Guha at the Maudsley's Institute of Psychiatry library, University of London, guided me to key information and sources, and Gary McMillan at the American Psychiatric Association in Arlington, Virginia, gave me unprecedented access to the vast archive of unpublished *DSM-III* memos and letters in Robert Spitzer's papers.

Among colleagues at Northwestern, I owe particular debts to Galen Bodenhausen, interim Chair of Psychology, and Ron Krasner, Chair of Psychiatry, who shared their work with me and offered many helpful counterpoints. I am also grateful to colleagues in English, especially Wendy Wall, chair of the department, Chris Herbert, and Julia Stern; to the dean's office in the Weinberg College of Arts and Sciences; and to Angela Nuzzarello, Chau Wu, and other colleagues in the Feinberg School of Medicine, who let me audit their lectures on neuropharmacology, gave invaluable feedback about medicine and clinical work, and responded gracefully to follow-up questions. Michelle Frisque and especially Jim Shedlock at Northwestern's Health Sciences library made an array of journals available to me in Europe, where I wrote large portions of this book.

Jeffrey Perl, editor of *Common Knowledge*, helped crystallize my thoughts by soliciting an essay for a special issue on "unsocial thought," fragments of which I have reprinted here with permission. My thanks to him and to Aden Bar-Tura, the journal's managing editor. For related invitations that generated welcome debate and reflection, I am grateful to Jim Anderson, Robert Gordon, and Christine Kieffer at the Chicago Psychoanalytic Institute; to Virginia Blum and colleagues at the University of Kentucky's Committee on Social Theory; to Dan Born and Don Whitfield at the Great Books Foundation, Chicago; to Paola Mieli and other analysts at Après Coup in New York; and to Gabrielle Weinberger and colleagues for the opportunity, at the University of Malta, to discuss fear.

I warmly thank Jorge Ribeiro in Guimarães and Isabel Botto at the University of Coimbra for helping to make my time in Portugal so productive and enjoyable. I am deeply grateful to my family in England, who followed my progress, sometimes page by page. Among close friends in the United States, I extend heartfelt thanks to Tim Dean, Carol Donnelly, Tom Downar, and especially Mark Bauerlein and Ed Hirschland for their advice and copyediting expertise. My thanks also to Leo Bersani, Robert Caserio, Tod Chambers, Dolan Cummings, Jonathan Franzen, Patricia Gherovici, Gretchen Helfrich, Richard Kaye, Deborah Luepnitz, Sue Mineka, Adam Phillips, and Kaja Silverman. Fehmi Yalsin kept me laughing by asking when I'd *finally* stop writing about "depressed Victorians."

A fellowship from the John S. Guggenheim Foundation gave me the time to complete this book. Dan O'Connell and Wendy Strothman at the Strothman Agency, Boston, offered wonderful support, encouragement, and feedback at all stages. So did Jean Thomson Black, my editor at Yale, as well as Matthew Laird, her assistant, and Vivian Wheeler, the Press's superb freelance manuscript editor. I thank the Press's anonymous readers for incisive comments that helped me greatly in revising the manuscript. Jorge Arce, a constant source of comfort and inspiration, deserves far more thanks than he could know.

With one exception (a previously confidential memo distributed among GlaxoSmithKline executives) all unpublished documents and correspondence quoted in this book appear courtesy of the American Psychiatric Association and are reprinted with permission. I thank Duke University Press for permission to reproduce several paragraphs from my essay "How Shyness Became an Illness: A Brief History of Social Phobia," *Common Knowledge* 12.3 (Fall 2006), 388–409.

INDEX

abnormal behavior, and diagnostic thresholds, 66

abulia, and overmedication, 107

acronyms, and marketing of medical conditions, 135

adolescents, and antidepressants, 198–99, 205–6

Adult Anxiety Clinic, Temple University, 7, 136

advertising: by drug companies, 105, 106–17; for Paxil, 105, 121–34. *See also* marketing, pharmaceutical

advocacy groups, and marketing, 136–37

agoraphobia, 15, 30, 42, 71–72, 76

Akiskal, Hagop, 27

alizarin (mordant red), 37

American Psychiatric Association (APA): archives, 6; biomedical emphasis of, 104; and *DSM-III*, 2–3, 39–42, 47–48; and DSM-III Task Force on Nomenclature and Statistics, 42–47, 51–56; and *DSM-IIIR*, 97; maintaining *DSM* categories, 202; and marketing of social anxiety disorder, 123, 125

American Psychoanalytic Association, ad hoc committee on *DSM-III*, 54–55

Amitriptyline hydrochloride, as tricyclic antidepressant, 106

anger, expression of, and social anxiety disorder, 162, 163, 164, 166. *See also* intermittent explosive disorder (IED)

anticholinergic drugs, 142, 146–47, 174. *See also* Paxil (paroxetine hydrochloride)

antidepressants: for children and adolescents, 198–99, 205–6; and emotional blunting, 8; marketing of, 4, 17, 106–17, 121; risks of, 117–18, 198; for social anxiety disorder, 120–21. *See also* Paxil (paroxetine hydrochloride); selective serotonin-reuptake inhibitors (SSRIs)

antisocial behavior, and conformism, 245–46n42

Antisocial Behaviour Orders (ASBOs in Britain), 207, 245n42

antisocial personality disorder (ASPD), 15–16, 17

anxiety: causes and effects of, 19–20, 149–53; drug treatments for, 140–41, 151, 161, 166–68; and expression of anger, 162–63; Freudian views of, 31–35, 154–55, 157, 160; historic views of, 8, 9, 11–14; and marketing of Paxil, 121; as rational response to stress, 139, 168; sociological perspectives of, 155–61

anxiety disorders: and "chemical imbalance," 159; drug treatments for, 105, 139; Freudian view of, 32–34; and marketing campaigns, 134–38; naming and